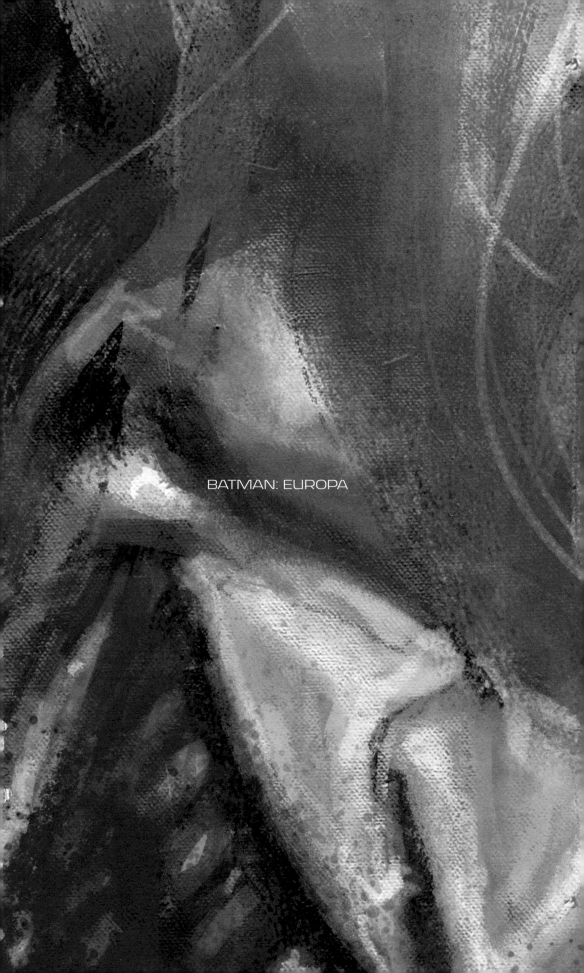

BATMAN: EUROPA

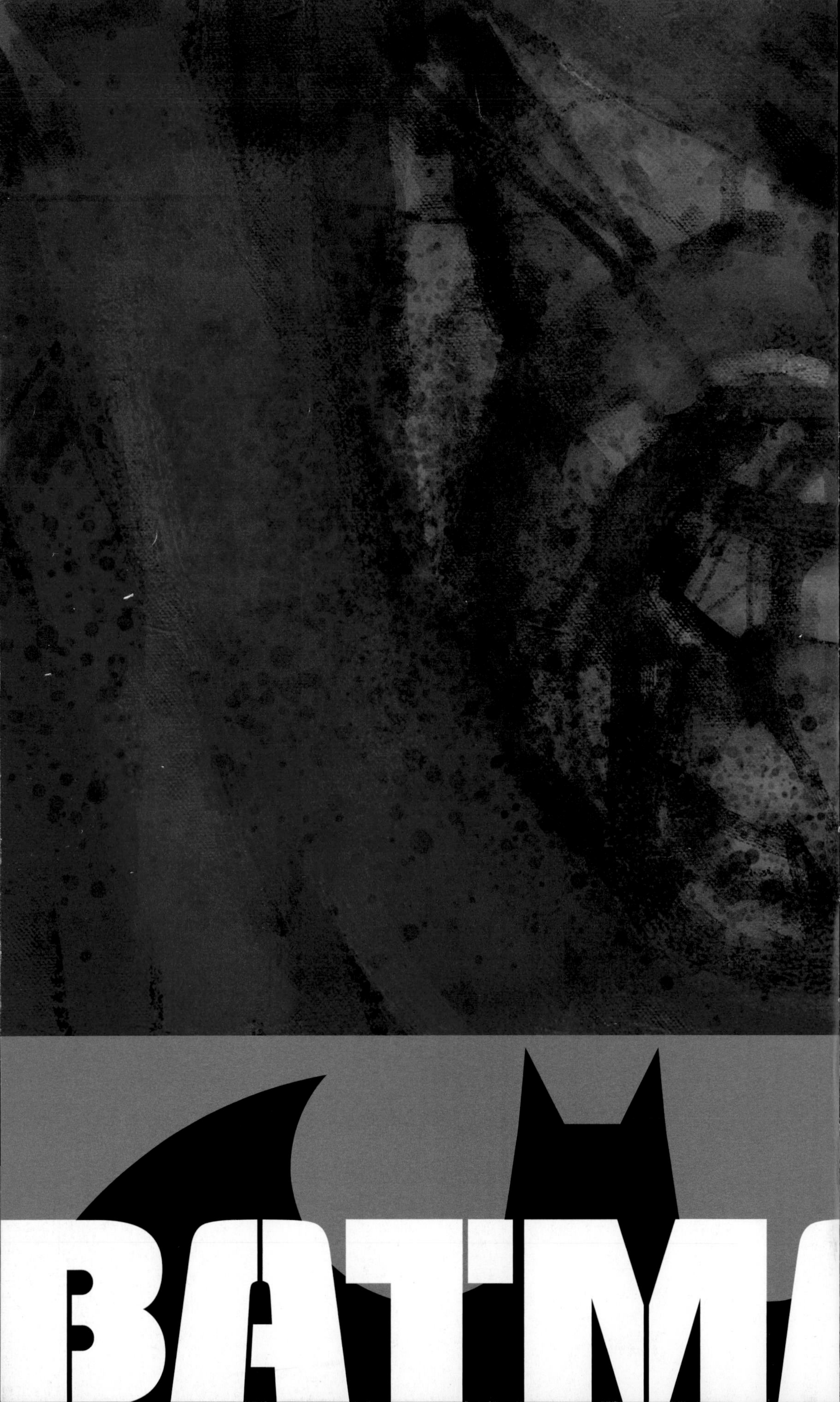

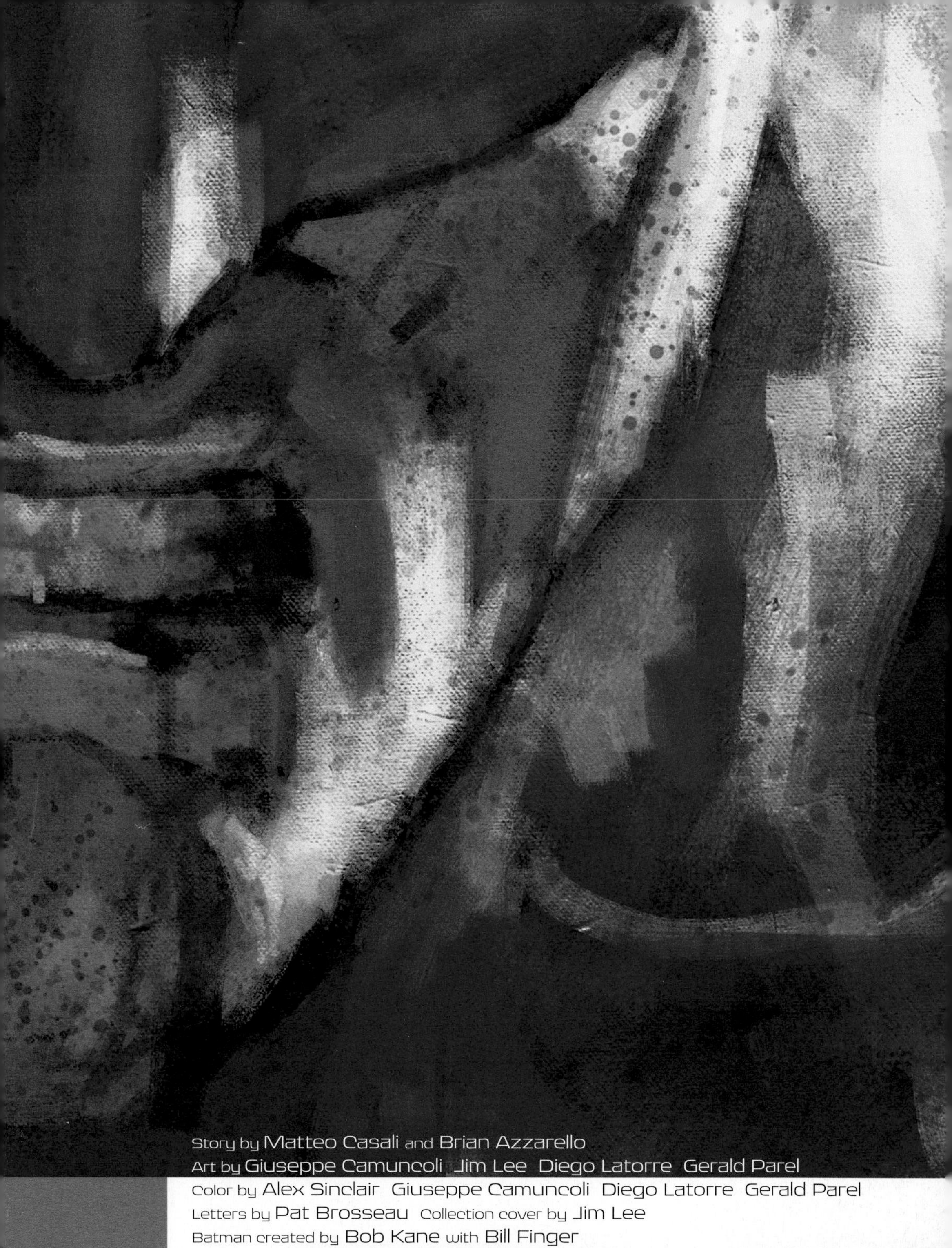

Story by Matteo Casali and Brian Azzarello

Art by Giuseppe Camuncoli Jim Lee Diego Latorre Gerald Parel

Color by Alex Sinclair Giuseppe Camuncoli Diego Latorre Gerald Parel

Letters by Pat Brosseau Collection cover by Jim Lee

Batman created by Bob Kane with Bill Finger

EUROPA

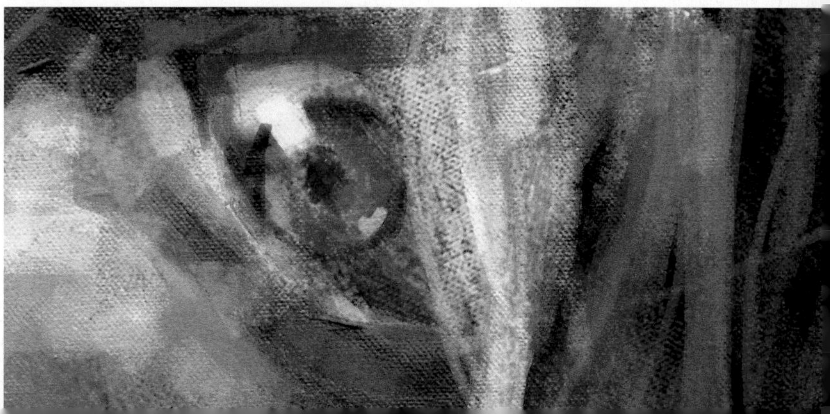

Jim Chadwick Editor – Original Series **David Piña** Assistant Editor – Original Series
Jeb Woodard Group Editor – Collected Editions **Robin Wildman** Editor – Collected Edition
Steve Cook Design Director – Books **Louis Prandi** Publication Design

Bob Harras Senior VP – Editor-in-Chief, DC Comics

Diane Nelson President **Dan DiDio** and **Jim Lee** Co-Publishers
Geoff Johns Chief Creative Officer **Amit Desai** Senior VP – Marketing & Global Franchise Management
Nairi Gardiner Senior VP – Finance **Sam Ades** VP – Digital Marketing
Bobbie Chase VP – Talent Development **Mark Chiarello** Senior VP – Art, Design & Collected Editions
John Cunningham VP – Content Strategy **Anne DePies** VP – Strategy Planning & Reporting
Don Falletti VP – Manufacturing Operations **Lawrence Ganem** VP – Editorial Administration & Talent Relations
Alison Gill Senior VP – Manufacturing & Operations **Hank Kanalz** Senior VP – Editorial Strategy & Administration
Jay Kogan VP – Legal Affairs **Derek Maddalena** Senior VP – Sales & Business Development
Jack Mahan VP – Business Affairs **Dan Miron** VP – Sales Planning & Trade Development
Nick Napolitano VP – Manufacturing Administration **Carol Roeder** VP – Marketing
Eddie Scannell VP – Mass Account & Digital Sales **Courtney Simmons** Senior VP – Publicity & Communications
Jim (Ski) Sokolowski VP – Comic Book Specialty & Newsstand Sales **Sandy Yi** Senior VP – Global Franchise Management

BATMAN: EUROPA

Published by DC Comics. Compilation and all new material
Copyright © 2016 DC Comics. All Rights Reserved.

Originally published in single magazine form in BATMAN: EUROPA
1-4 Copyright © 2015, 2016 DC Comics. All Rights Reserved.
All characters, their distinctive likenesses and related elements
featured in this publication are trademarks of DC Comics.

The stories, characters and incidents featured in this publication
are entirely fictional. DC Comics does not read or accept
unsolicited submissions of ideas, stories or artwork.

DC Comics, 2900 West Alameda Avenue, Burbank, CA 91505
Printed by RR Donnelley, Salem, VA, USA. 3/11/16. First Printing.
ISBN: 978-1-4012-5970-9

Library of Congress Cataloging-In-Publication Data is available.

PEFC Certified

Printed on paper from
sustainably managed
forests and controlled
sources

PEFC™

PEFC/29-31-75 www.pefc.org

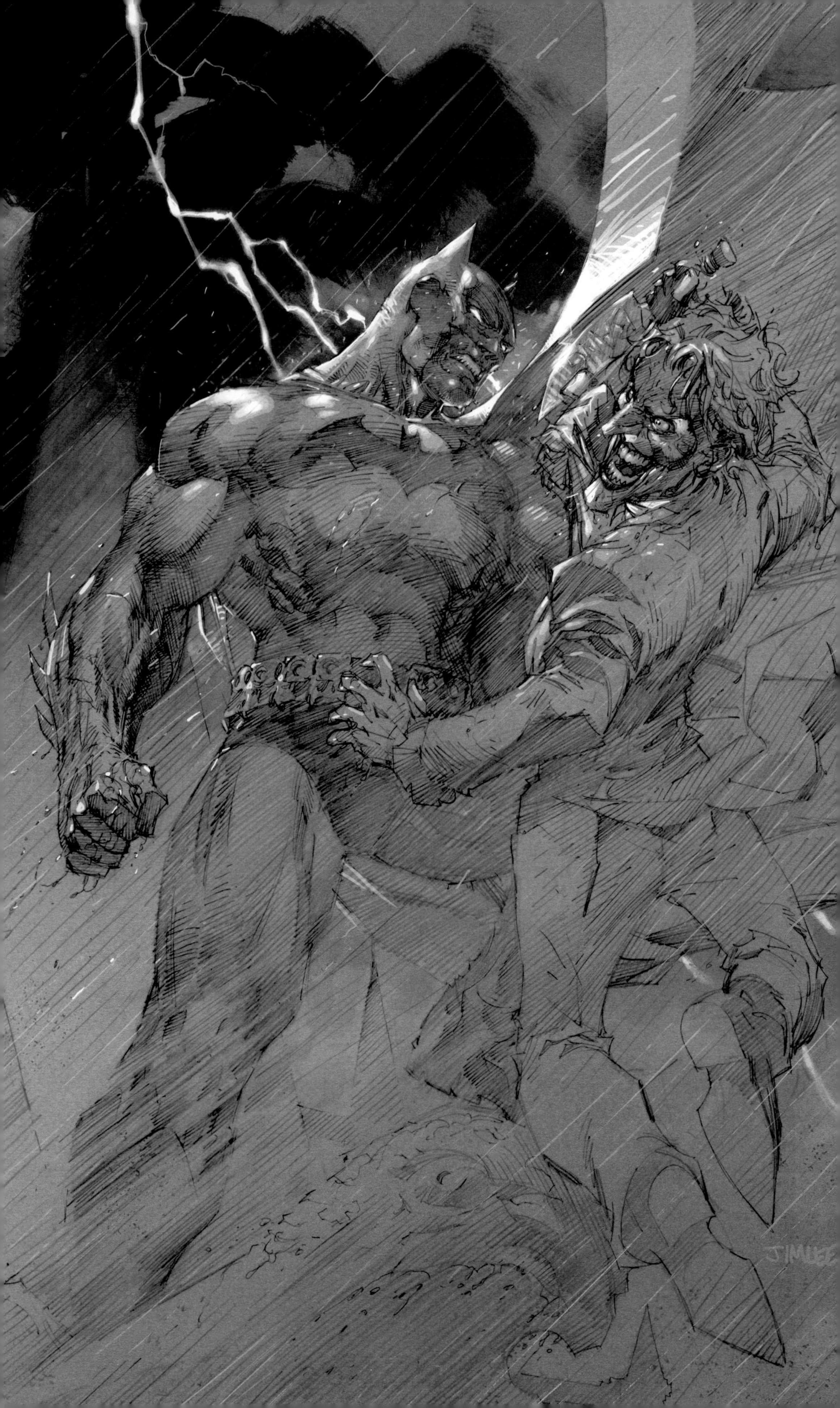

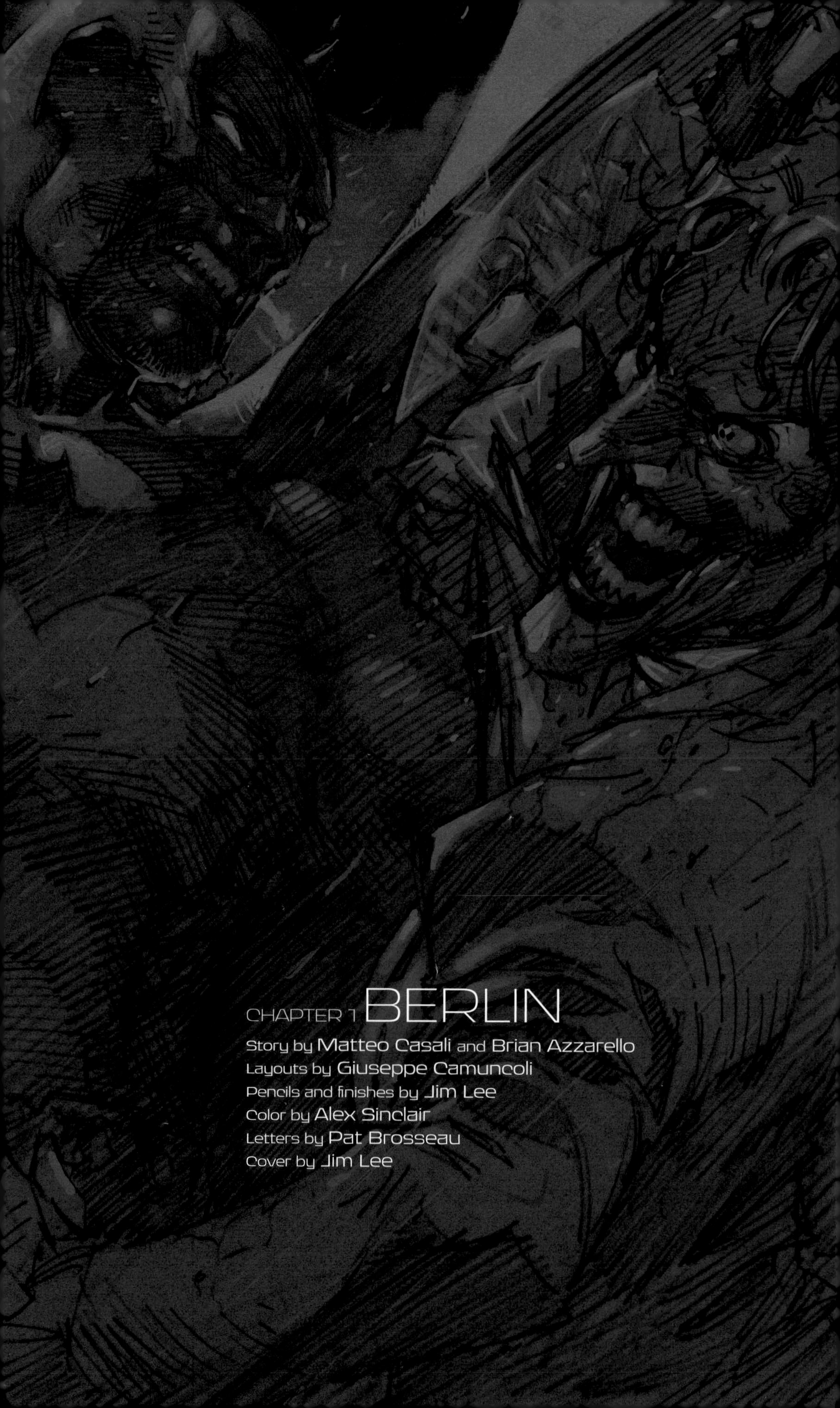

CHAPTER 1 BERLIN

Story by Matteo Casali and Brian Azzarello
Layouts by Giuseppe Camuncoli
Pencils and finishes by Jim Lee
Color by Alex Sinclair
Letters by Pat Brosseau
Cover by Jim Lee

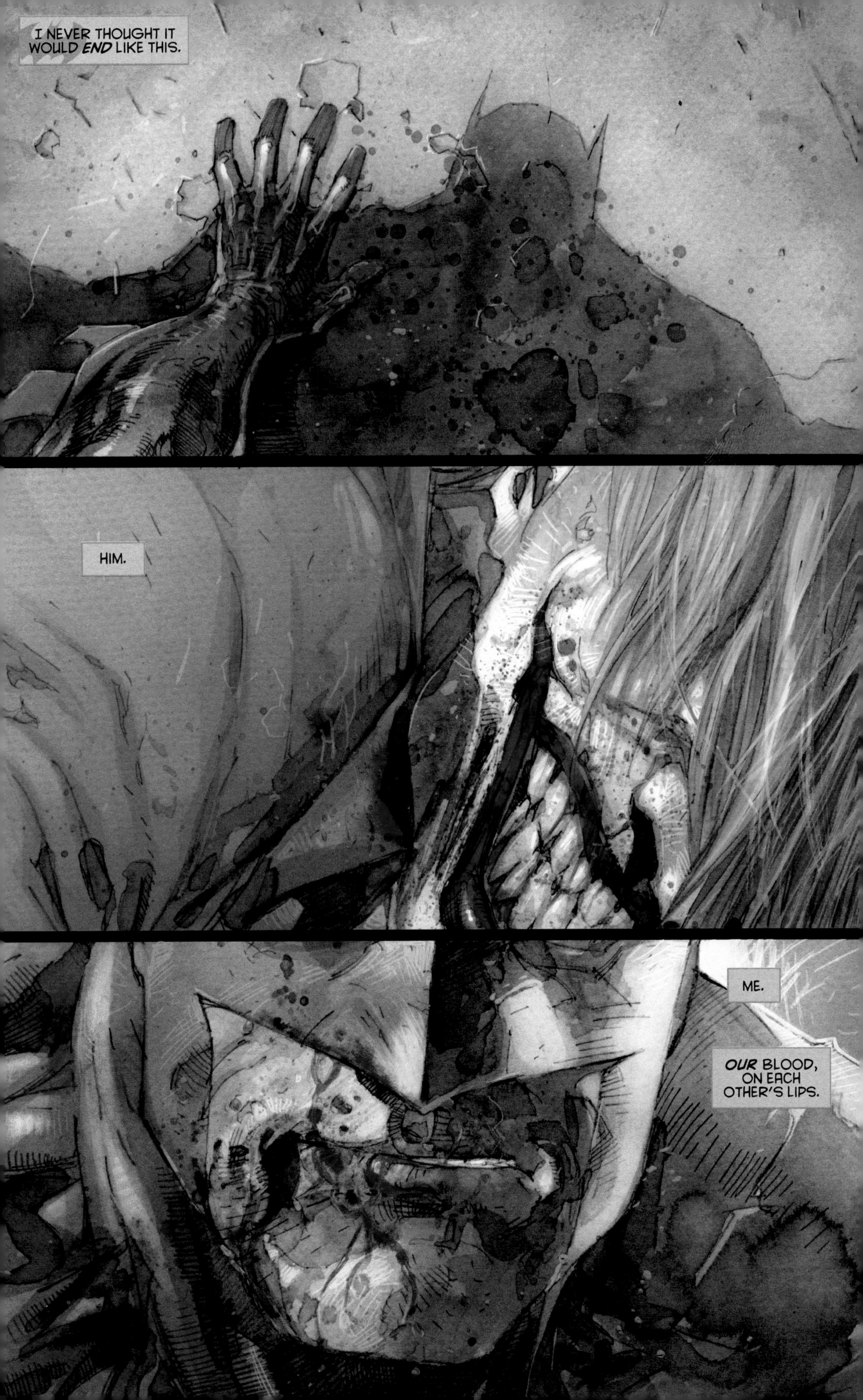
I NEVER THOUGHT IT WOULD END LIKE THIS.
HIM.
ME.
OUR BLOOD, ON EACH OTHER'S LIPS.

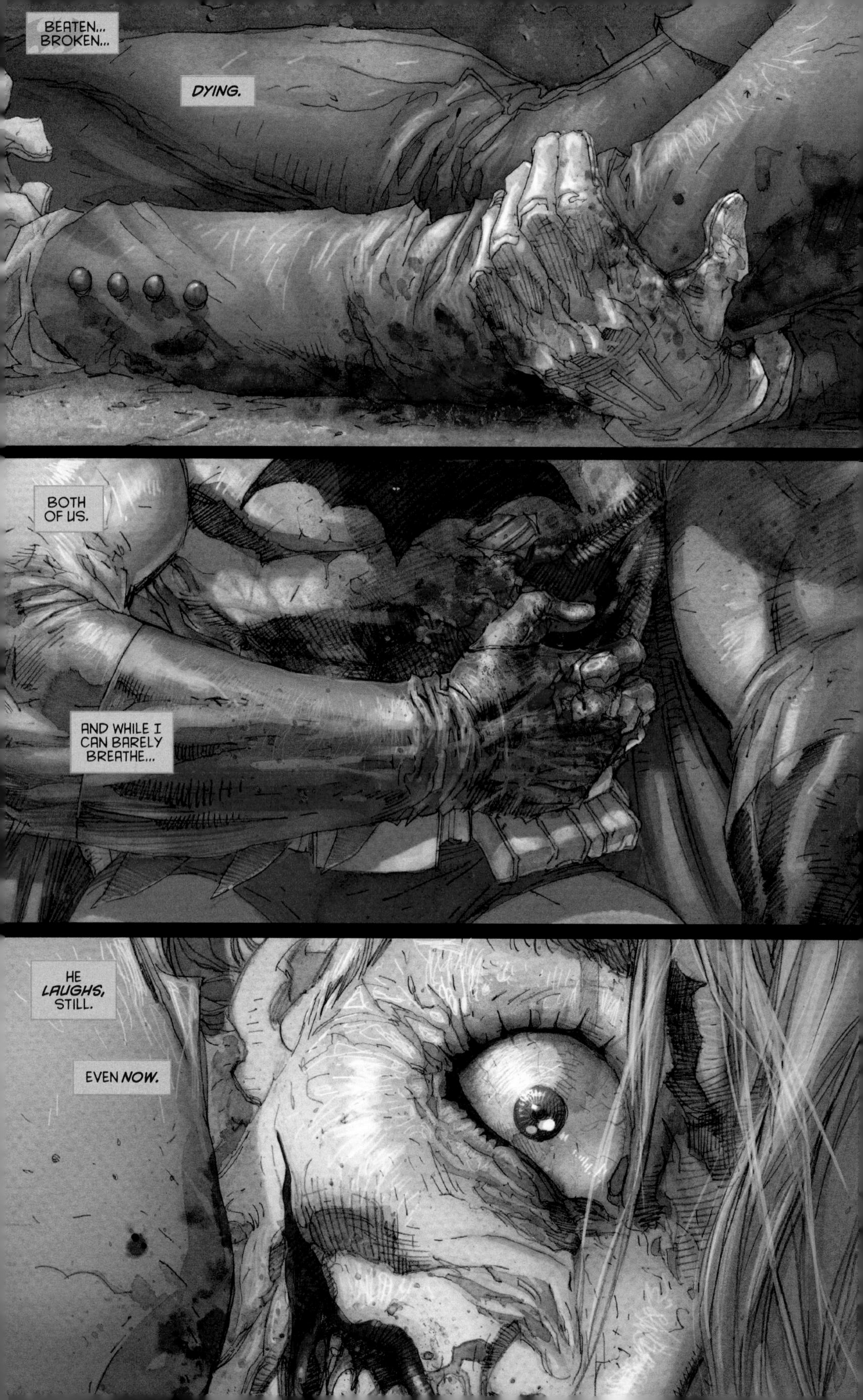
BEATEN... BROKEN...
DYING.
BOTH OF US.
AND WHILE I CAN BARELY BREATHE...
HE *LAUGHS,* STILL.
EVEN *NOW.*

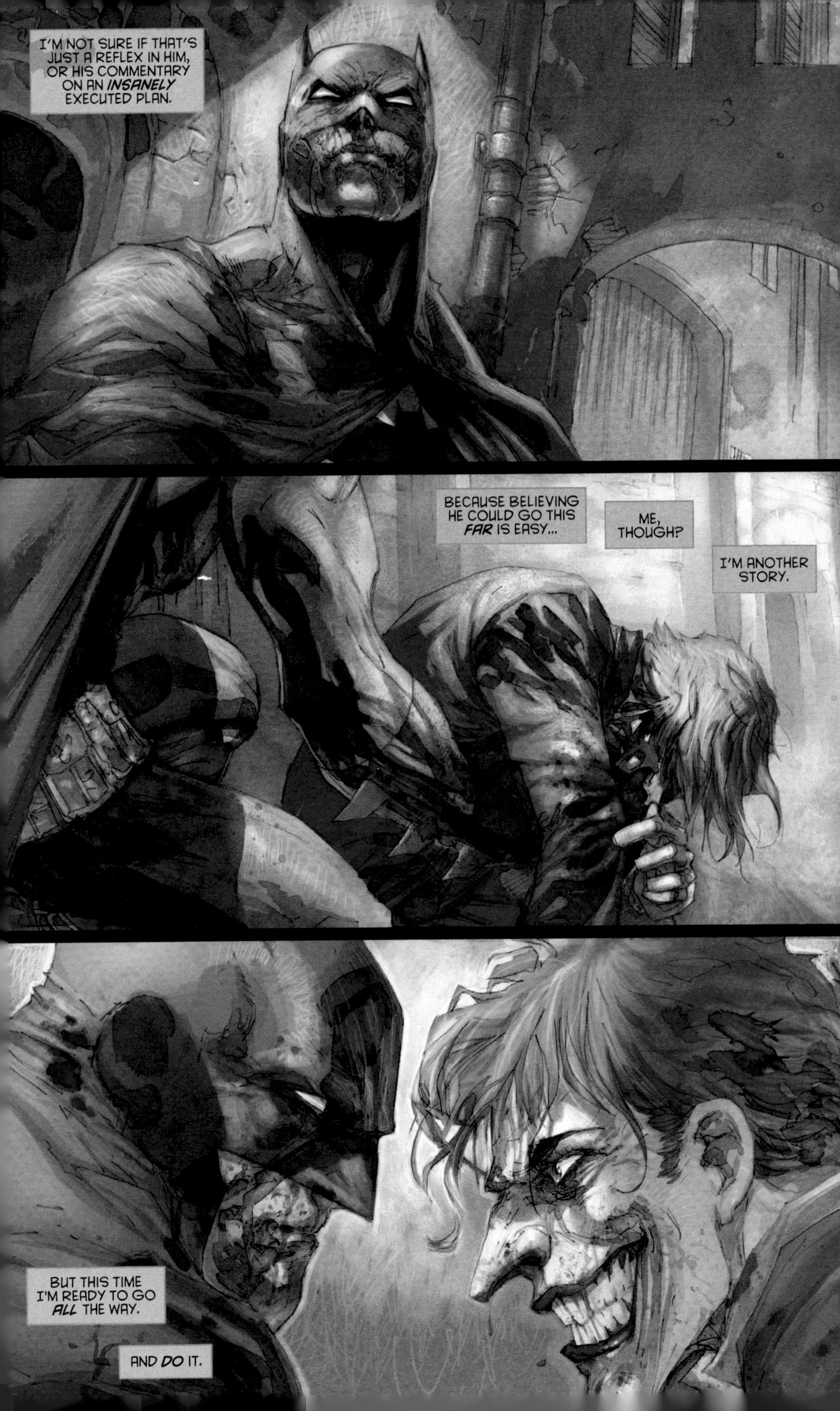
I'M NOT SURE IF THAT'S JUST A REFLEX IN HIM, OR HIS COMMENTARY ON AN *INSANELY* EXECUTED PLAN.
BECAUSE BELIEVING HE COULD GO THIS *FAR* IS EASY...
ME, THOUGH?
I'M ANOTHER STORY.
BUT THIS TIME I'M READY TO GO *ALL* THE WAY.
AND *DO* IT.

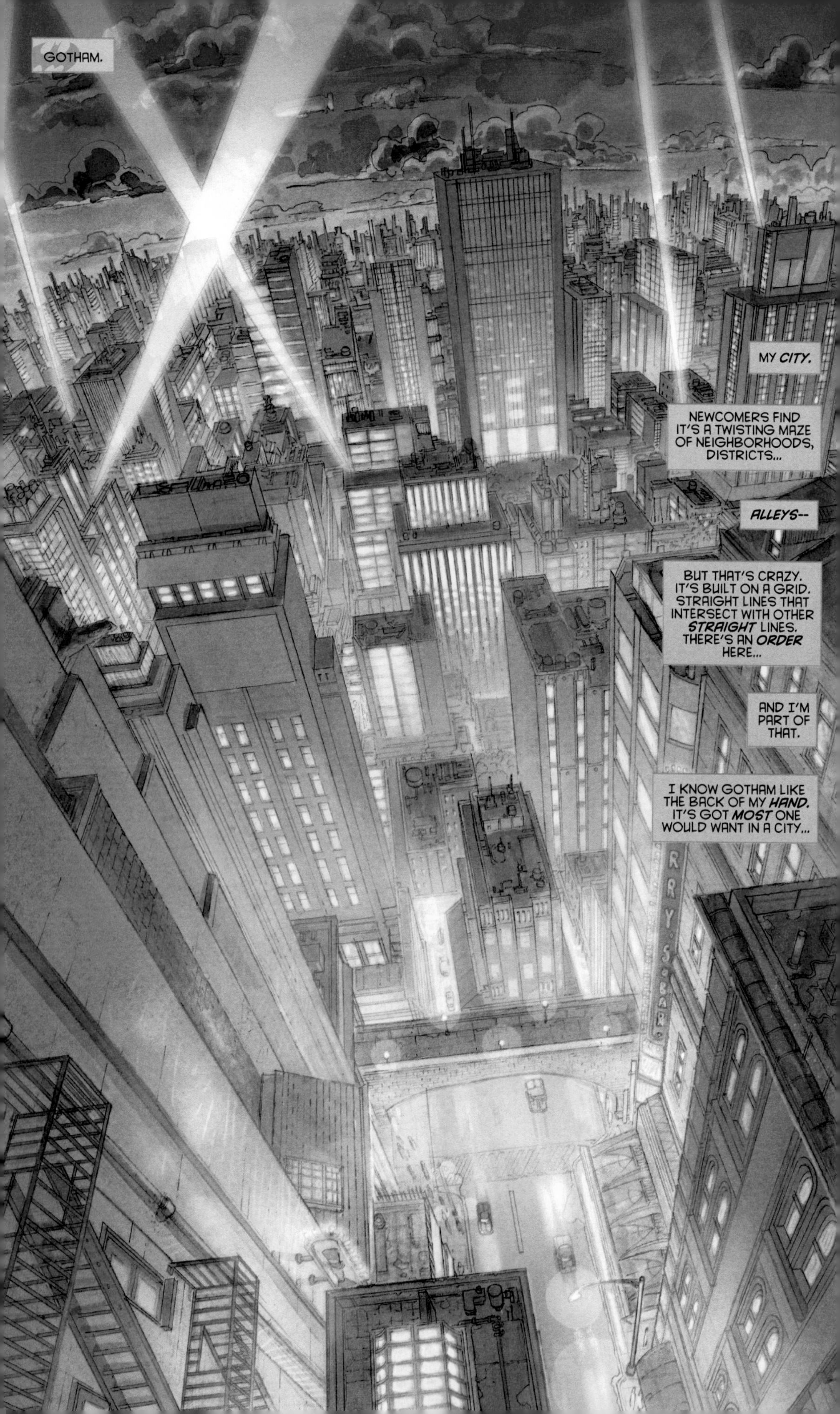
GOTHAM.
MY *CITY.*
NEWCOMERS FIND IT'S A TWISTING MAZE OF NEIGHBORHOODS, DISTRICTS...
ALLEYS--
BUT THAT'S CRAZY. IT'S BUILT ON A GRID. STRAIGHT LINES THAT INTERSECT WITH OTHER *STRAIGHT* LINES. THERE'S AN *ORDER* HERE...
AND I'M PART OF THAT.
I KNOW GOTHAM LIKE THE BACK OF MY *HAND.* IT'S GOT *MOST* ONE WOULD WANT IN A CITY...

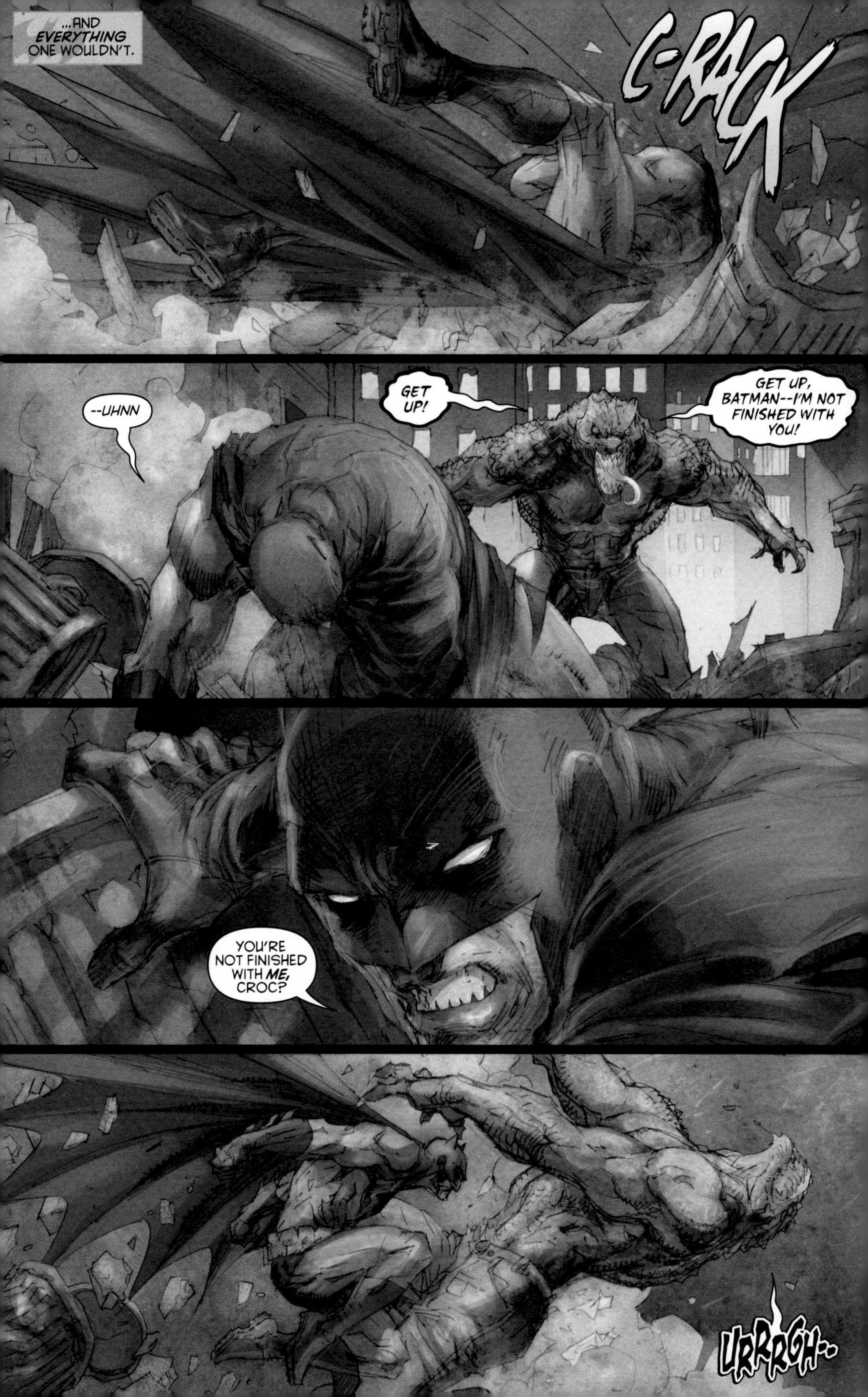
...AND EVERYTHING ONE WOULDN'T.
C-RACK
--UHNN
GET UP!
GET UP, BATMAN--I'M NOT FINISHED WITH YOU!
YOU'RE NOT FINISHED WITH ME, CROC?
URRRGH..

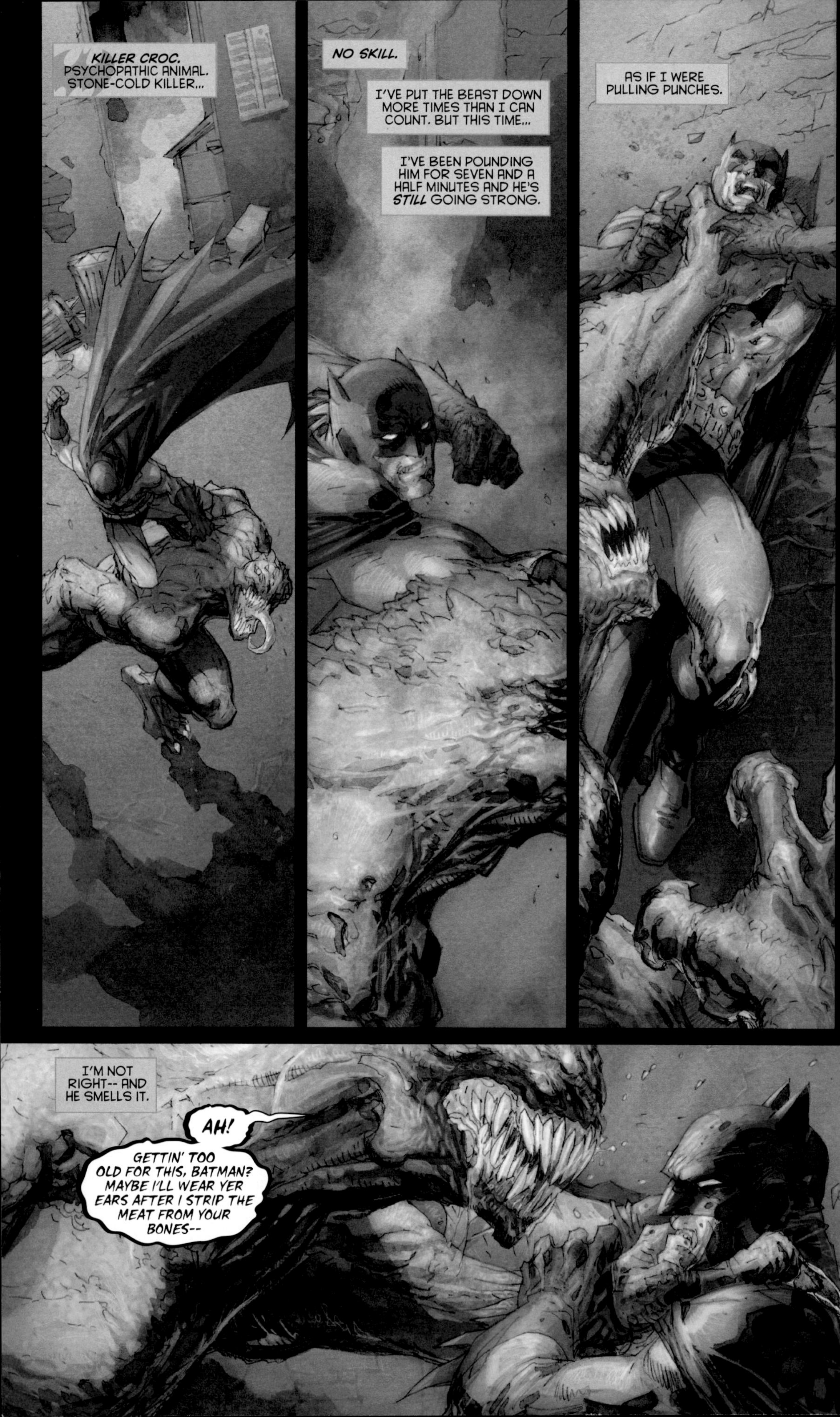
KILLER CROC. PSYCHOPATHIC ANIMAL. STONE-COLD KILLER...
NO SKILL.
I'VE PUT THE BEAST DOWN MORE TIMES THAN I CAN COUNT. BUT THIS TIME...
I'VE BEEN POUNDING HIM FOR SEVEN AND A HALF MINUTES AND HE'S STILL GOING STRONG.
AS IF I WERE PULLING PUNCHES.
I'M NOT RIGHT-- AND HE SMELLS IT.
AH!
GETTIN' TOO OLD FOR THIS, BATMAN? MAYBE I'LL WEAR YER EARS AFTER I STRIP THE MEAT FROM YOUR BONES--

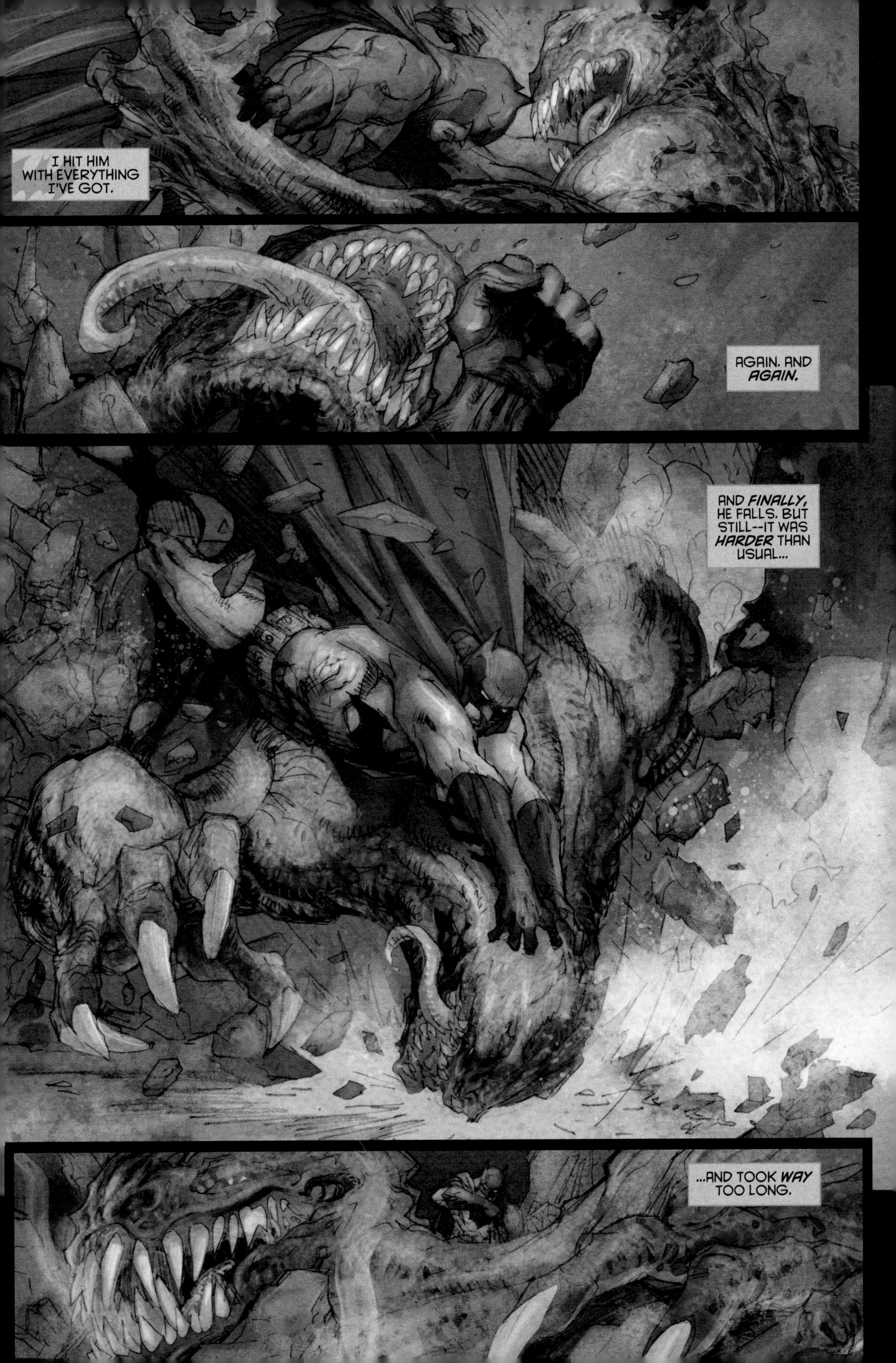
I HIT HIM WITH EVERYTHING I'VE GOT.
AGAIN. AND AGAIN.
AND FINALLY, HE FALLS. BUT STILL--IT WAS HARDER THAN USUAL...
...AND TOOK WAY TOO LONG.

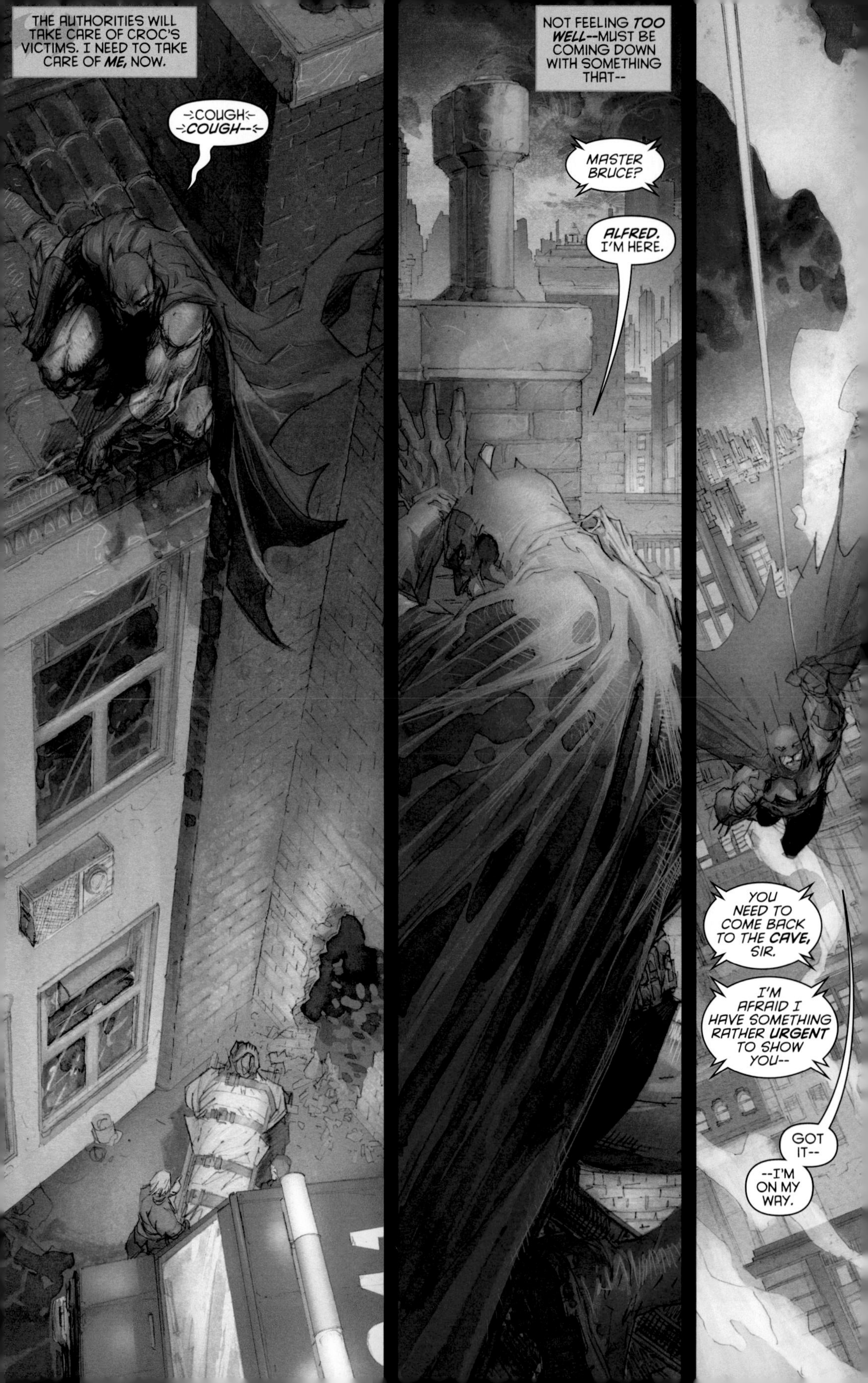
THE AUTHORITIES WILL TAKE CARE OF CROC'S VICTIMS. I NEED TO TAKE CARE OF ME, NOW.
COUGH COUGH--
NOT FEELING TOO WELL--MUST BE COMING DOWN WITH SOMETHING THAT--
MASTER BRUCE?
ALFRED. I'M HERE.
YOU NEED TO COME BACK TO THE CAVE, SIR.
I'M AFRAID I HAVE SOMETHING RATHER URGENT TO SHOW YOU--
GOT IT--
--I'M ON MY WAY.

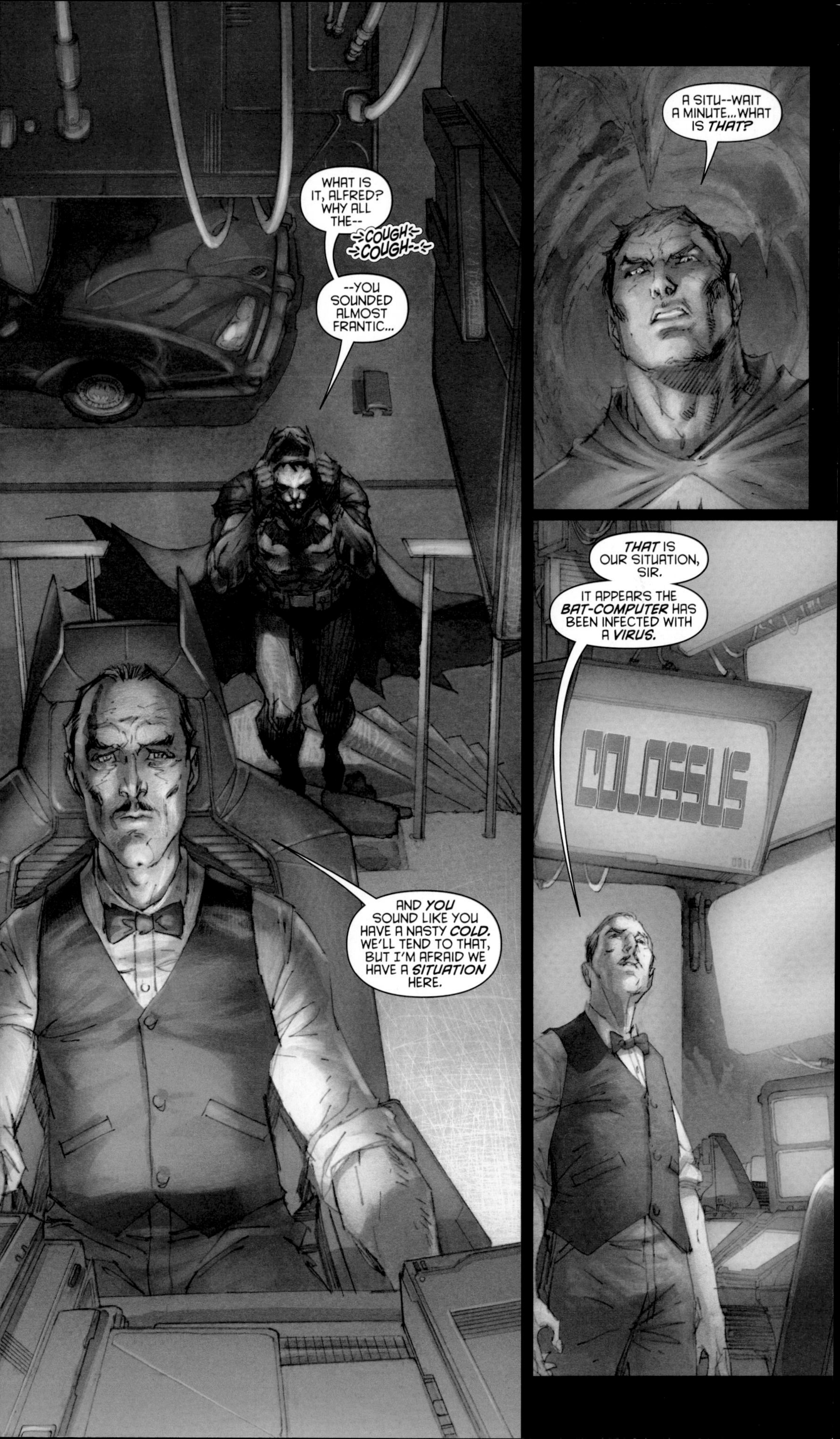
WHAT IS IT, ALFRED? WHY ALL THE--
COUGH COUGH
--YOU SOUNDED ALMOST FRANTIC...
AND *YOU* SOUND LIKE YOU HAVE A NASTY *COLD.* WE'LL TEND TO THAT, BUT I'M AFRAID WE HAVE A *SITUATION* HERE.
A SITU--WAIT A MINUTE...WHAT IS *THAT?*
THAT IS OUR SITUATION, SIR.
IT APPEARS THE *BAT-COMPUTER* HAS BEEN INFECTED WITH A *VIRUS.*
COLOSSUS

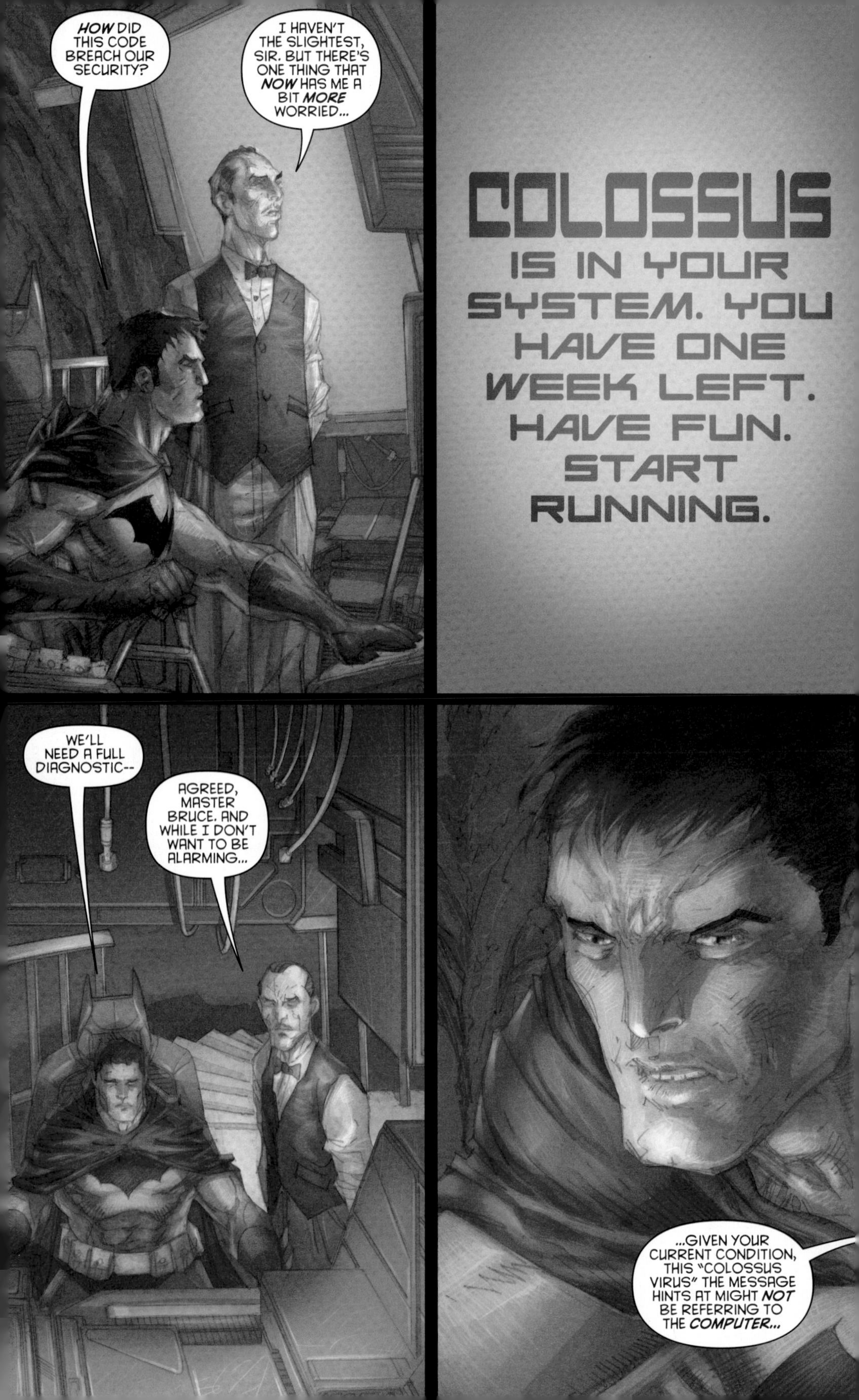
HOW DID THIS CODE BREACH OUR SECURITY?
I HAVEN'T THE SLIGHTEST, SIR. BUT THERE'S ONE THING THAT NOW HAS ME A BIT MORE WORRIED...
COLOSSUS IS IN YOUR SYSTEM. YOU HAVE ONE WEEK LEFT. HAVE FUN. START RUNNING.
WE'LL NEED A FULL DIAGNOSTIC--
AGREED, MASTER BRUCE. AND WHILE I DON'T WANT TO BE ALARMING...
...GIVEN YOUR CURRENT CONDITION, THIS "COLOSSUS VIRUS" THE MESSAGE HINTS AT MIGHT NOT BE REFERRING TO THE COMPUTER...

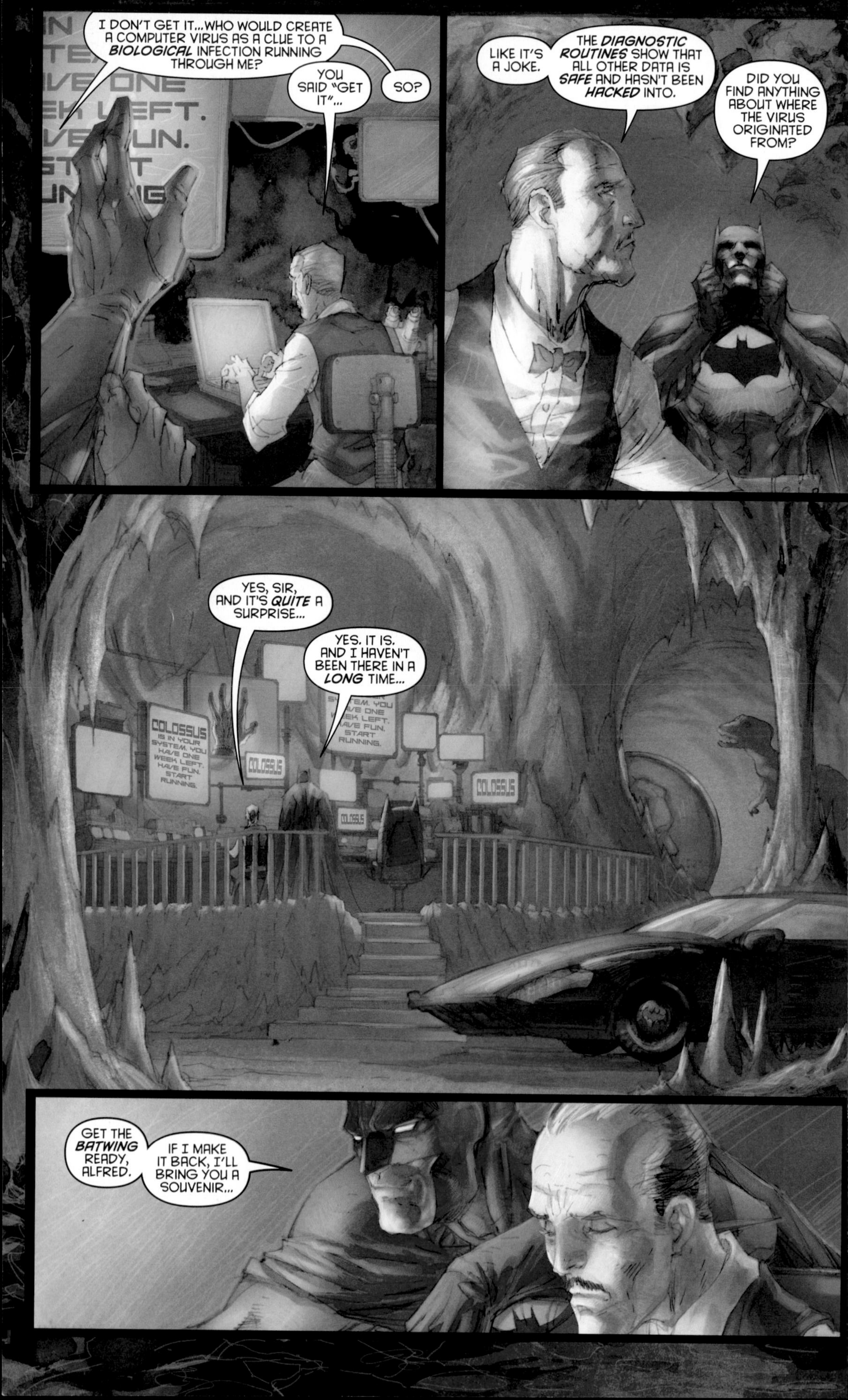

I DON'T GET IT...WHO WOULD CREATE A COMPUTER VIRUS AS A CLUE TO A *BIOLOGICAL* INFECTION RUNNING THROUGH ME?
YOU SAID "GET IT"...
SO?
LIKE IT'S A JOKE.
THE *DIAGNOSTIC ROUTINES* SHOW THAT ALL OTHER DATA IS *SAFE* AND HASN'T BEEN *HACKED* INTO.
DID YOU FIND ANYTHING ABOUT WHERE THE VIRUS ORIGINATED FROM?
YES, SIR, AND IT'S *QUITE* A SURPRISE...
YES. IT IS. AND I HAVEN'T BEEN THERE IN A *LONG* TIME...
COLOSSUS IS IN YOUR SYSTEM. YOU HAVE ONE WEEK LEFT. HAVE FUN. START RUNNING.
COLOSSUS
COLOSSUS
GET THE *BATWING* READY, ALFRED.
IF I MAKE IT BACK, I'LL BRING YOU A SOUVENIR...

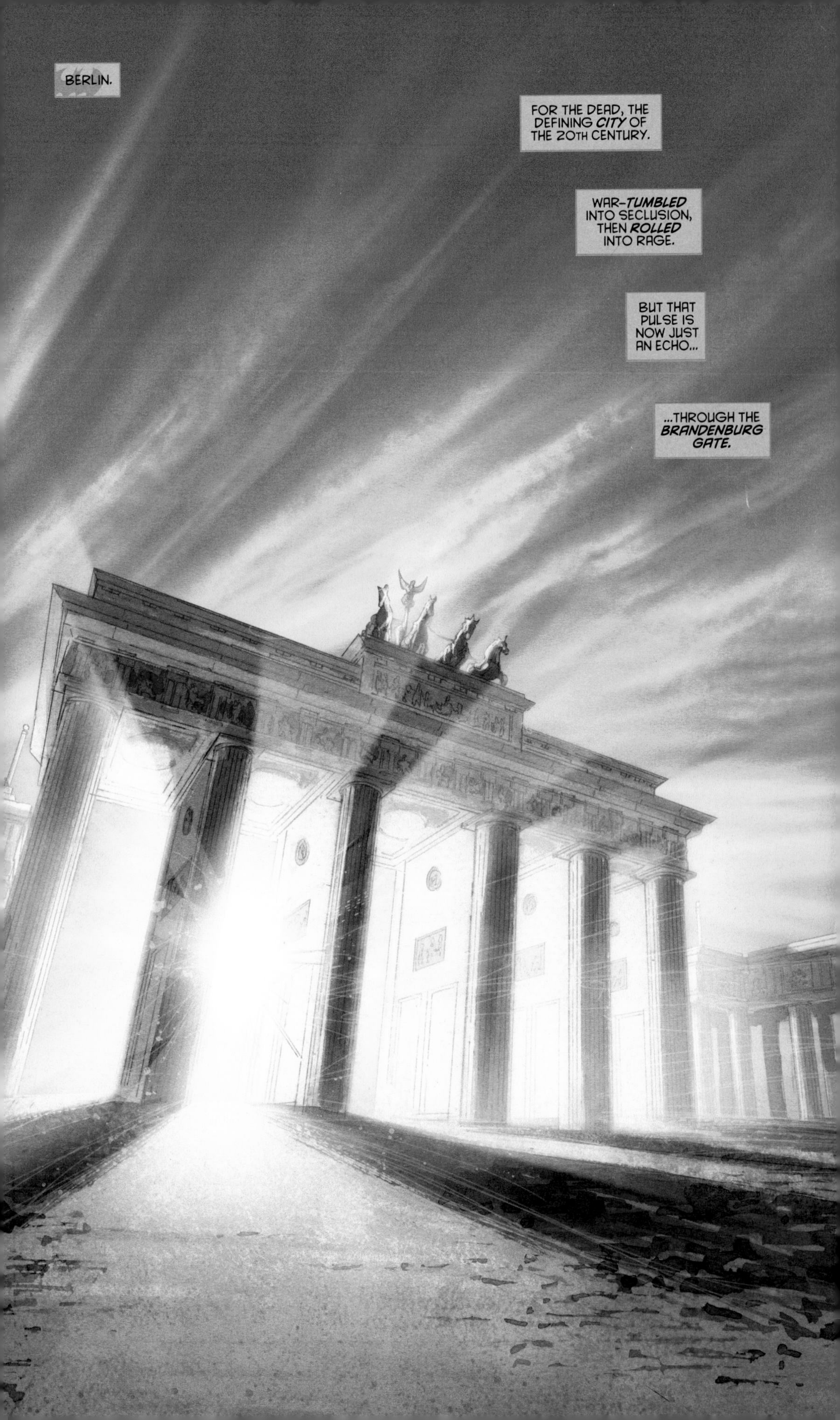
BERLIN.
FOR THE DEAD, THE DEFINING CITY OF THE 20TH CENTURY.
WAR-TUMBLED INTO SECLUSION, THEN ROLLED INTO RAGE.
BUT THAT PULSE IS NOW JUST AN ECHO...
...THROUGH THE BRANDENBURG GATE.

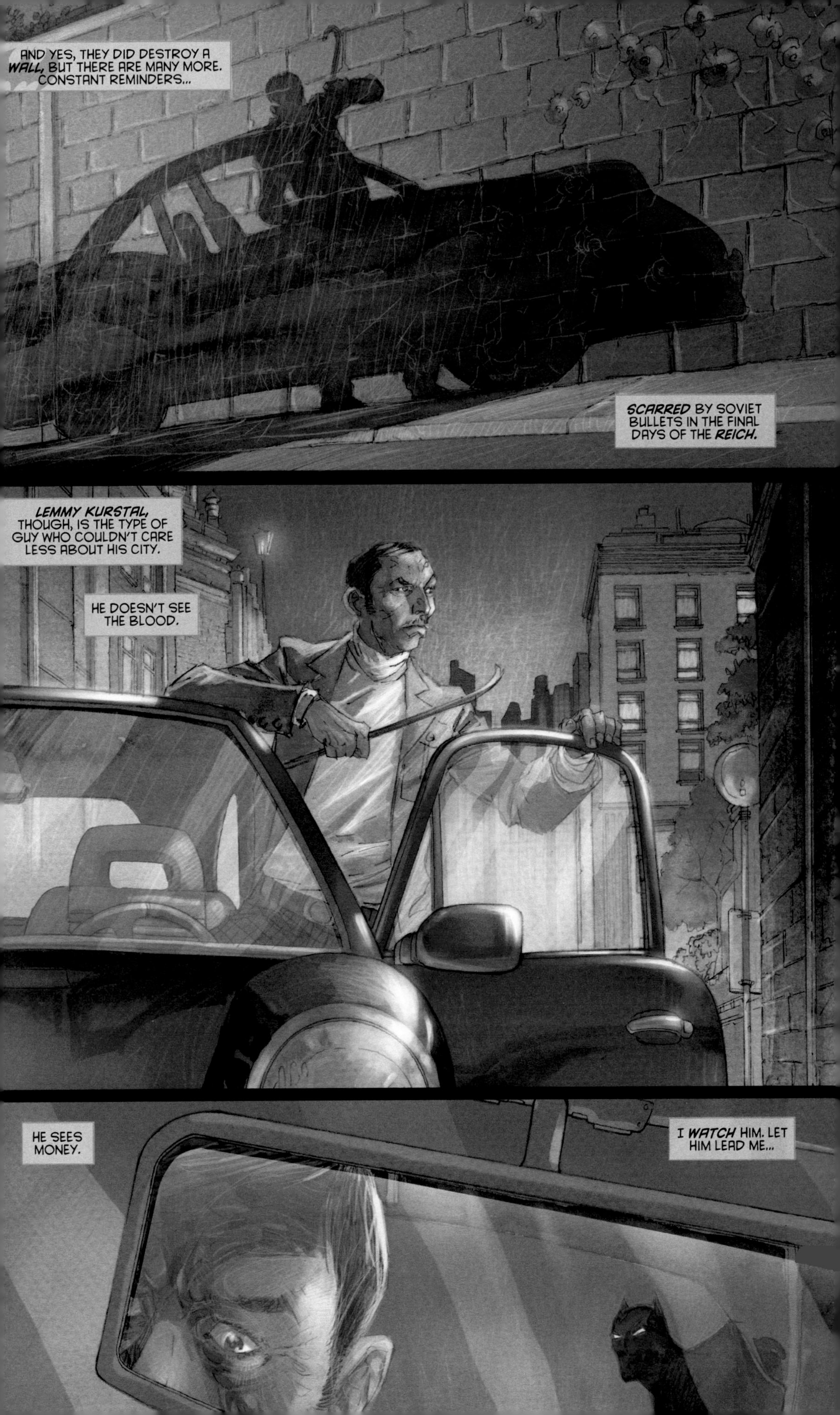
AND YES, THEY DID DESTROY A *WALL*, BUT THERE ARE MANY MORE. CONSTANT REMINDERS...
SCARRED BY SOVIET BULLETS IN THE FINAL DAYS OF THE *REICH.*
LEMMY KURSTAL, THOUGH, IS THE TYPE OF GUY WHO COULDN'T CARE LESS ABOUT HIS CITY.
HE DOESN'T SEE THE BLOOD.
HE SEES MONEY.
I *WATCH* HIM. LET HIM LEAD ME...

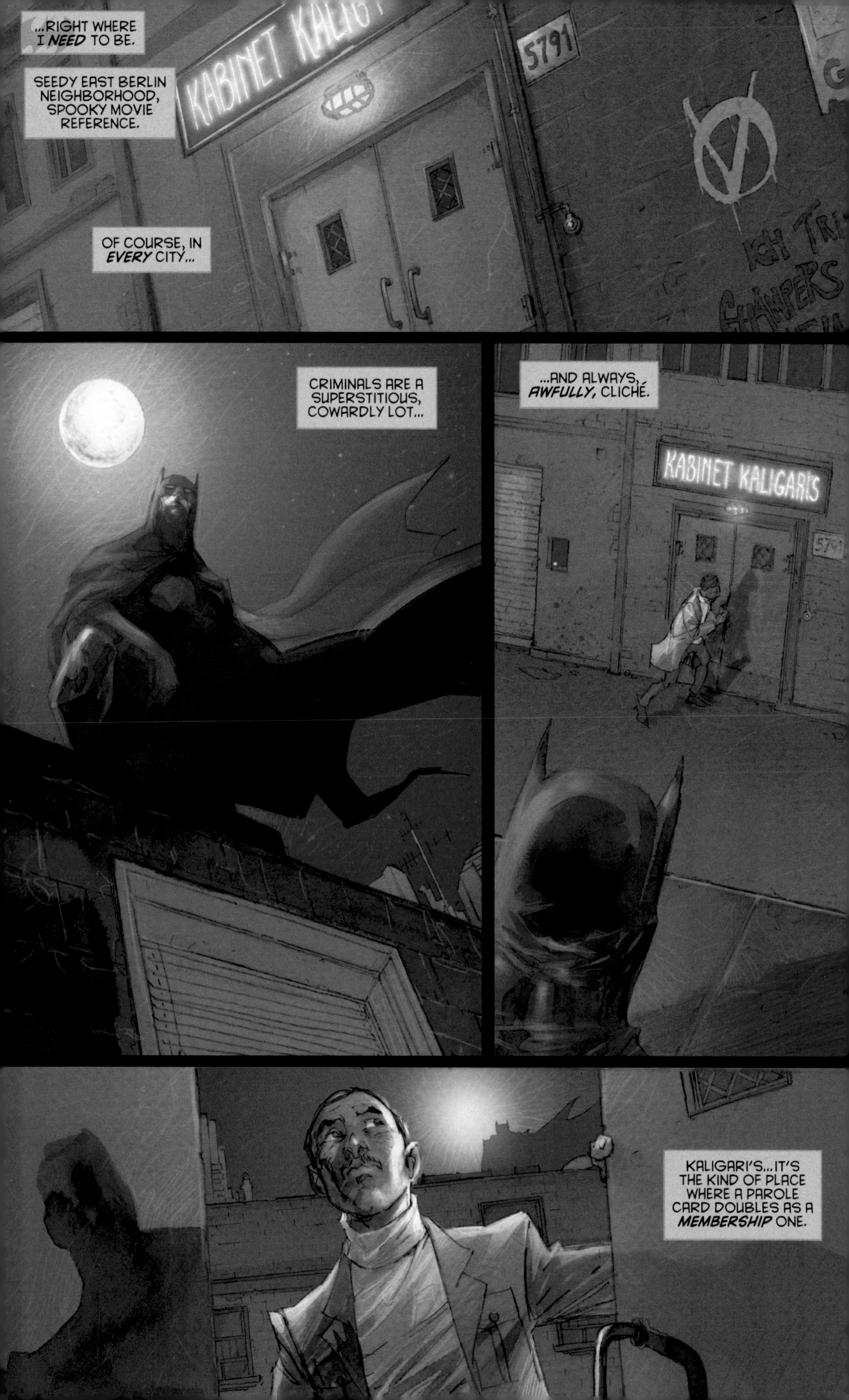
...RIGHT WHERE I *NEED* TO BE.
KABINET KALIG
5791
SEEDY EAST BERLIN NEIGHBORHOOD, SPOOKY MOVIE REFERENCE.
OF COURSE, IN *EVERY* CITY...
CRIMINALS ARE A SUPERSTITIOUS, COWARDLY LOT...
...AND ALWAYS, *AWFULLY,* CLICHÉ.
KABINET KALIGARIS
5791
KALIGARI'S...IT'S THE KIND OF PLACE WHERE A PAROLE CARD DOUBLES AS A *MEMBERSHIP* ONE.

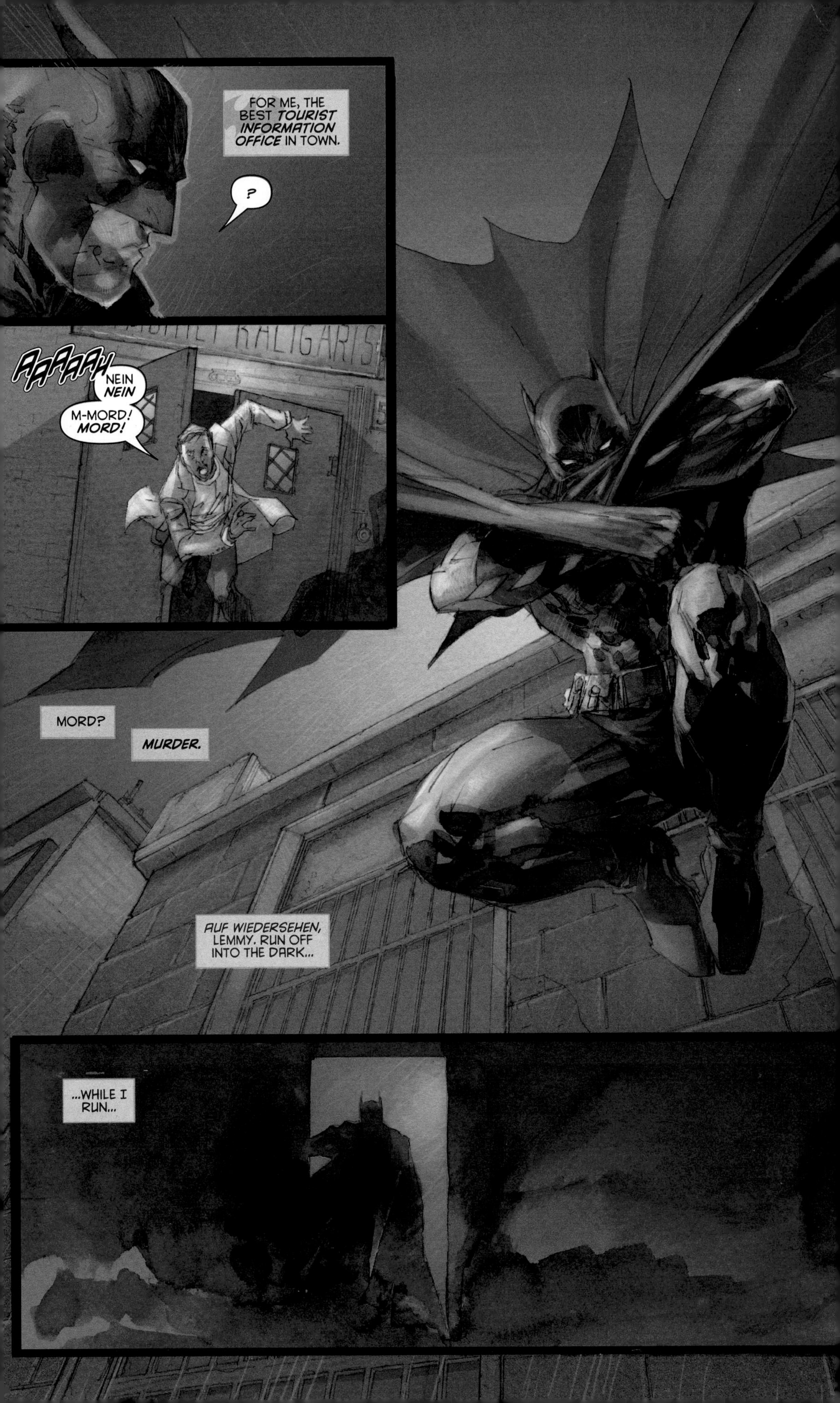

FOR ME, THE BEST TOURIST INFORMATION OFFICE IN TOWN.
?
AAAAAH
NEIN NEIN
M-MORD! MORD!
MORD?
MURDER.
AUF WIEDERSEHEN, LEMMY. RUN OFF INTO THE DARK...
...WHILE I RUN...

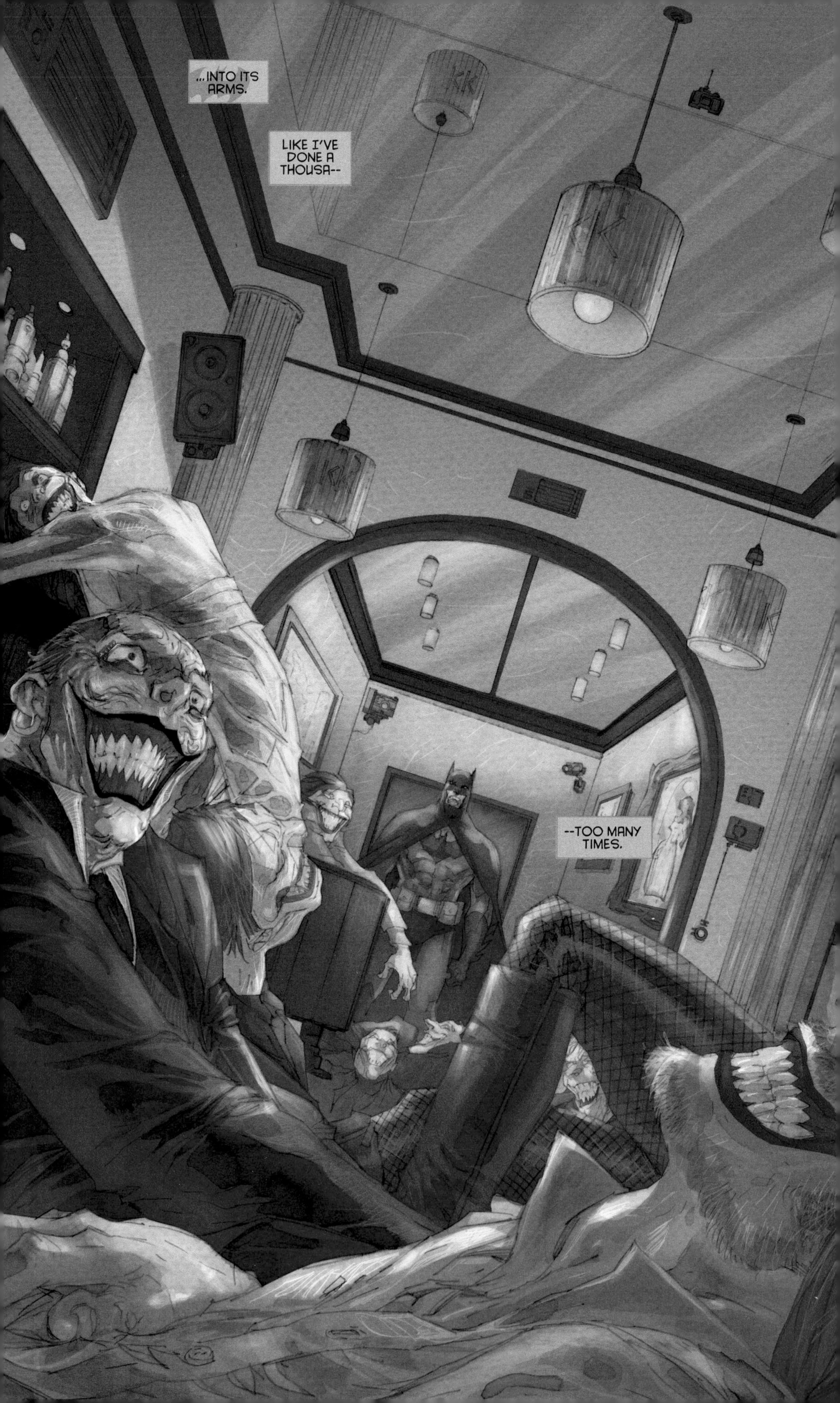
...INTO ITS ARMS.
LIKE I'VE DONE A THOUSA--
--TOO MANY TIMES.

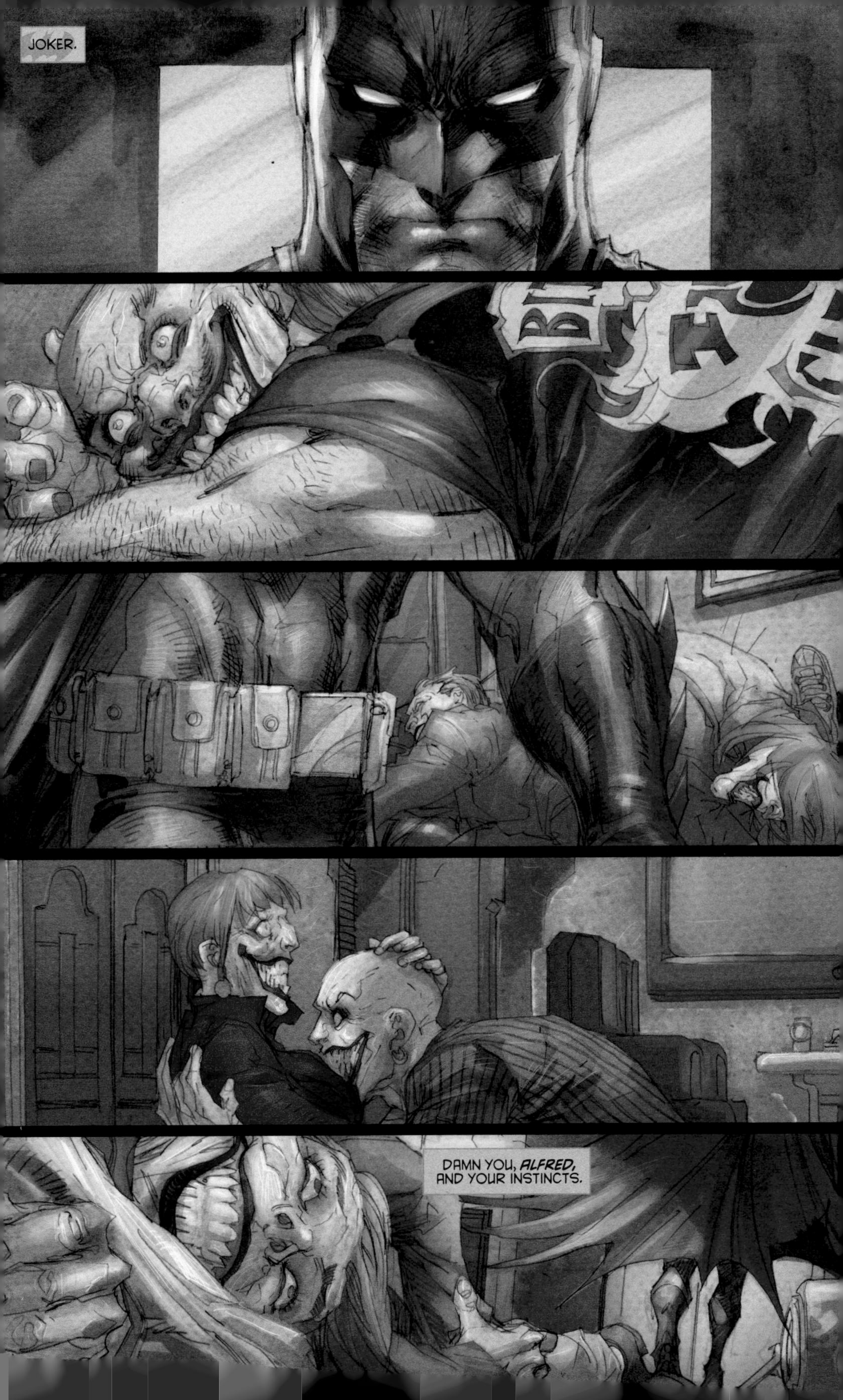
JOKER.
DAMN YOU, ALFRED, AND YOUR INSTINCTS.

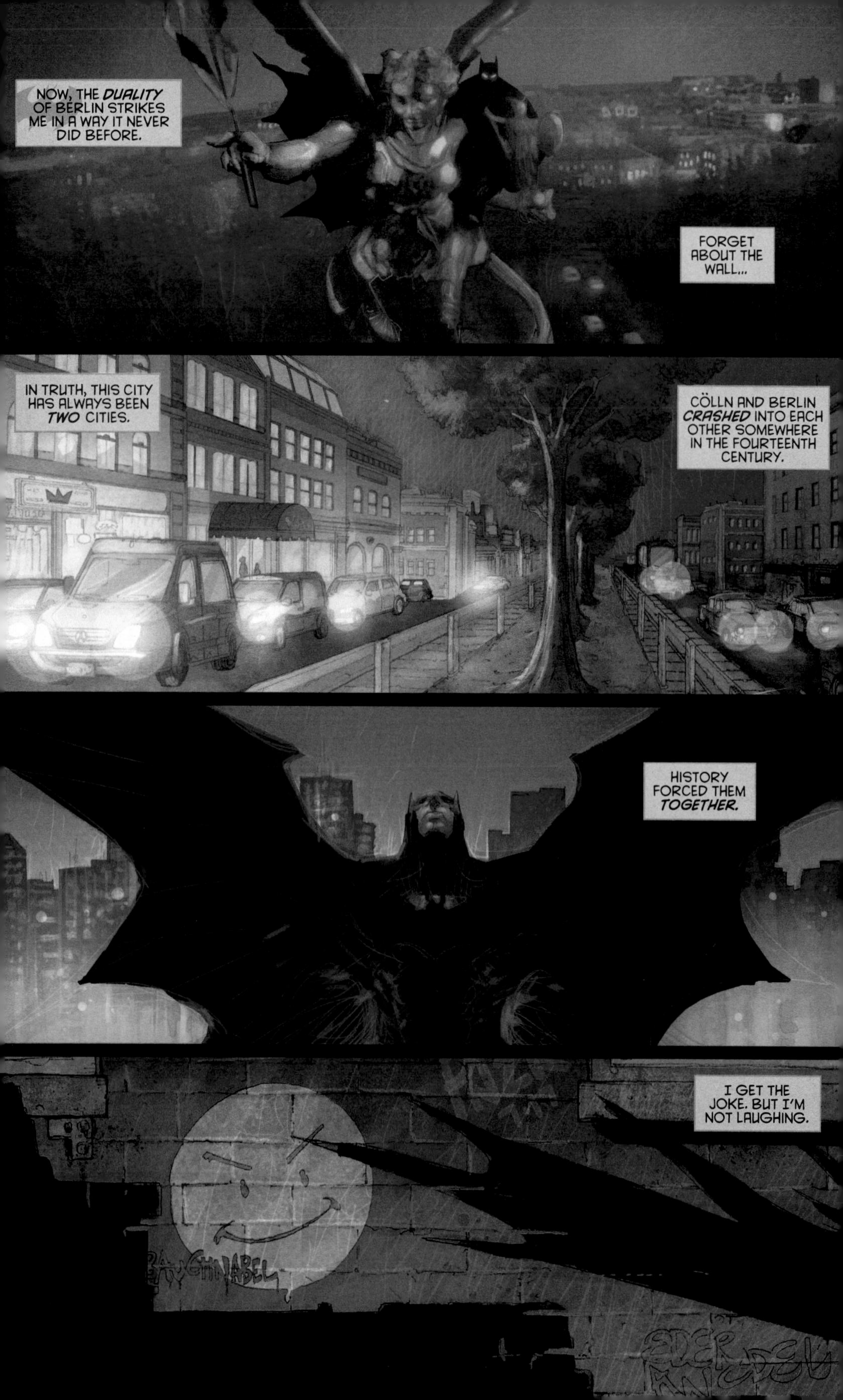
NOW, THE *DUALITY* OF BERLIN STRIKES ME IN A WAY IT NEVER DID BEFORE.
FORGET ABOUT THE WALL...
IN TRUTH, THIS CITY HAS ALWAYS BEEN *TWO* CITIES.
CÖLLN AND BERLIN *CRASHED* INTO EACH OTHER SOMEWHERE IN THE FOURTEENTH CENTURY.
HISTORY FORCED THEM *TOGETHER.*
I GET THE JOKE. BUT I'M NOT LAUGHING.

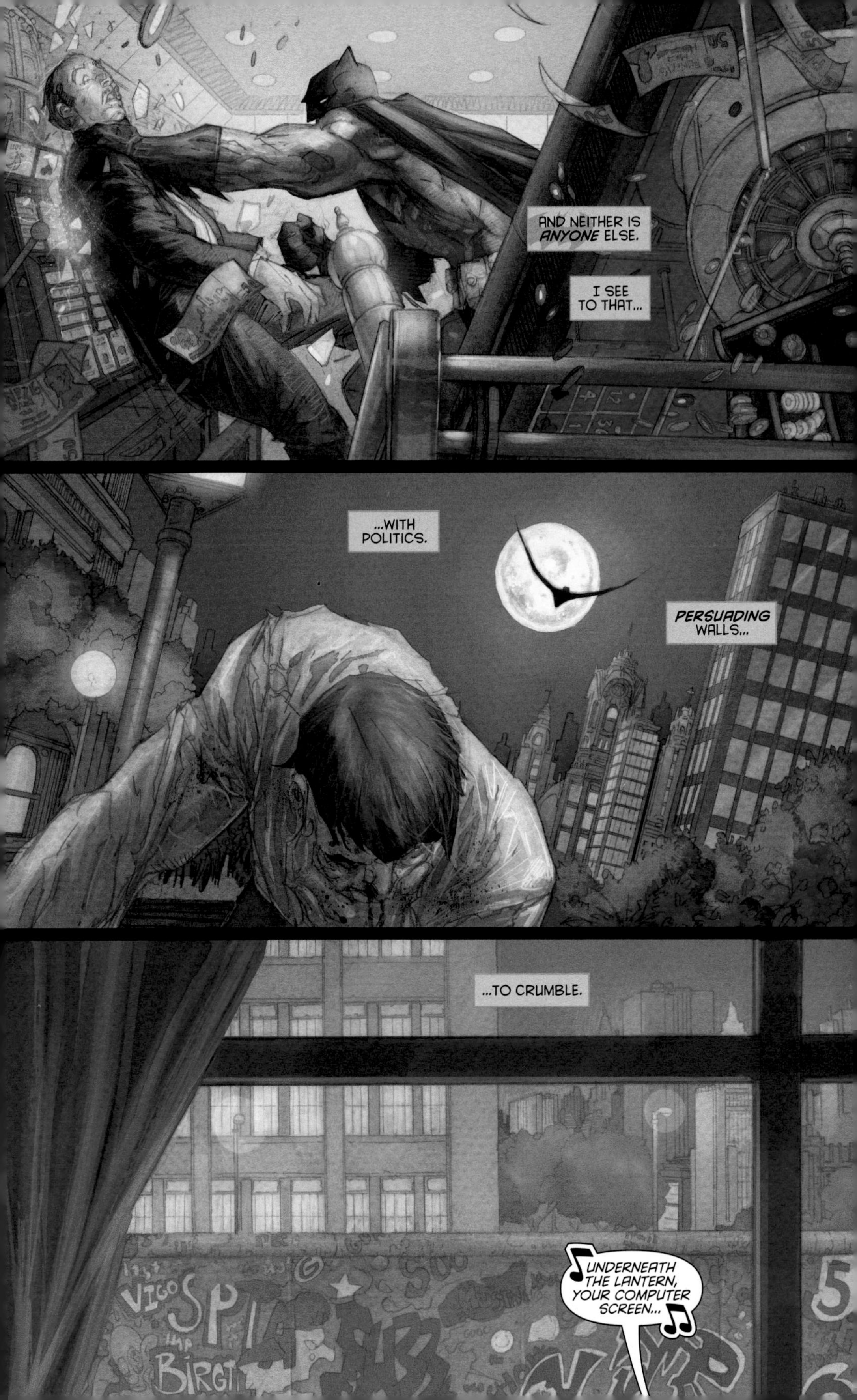
AND NEITHER IS ANYONE ELSE.
I SEE TO THAT...
...WITH POLITICS.
PERSUADING WALLS...
...TO CRUMBLE.
UNDERNEATH THE LANTERN, YOUR COMPUTER SCREEN...

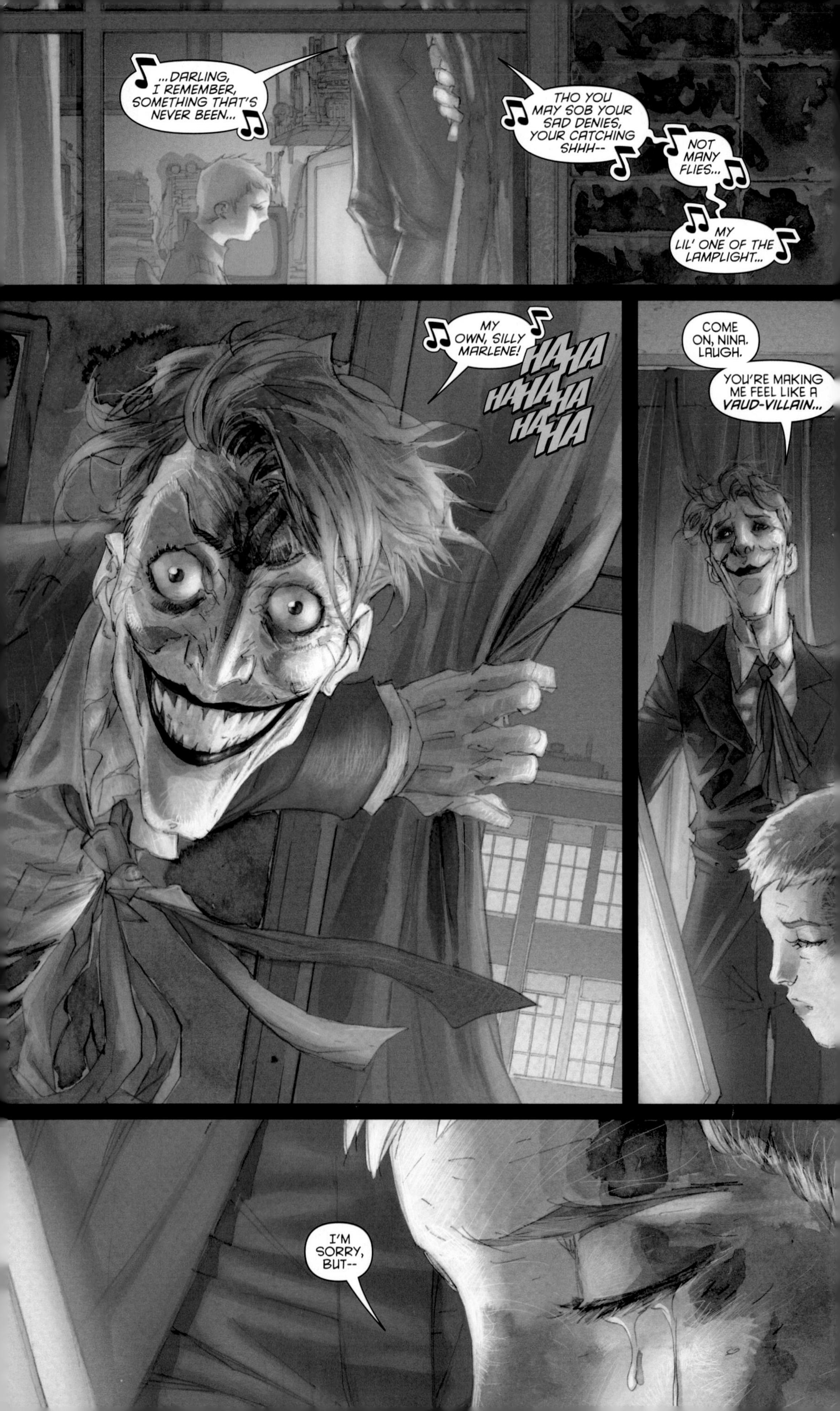
...DARLING, I REMEMBER, SOMETHING THAT'S NEVER BEEN...
THO YOU MAY SOB YOUR SAD DENIES, YOUR CATCHING SHHH--
NOT MANY FLIES...
MY LIL' ONE OF THE LAMPLIGHT...
MY OWN, SILLY MARLENE!
HAHA HAHAHA HAHA
COME ON, NINA. LAUGH.
YOU'RE MAKING ME FEEL LIKE A VAUD-VILLAIN...
I'M SORRY, BUT--

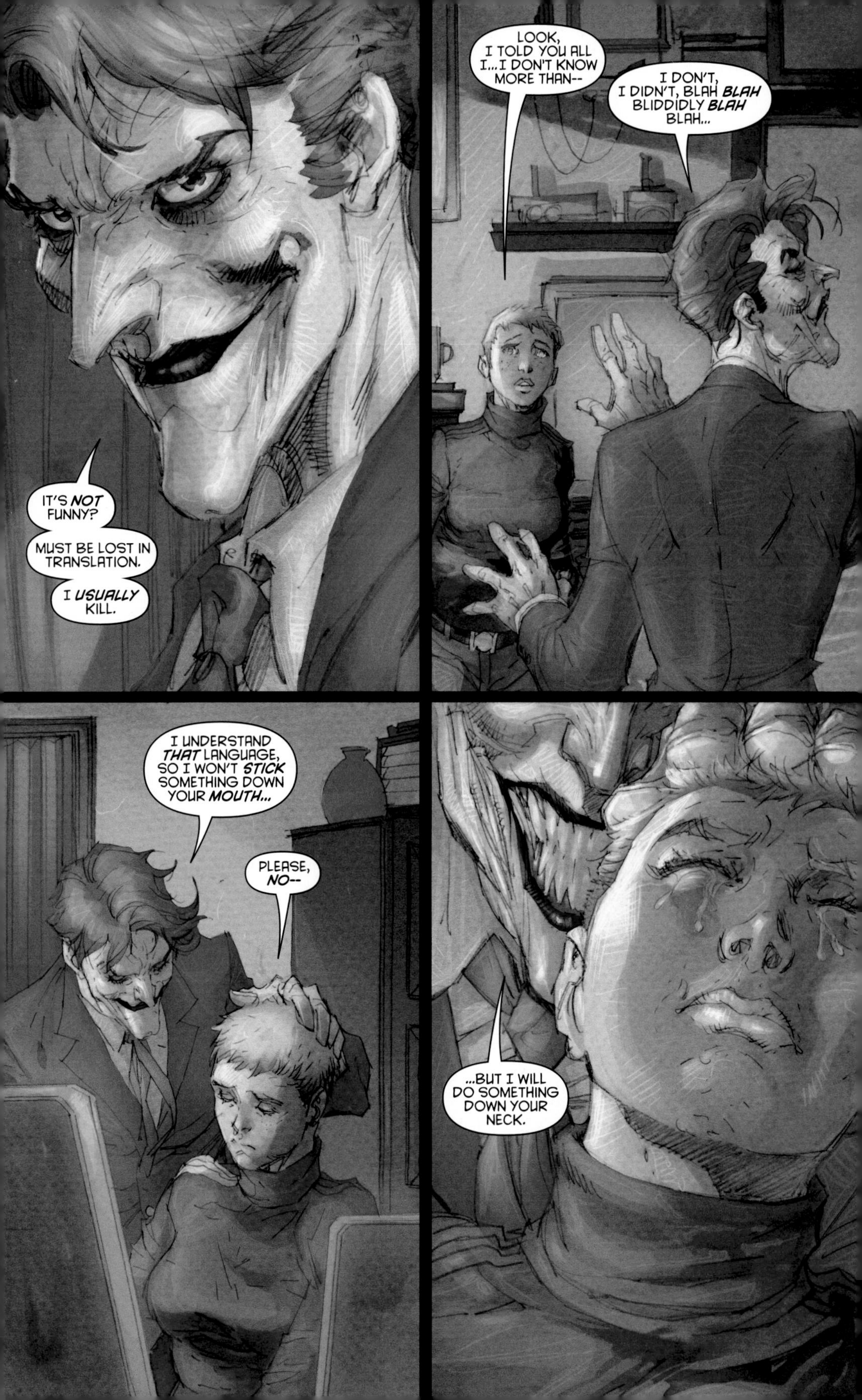
IT'S NOT FUNNY?
MUST BE LOST IN TRANSLATION.
I USUALLY KILL.
LOOK, I TOLD YOU ALL I...I DON'T KNOW MORE THAN--
I DON'T, I DIDN'T, BLAH BLAH BLIDDIDLY BLAH BLAH...
I UNDERSTAND THAT LANGUAGE, SO I WON'T STICK SOMETHING DOWN YOUR MOUTH...
PLEASE, NO--
...BUT I WILL DO SOMETHING DOWN YOUR NECK.

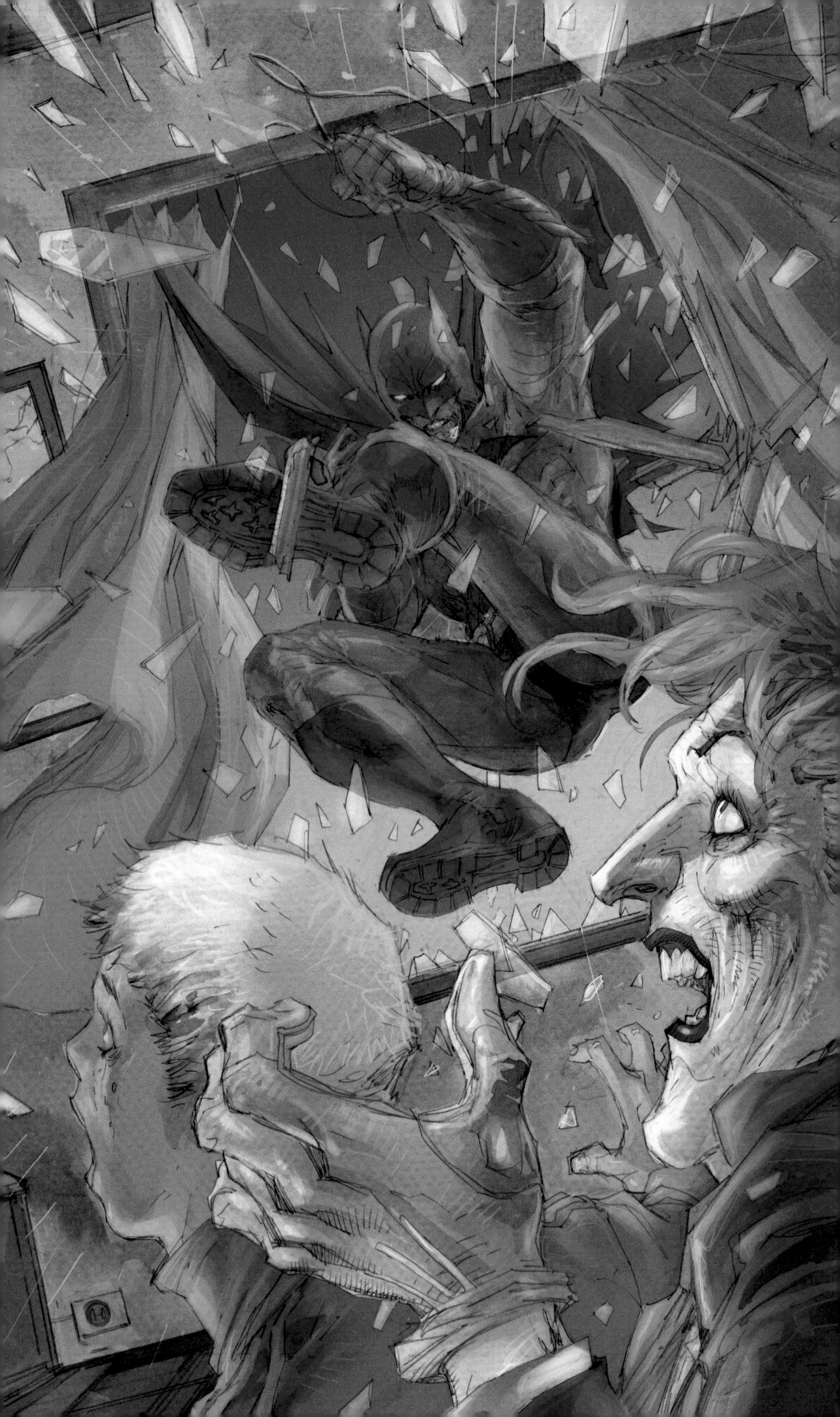

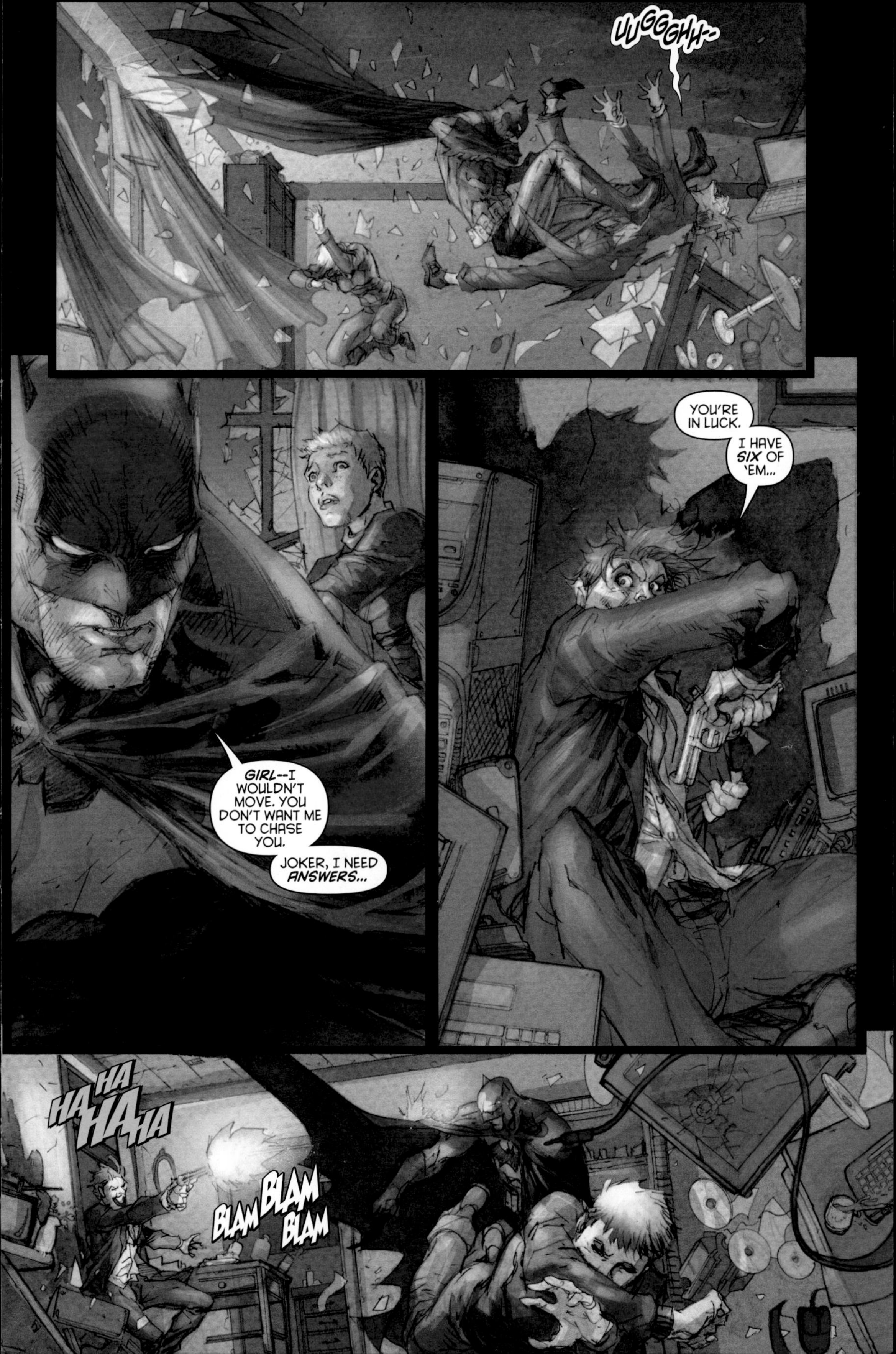

UUGGGHH--
GIRL--I WOULDN'T MOVE. YOU DON'T WANT ME TO CHASE YOU.
JOKER, I NEED ANSWERS...
YOU'RE IN LUCK.
I HAVE SIX OF 'EM...
HA HA HA HA
BLAM BLAM BLAM BLAM

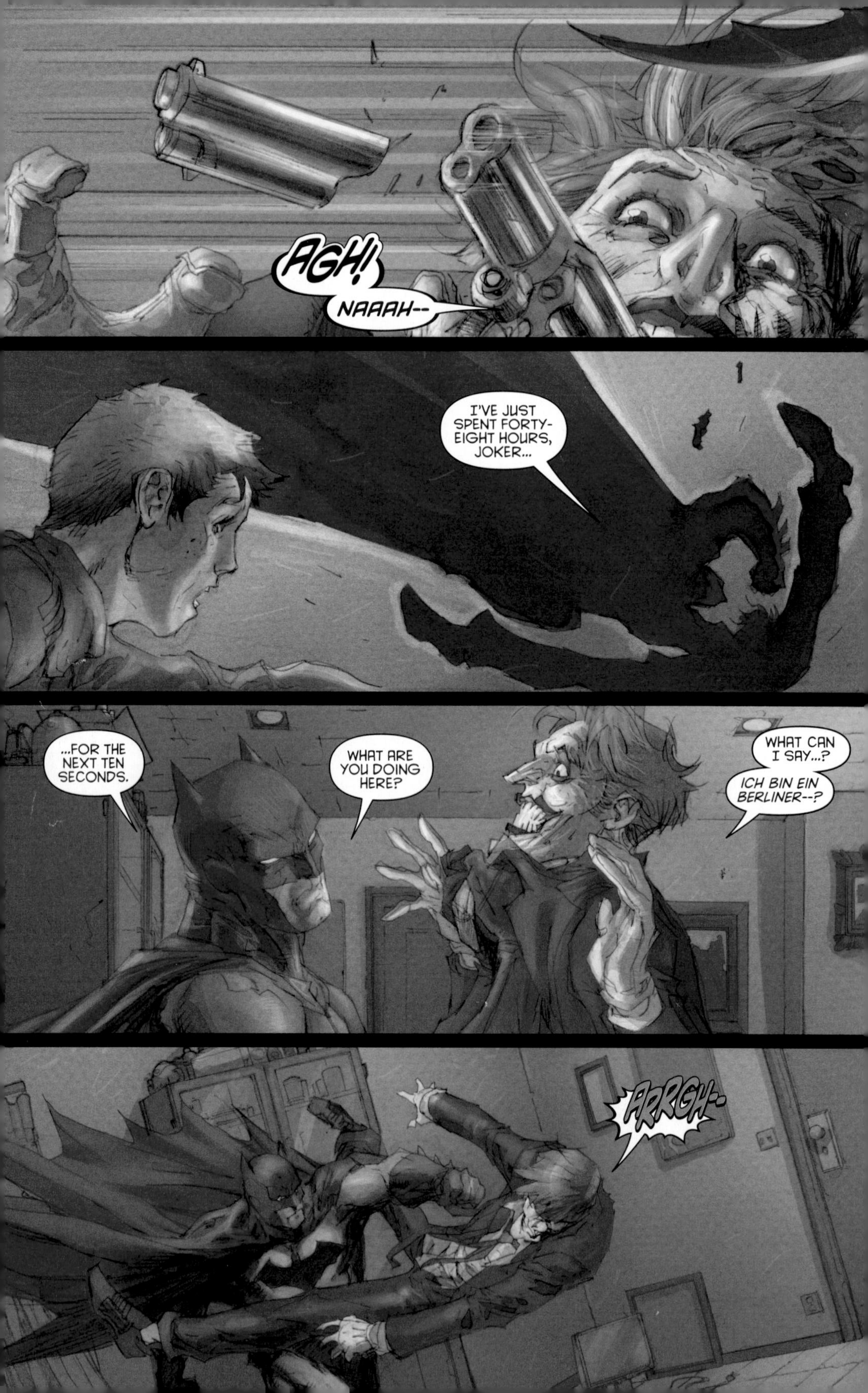
AGH!
NAAAH--
I'VE JUST SPENT FORTY-EIGHT HOURS, JOKER...
...FOR THE NEXT TEN SECONDS.
WHAT ARE YOU DOING HERE?
WHAT CAN I SAY...?
ICH BIN EIN BERLINER--?
ARRGH--

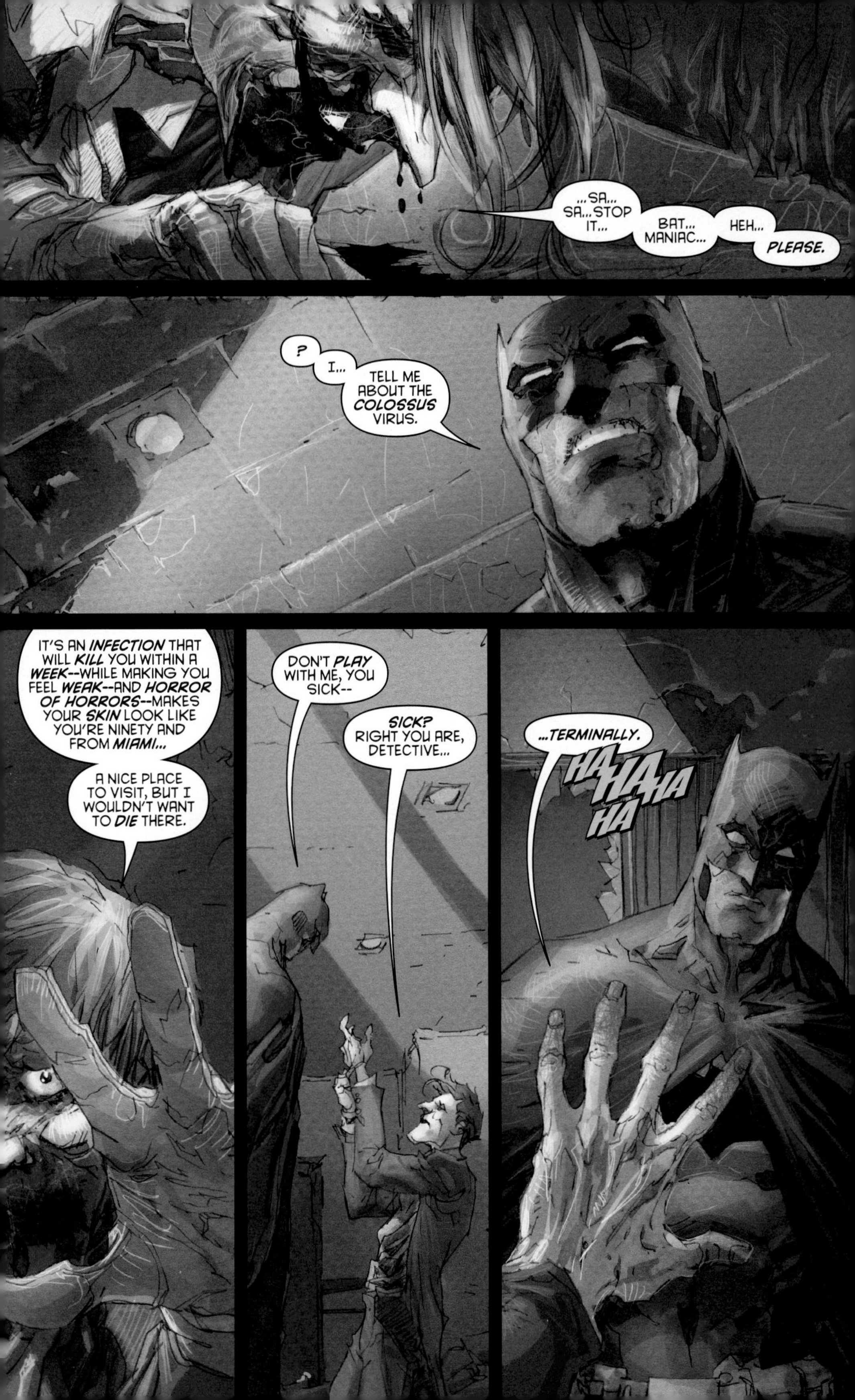
...SA... SA...STOP IT...
BAT... MANIAC...
HEH...
PLEASE.
?
I...
TELL ME ABOUT THE COLOSSUS VIRUS.
IT'S AN INFECTION THAT WILL KILL YOU WITHIN A WEEK--WHILE MAKING YOU FEEL WEAK--AND HORROR OF HORRORS--MAKES YOUR SKIN LOOK LIKE YOU'RE NINETY AND FROM MIAMI...
A NICE PLACE TO VISIT, BUT I WOULDN'T WANT TO DIE THERE.
DON'T PLAY WITH ME, YOU SICK--
SICK? RIGHT YOU ARE, DETECTIVE...
...TERMINALLY.
HA HA HA HA

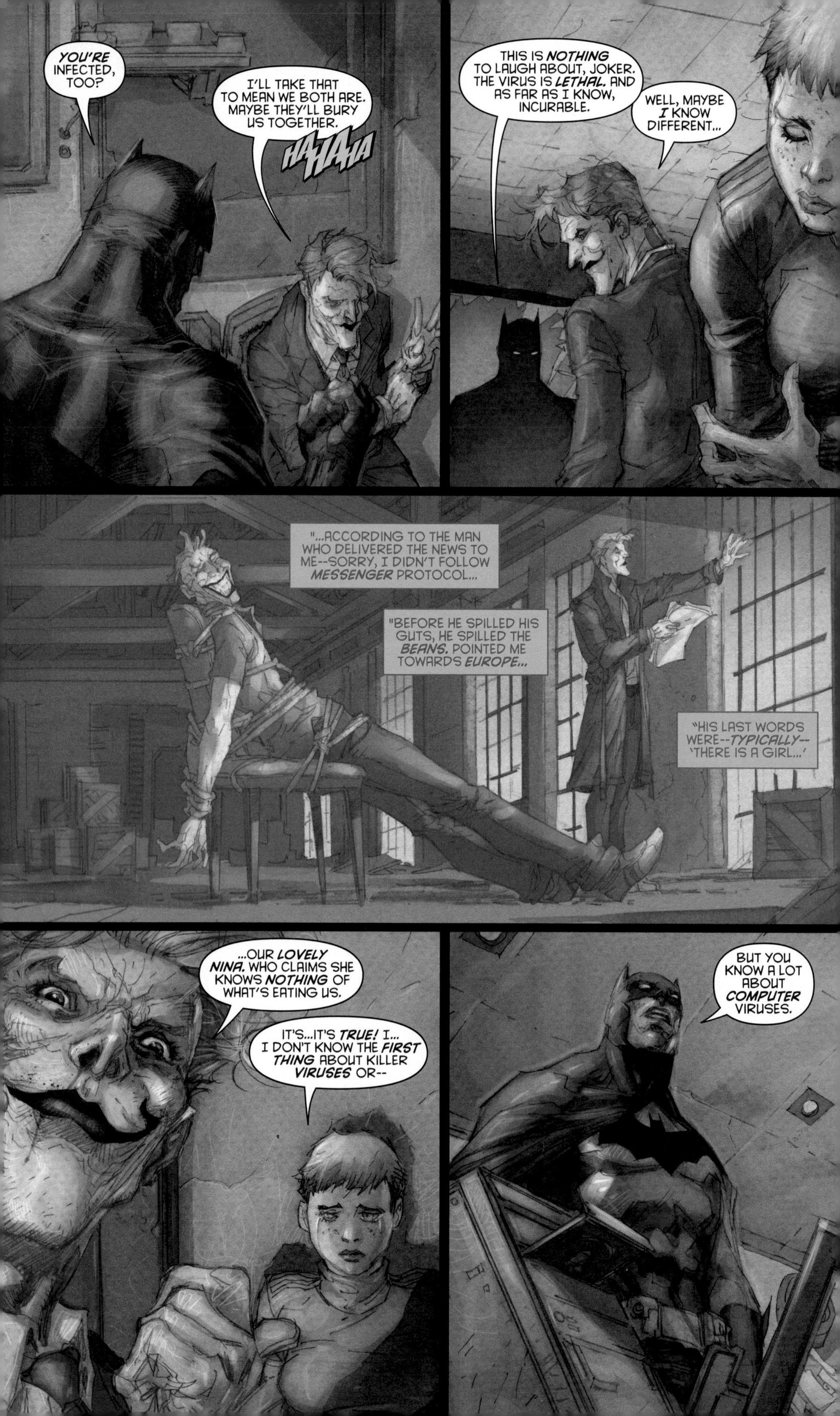
YOU'RE INFECTED, TOO?
I'LL TAKE THAT TO MEAN WE BOTH ARE. MAYBE THEY'LL BURY US TOGETHER.
HA HA HA
THIS IS NOTHING TO LAUGH ABOUT, JOKER. THE VIRUS IS LETHAL. AND AS FAR AS I KNOW, INCURABLE.
WELL, MAYBE I KNOW DIFFERENT...
"...ACCORDING TO THE MAN WHO DELIVERED THE NEWS TO ME--SORRY, I DIDN'T FOLLOW MESSENGER PROTOCOL...
"BEFORE HE SPILLED HIS GUTS, HE SPILLED THE BEANS. POINTED ME TOWARDS EUROPE...
"HIS LAST WORDS WERE--TYPICALLY-- 'THERE IS A GIRL...'
...OUR LOVELY NINA. WHO CLAIMS SHE KNOWS NOTHING OF WHAT'S EATING US.
IT'S...IT'S TRUE! I... I DON'T KNOW THE FIRST THING ABOUT KILLER VIRUSES OR--
BUT YOU KNOW A LOT ABOUT COMPUTER VIRUSES.

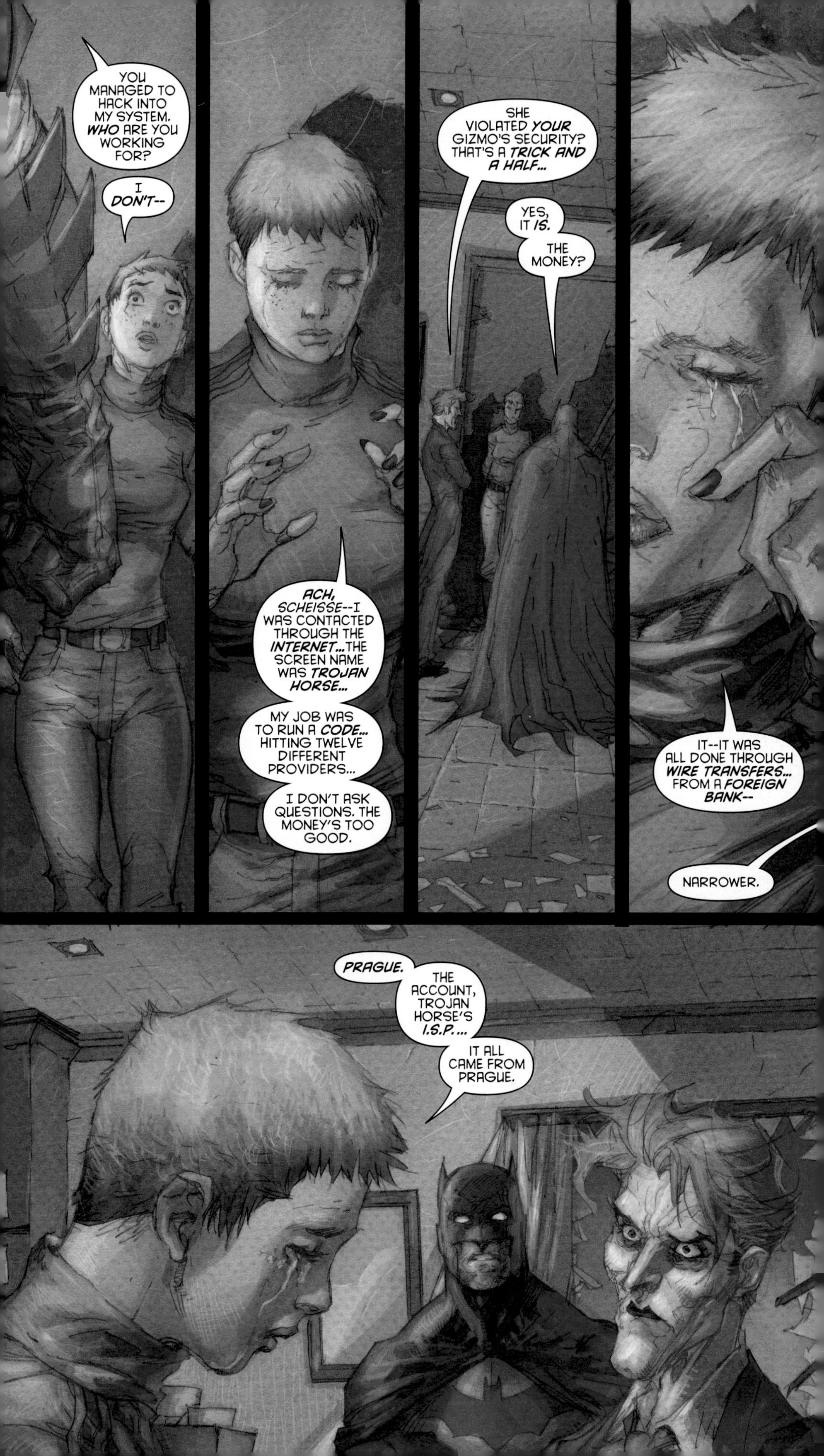
YOU MANAGED TO HACK INTO MY SYSTEM. WHO ARE YOU WORKING FOR?
I DON'T--
ACH, SCHEISSE--I WAS CONTACTED THROUGH THE INTERNET...THE SCREEN NAME WAS TROJAN HORSE...
MY JOB WAS TO RUN A CODE... HITTING TWELVE DIFFERENT PROVIDERS...
I DON'T ASK QUESTIONS. THE MONEY'S TOO GOOD.
SHE VIOLATED YOUR GIZMO'S SECURITY? THAT'S A TRICK AND A HALF...
YES, IT IS.
THE MONEY?
IT--IT WAS ALL DONE THROUGH WIRE TRANSFERS... FROM A FOREIGN BANK--
NARROWER.
PRAGUE.
THE ACCOUNT, TROJAN HORSE'S I.S.P. ...
IT ALL CAME FROM PRAGUE.

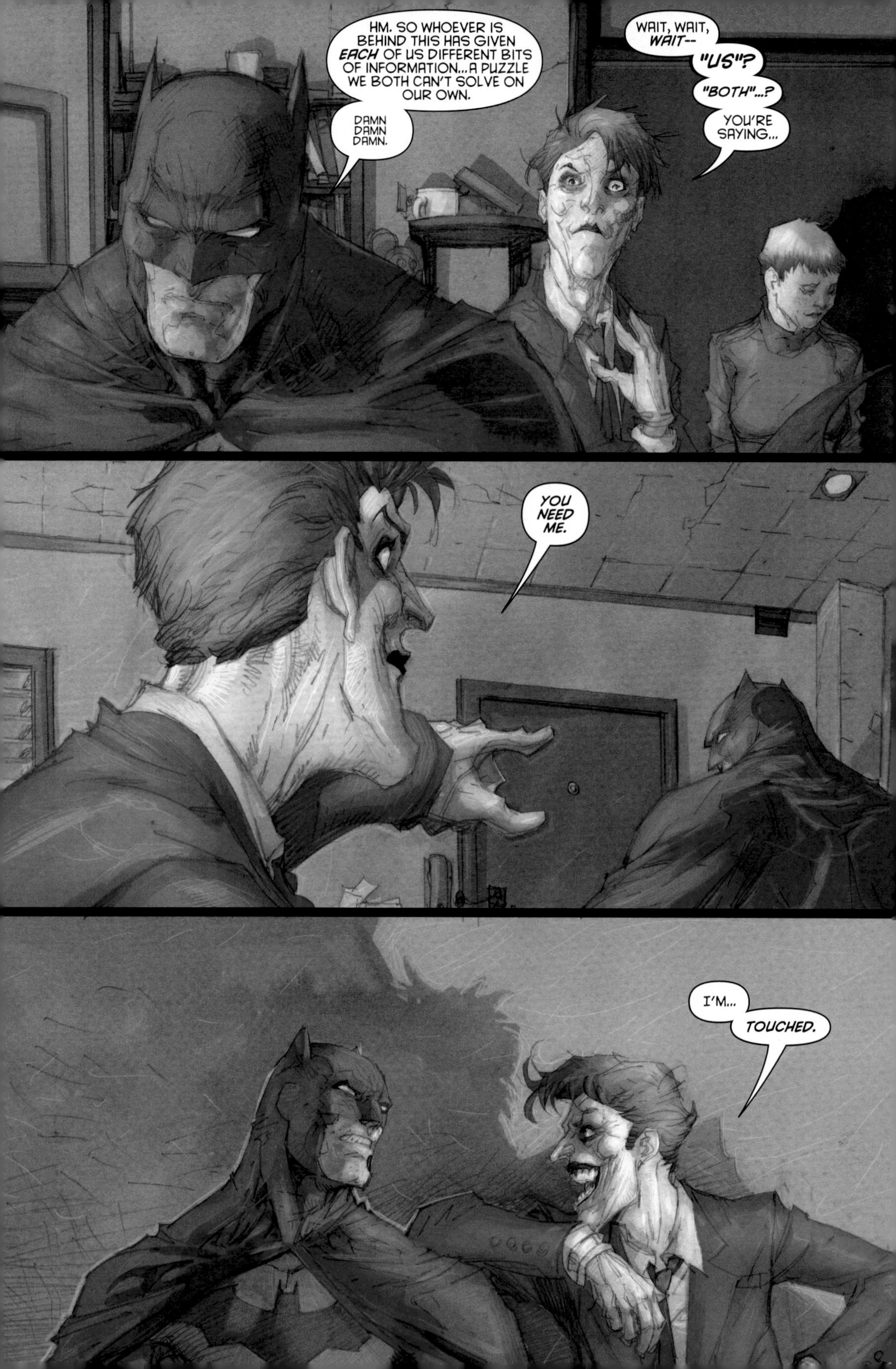
HM. SO WHOEVER IS BEHIND THIS HAS GIVEN EACH OF US DIFFERENT BITS OF INFORMATION...A PUZZLE WE BOTH CAN'T SOLVE ON OUR OWN.
DAMN DAMN DAMN.
WAIT, WAIT, WAIT--
"US"?
"BOTH"...?
YOU'RE SAYING...
YOU NEED ME.
I'M...
TOUCHED.

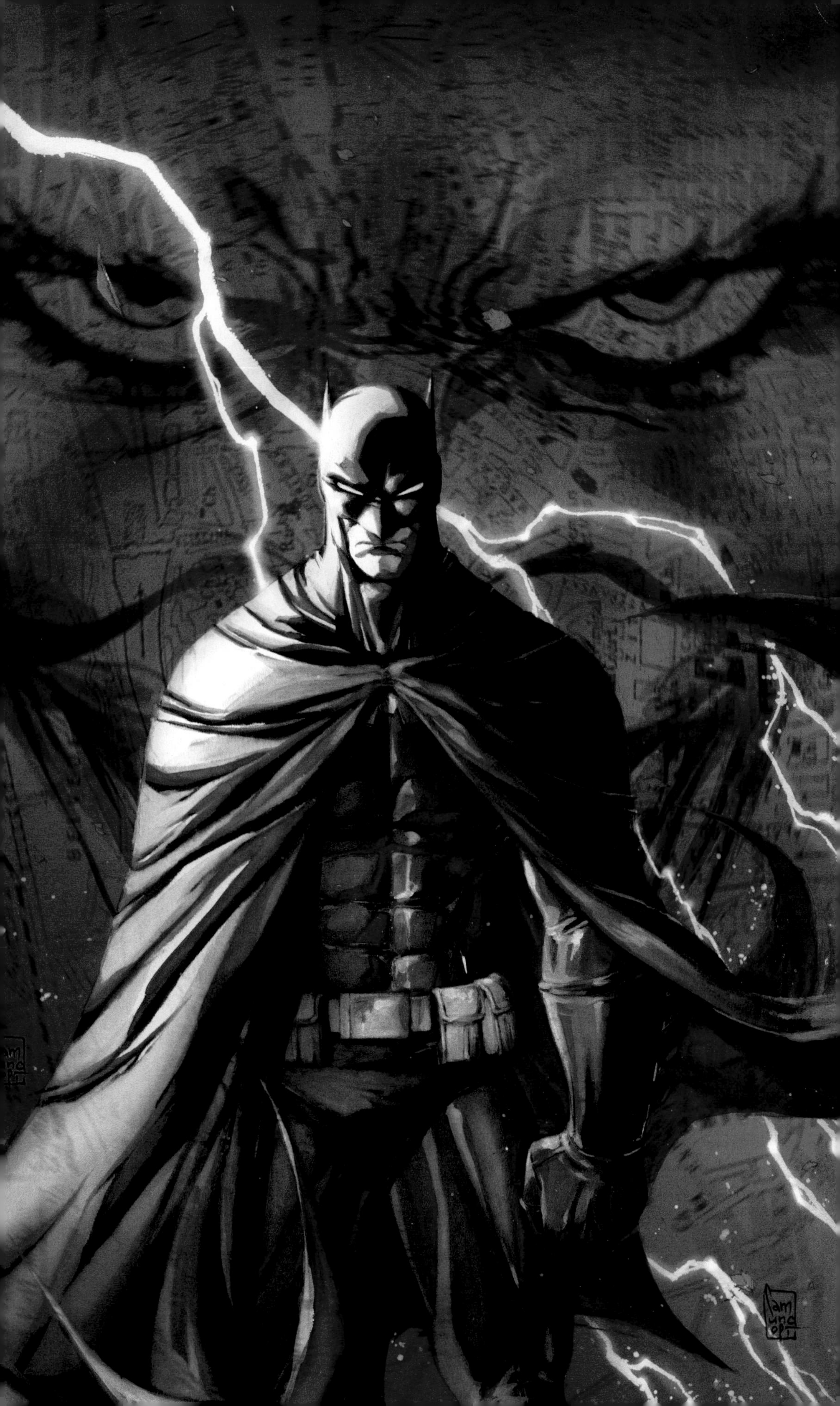

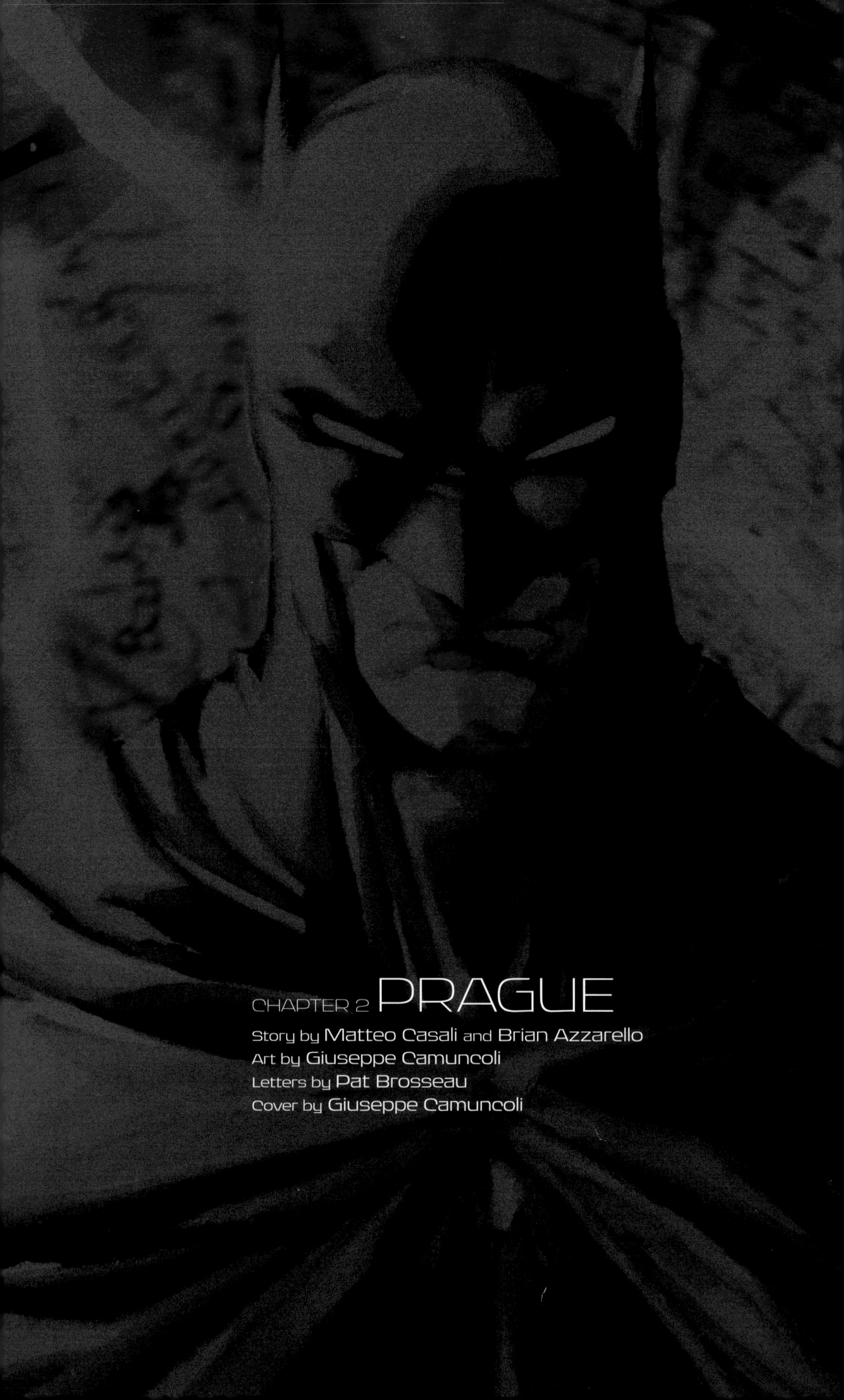

CHAPTER 2 PRAGUE

Story by Matteo Casali and Brian Azzarello
Art by Giuseppe Camuncoli
Letters by Pat Brosseau
Cover by Giuseppe Camuncoli

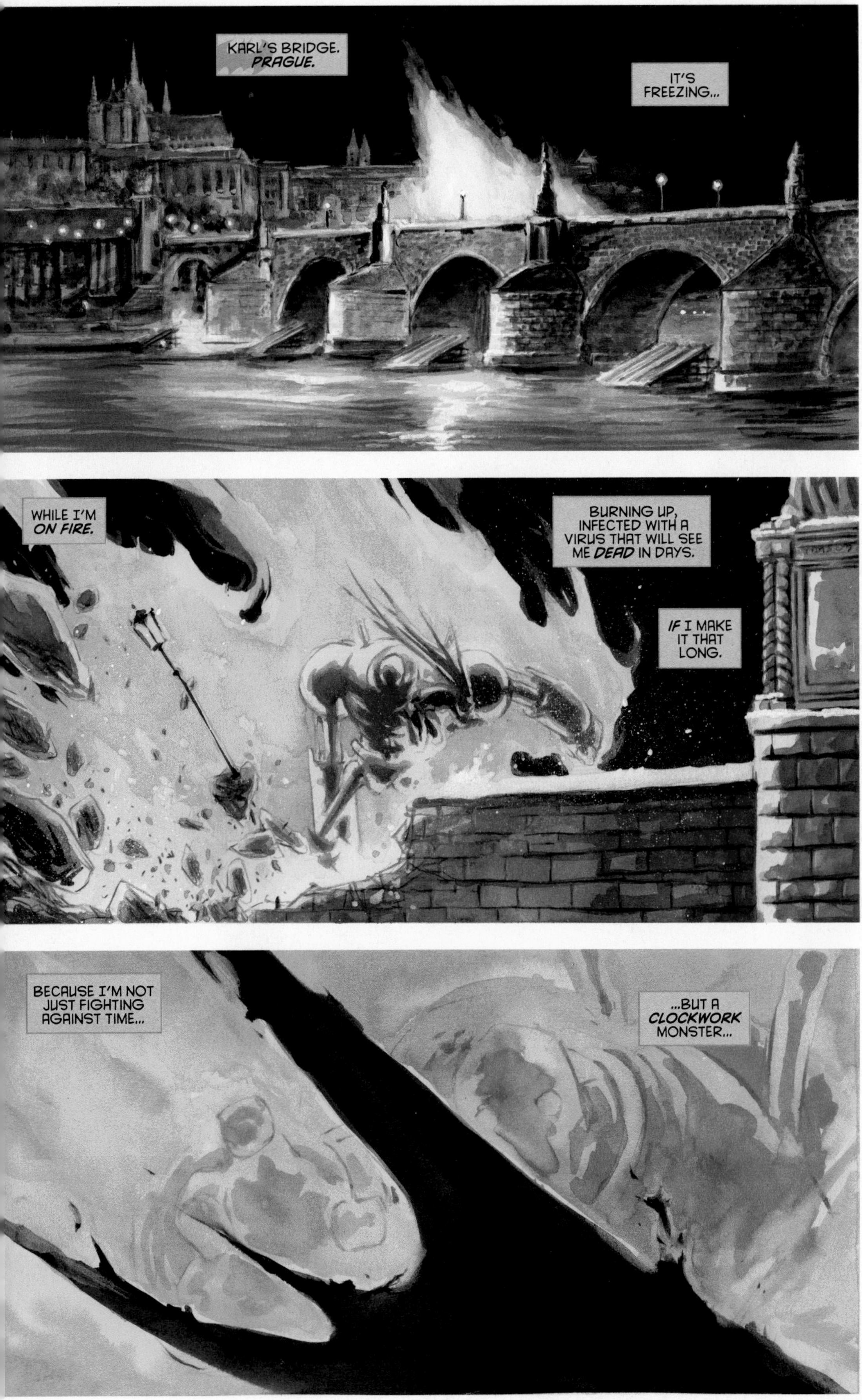
KARL'S BRIDGE. PRAGUE.
IT'S FREEZING...
WHILE I'M ON FIRE.
BURNING UP, INFECTED WITH A VIRUS THAT WILL SEE ME DEAD IN DAYS.
IF I MAKE IT THAT LONG.
BECAUSE I'M NOT JUST FIGHTING AGAINST TIME...
...BUT A CLOCKWORK MONSTER...

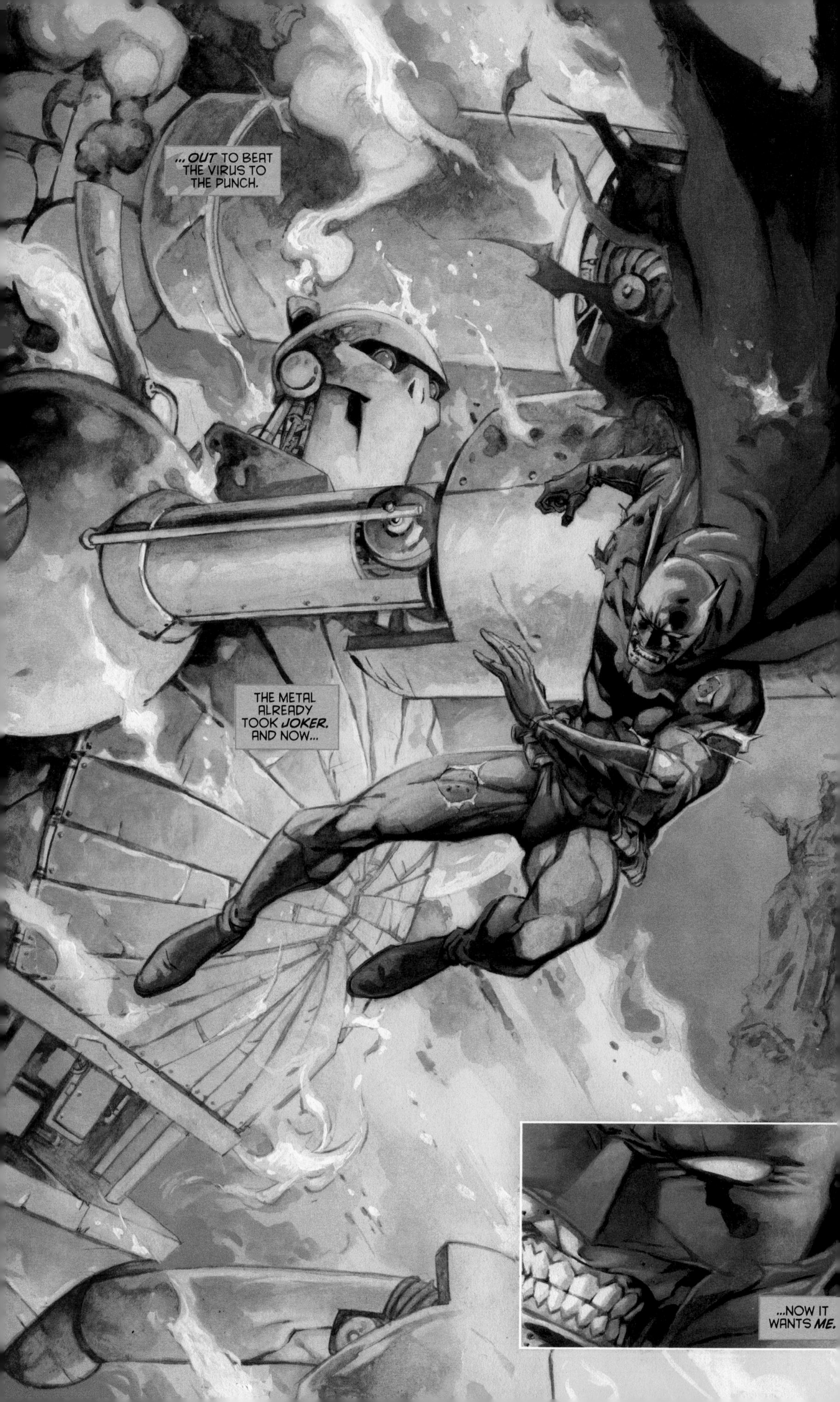

...OUT TO BEAT THE VIRUS TO THE PUNCH.
THE METAL ALREADY TOOK JOKER. AND NOW...
...NOW IT WANTS ME.

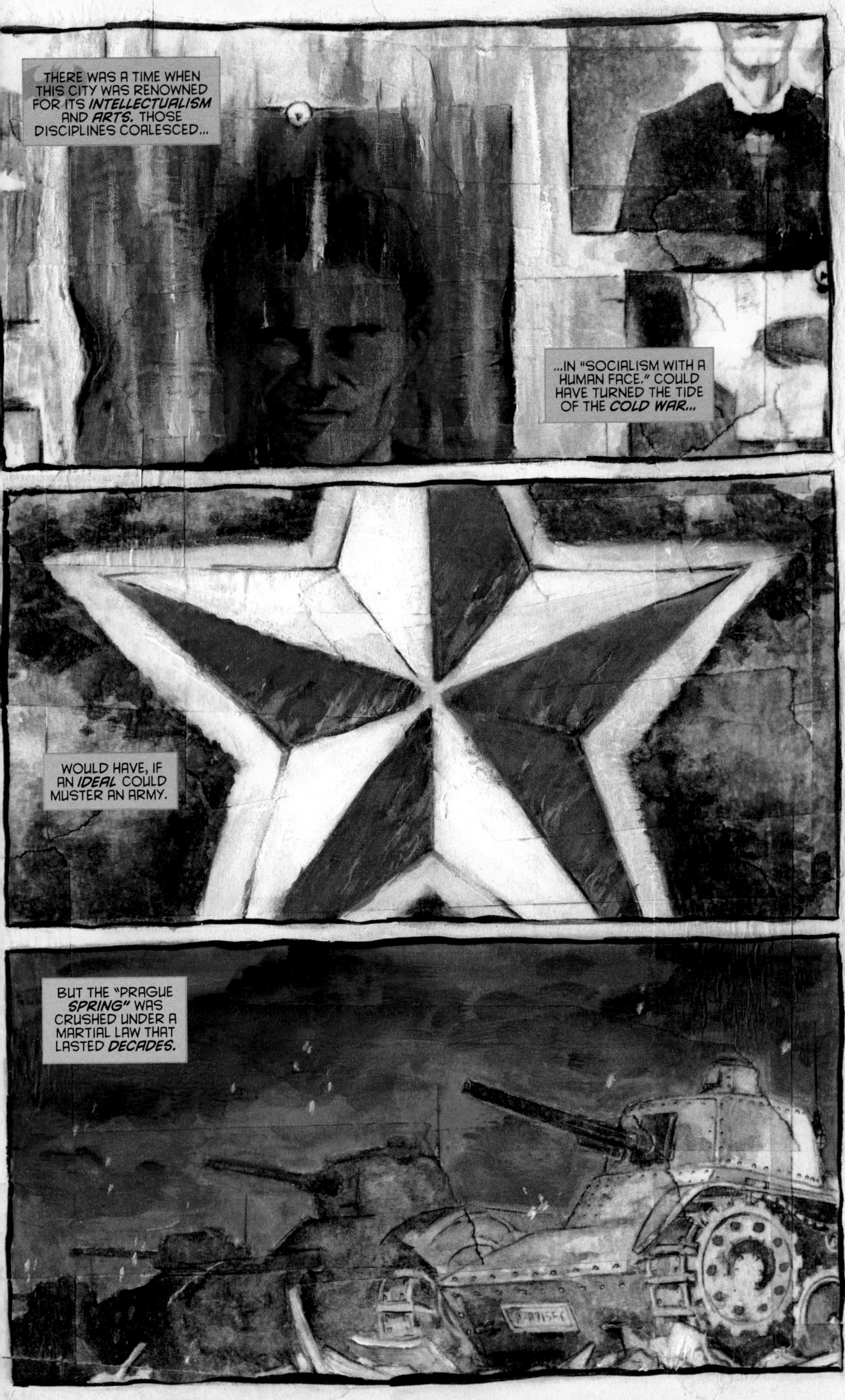
THERE WAS A TIME WHEN THIS CITY WAS RENOWNED FOR ITS *INTELLECTUALISM* AND *ARTS.* THOSE DISCIPLINES COALESCED...
...IN "SOCIALISM WITH A HUMAN FACE." COULD HAVE TURNED THE TIDE OF THE *COLD WAR...*
WOULD HAVE, IF AN *IDEAL* COULD MUSTER AN ARMY.
BUT THE "PRAGUE *SPRING*" WAS CRUSHED UNDER A MARTIAL LAW THAT LASTED *DECADES.*

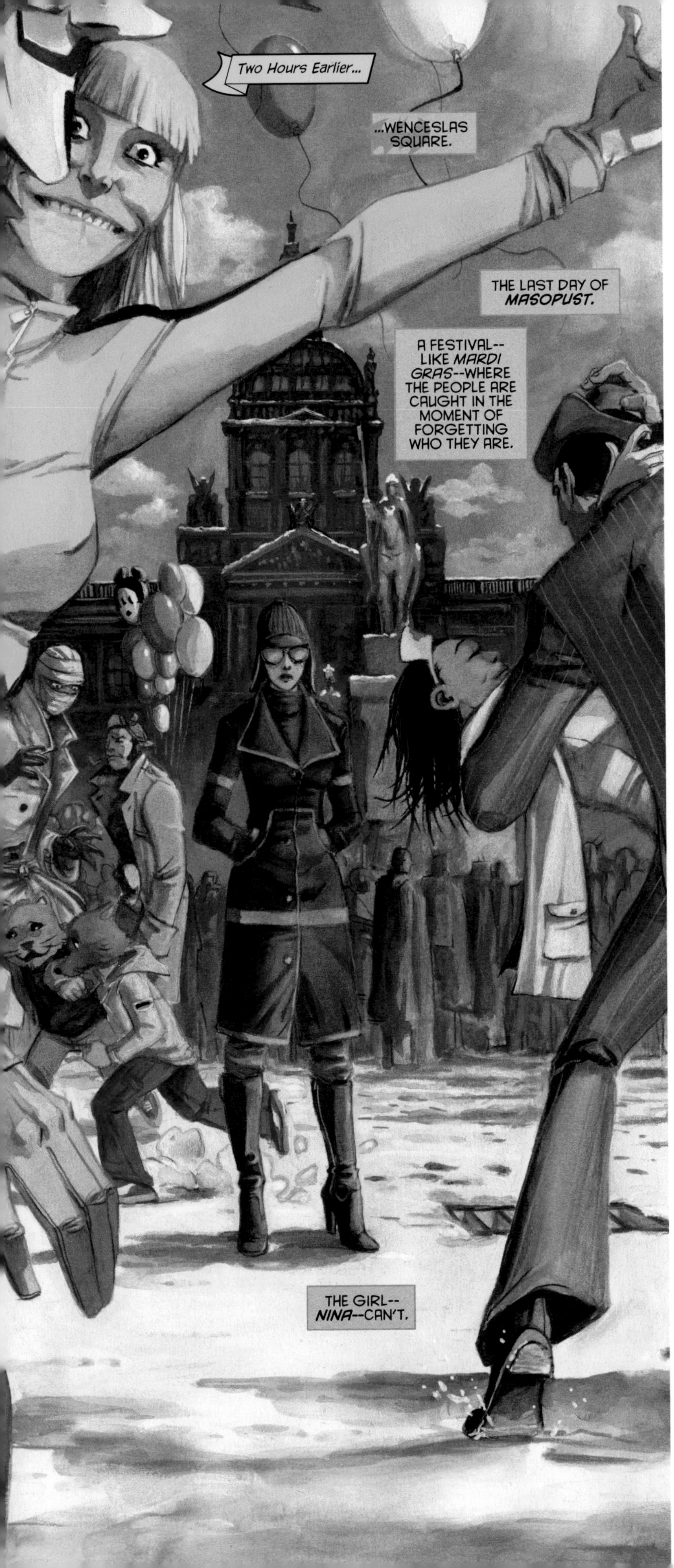
Two Hours Earlier...
...WENCESLAS SQUARE.
THE LAST DAY OF *MASOPUST.*
A FESTIVAL--LIKE *MARDI GRAS*--WHERE THE PEOPLE ARE CAUGHT IN THE MOMENT OF FORGETTING WHO THEY ARE.
THE GIRL--*NINA*--CAN'T.
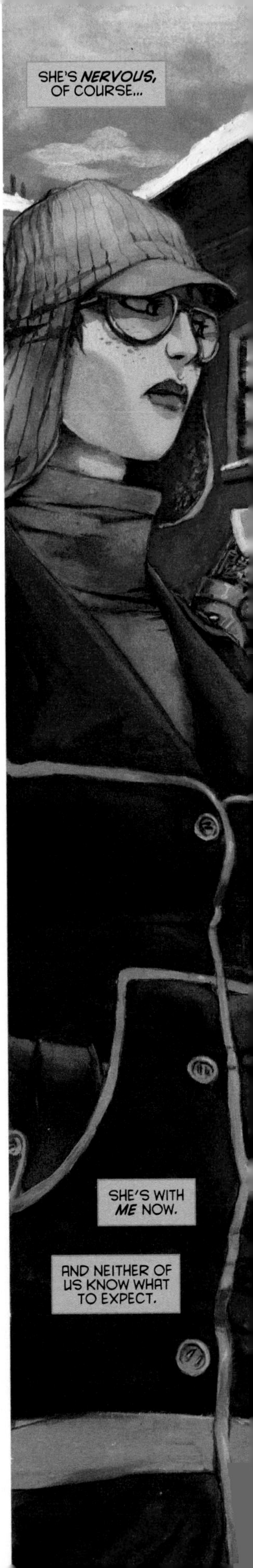
SHE'S *NERVOUS,* OF COURSE...
SHE'S WITH *ME* NOW.
AND NEITHER OF US KNOW WHAT TO EXPECT.

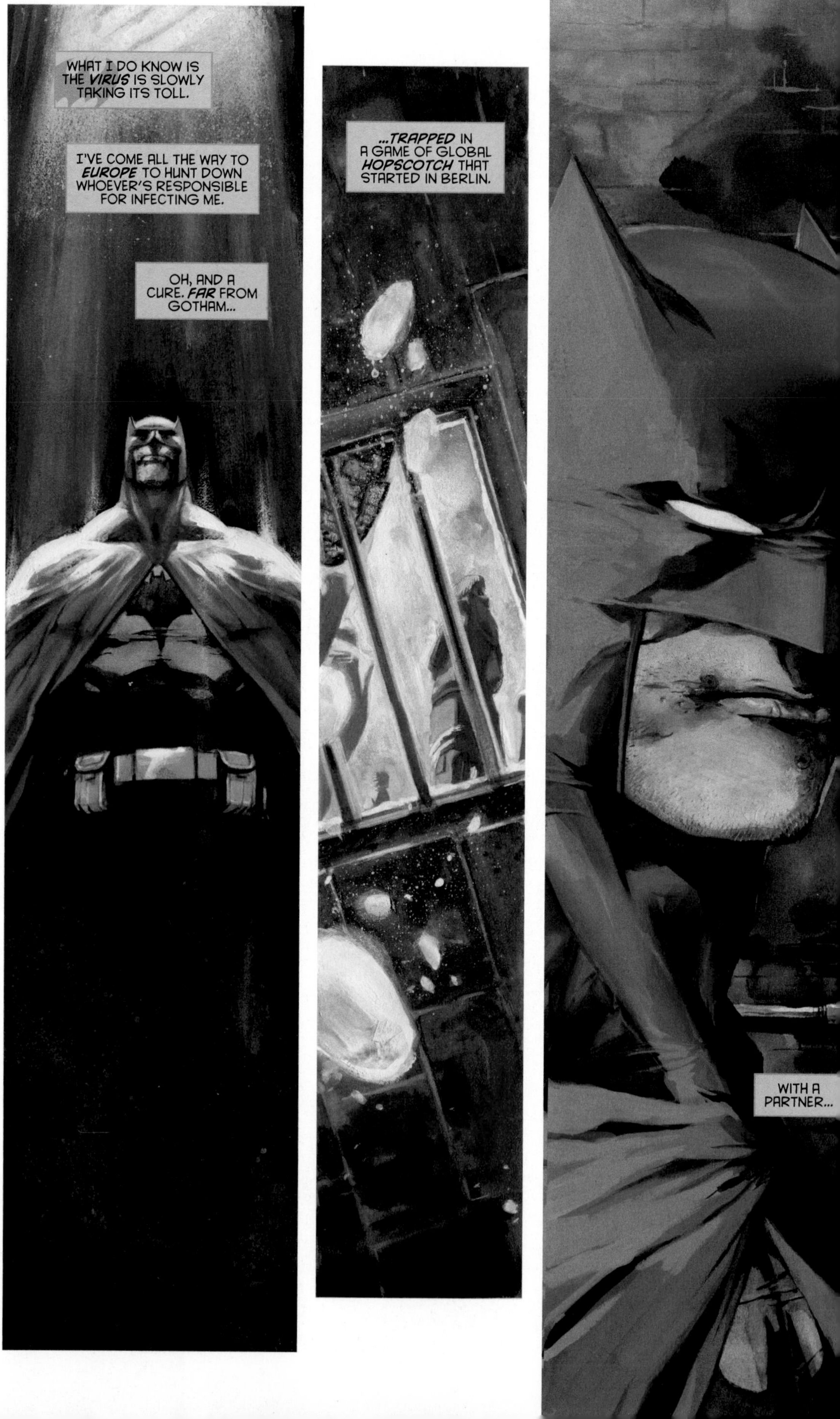
WHAT I DO KNOW IS THE *VIRUS* IS SLOWLY TAKING ITS TOLL.
I'VE COME ALL THE WAY TO *EUROPE* TO HUNT DOWN WHOEVER'S RESPONSIBLE FOR INFECTING ME.
OH, AND A CURE. *FAR* FROM GOTHAM...
...TRAPPED IN A GAME OF GLOBAL *HOPSCOTCH* THAT STARTED IN BERLIN.
WITH A PARTNER...

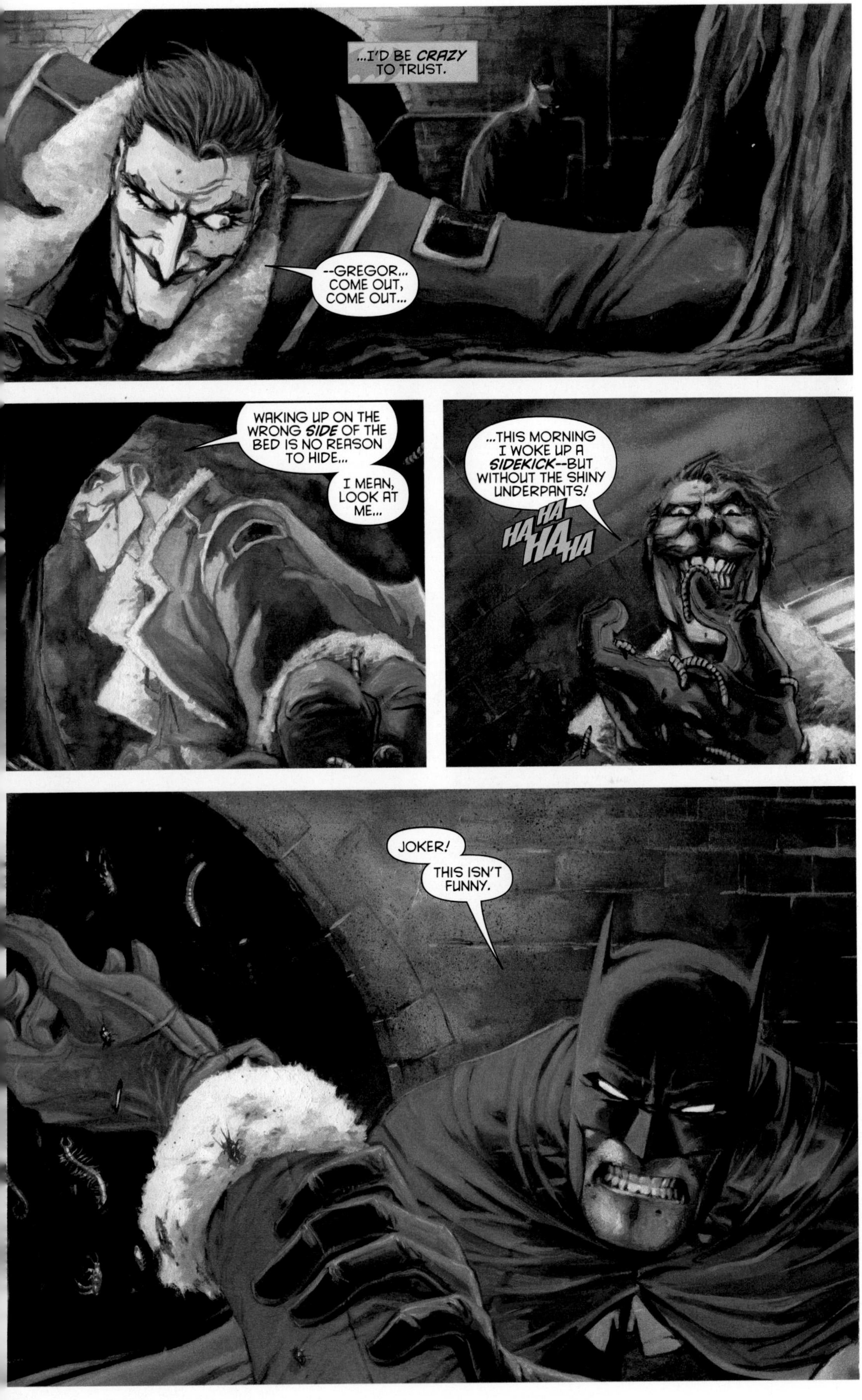

...I'D BE CRAZY TO TRUST.
--GREGOR... COME OUT, COME OUT...
WAKING UP ON THE WRONG SIDE OF THE BED IS NO REASON TO HIDE...
I MEAN, LOOK AT ME...
...THIS MORNING I WOKE UP A SIDEKICK--BUT WITHOUT THE SHINY UNDERPANTS!
HA HA HA HA
JOKER!
THIS ISN'T FUNNY.

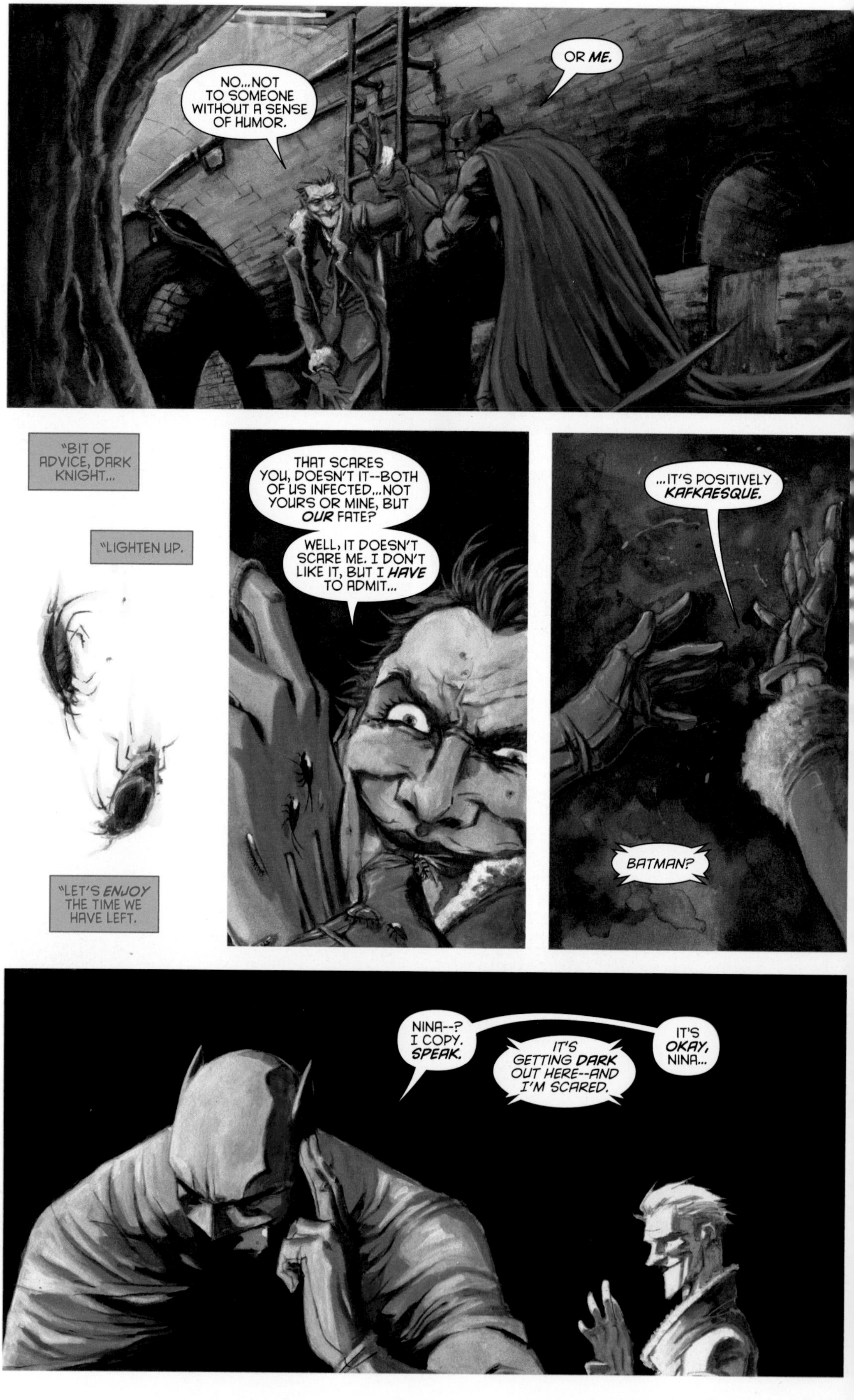
NO...NOT TO SOMEONE WITHOUT A SENSE OF HUMOR.
OR ME.
"BIT OF ADVICE, DARK KNIGHT...
"LIGHTEN UP.
"LET'S ENJOY THE TIME WE HAVE LEFT.
THAT SCARES YOU, DOESN'T IT--BOTH OF US INFECTED...NOT YOURS OR MINE, BUT OUR FATE?
WELL, IT DOESN'T SCARE ME. I DON'T LIKE IT, BUT I HAVE TO ADMIT...
...IT'S POSITIVELY KAFKAESQUE.
BATMAN?
NINA--? I COPY. SPEAK.
IT'S GETTING DARK OUT HERE--AND I'M SCARED.
IT'S OKAY, NINA...

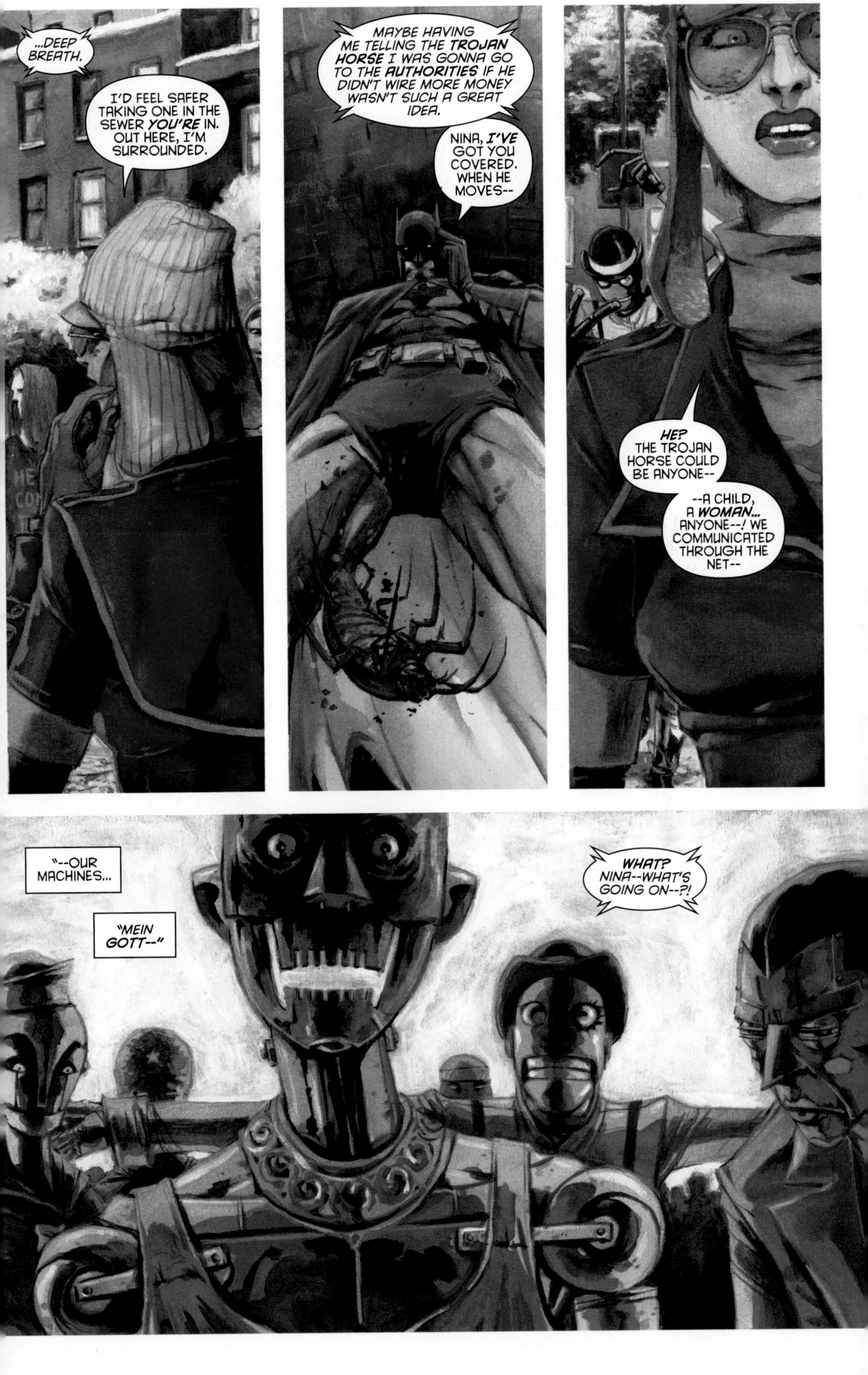
...DEEP BREATH.
I'D FEEL SAFER TAKING ONE IN THE SEWER YOU'RE IN. OUT HERE, I'M SURROUNDED.
MAYBE HAVING ME TELLING THE TROJAN HORSE I WAS GONNA GO TO THE AUTHORITIES IF HE DIDN'T WIRE MORE MONEY WASN'T SUCH A GREAT IDEA.
NINA, I'VE GOT YOU COVERED. WHEN HE MOVES--
HE? THE TROJAN HORSE COULD BE ANYONE--
--A CHILD, A WOMAN... ANYONE--! WE COMMUNICATED THROUGH THE NET--
"--OUR MACHINES...
"MEIN GOTT--"
WHAT? NINA--WHAT'S GOING ON--?!

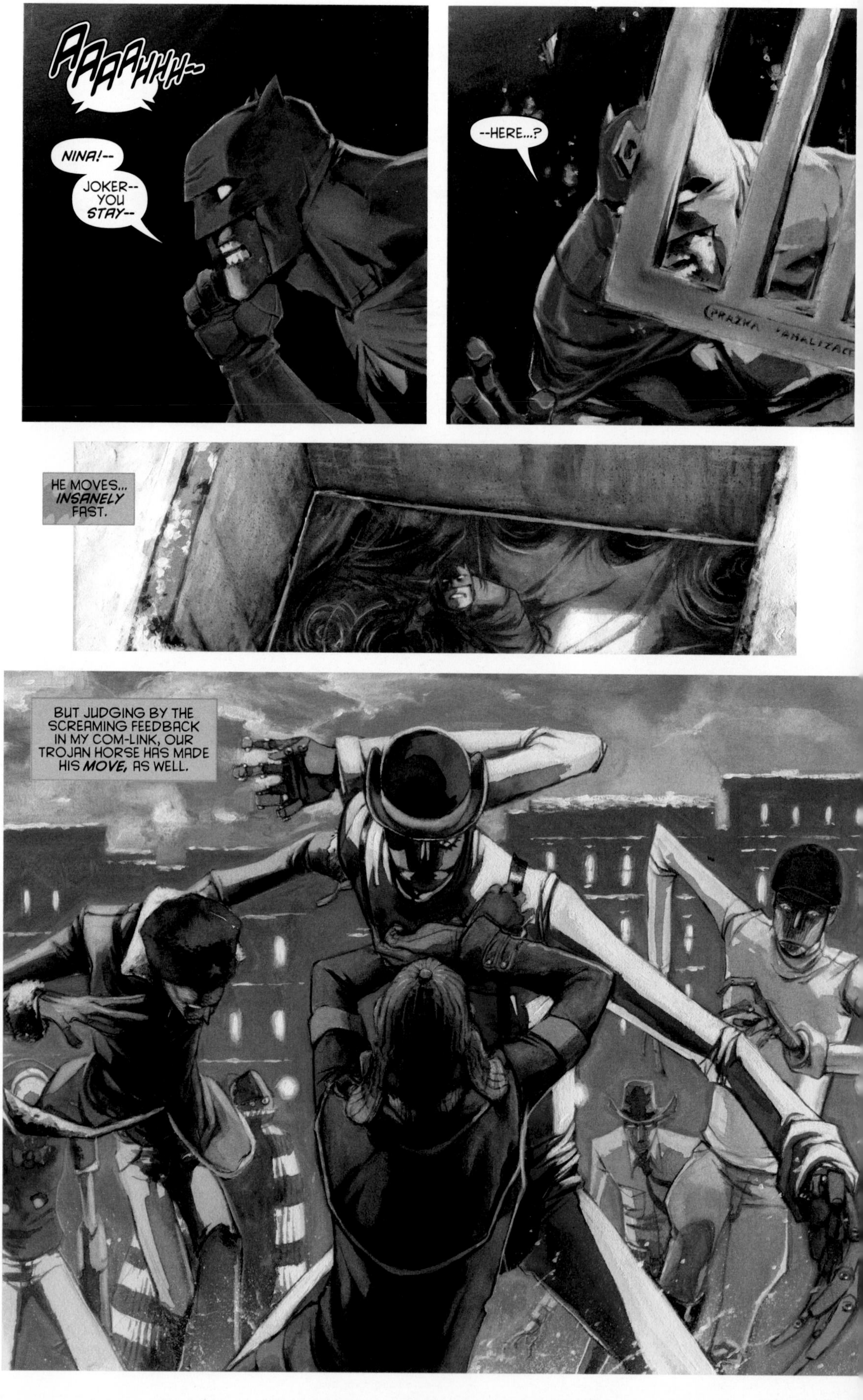
AAAAHHHH--
NINA!--
JOKER-- YOU STAY--
--HERE...?
HE MOVES... INSANELY FAST.
BUT JUDGING BY THE SCREAMING FEEDBACK IN MY COM-LINK, OUR TROJAN HORSE HAS MADE HIS MOVE, AS WELL.

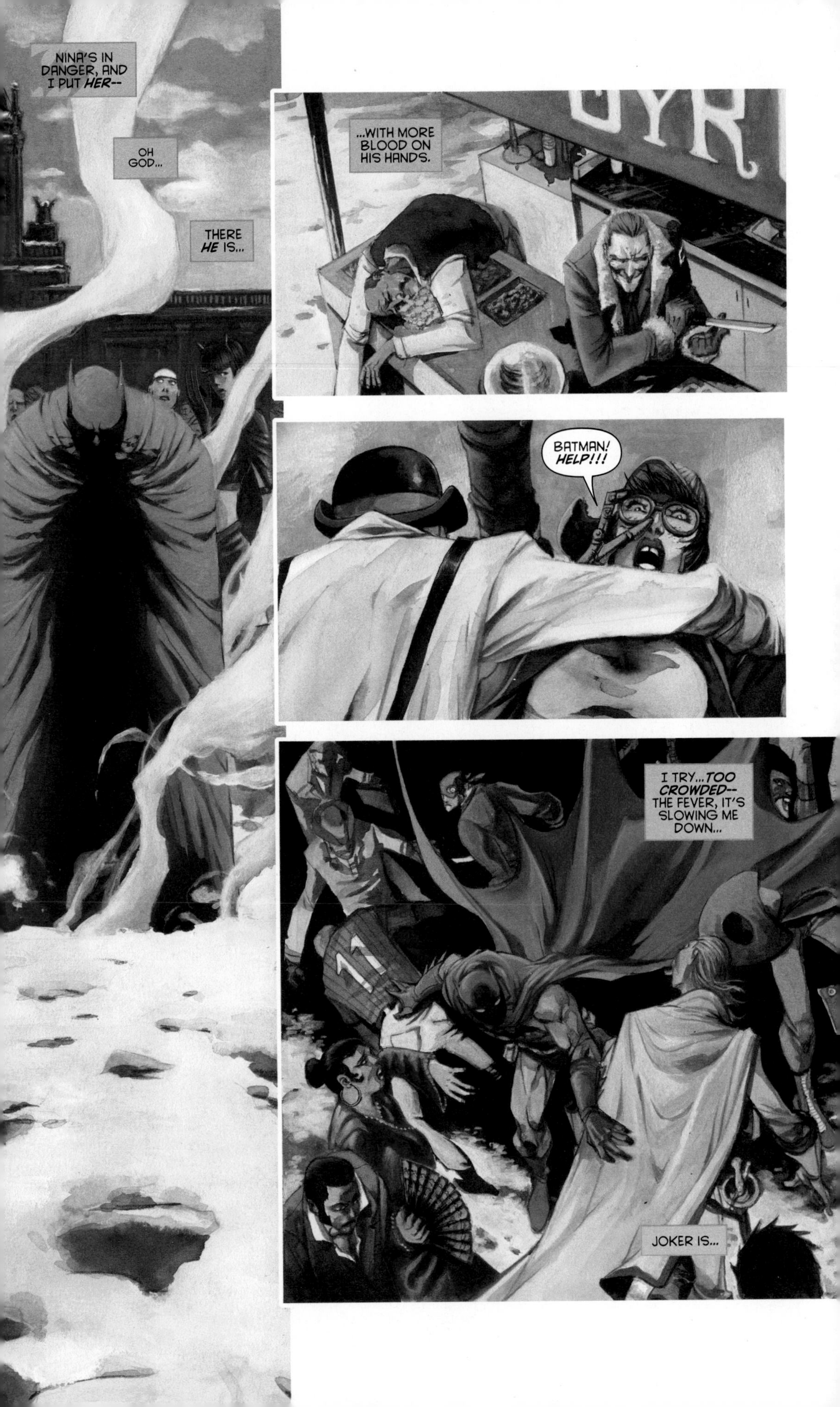

NINA'S IN DANGER, AND I PUT *HER*--
OH GOD...
THERE *HE* IS...
...WITH MORE BLOOD ON HIS HANDS.
BATMAN! *HELP!!!*
I TRY... *TOO CROWDED*-- THE FEVER, IT'S SLOWING ME DOWN...
JOKER IS...

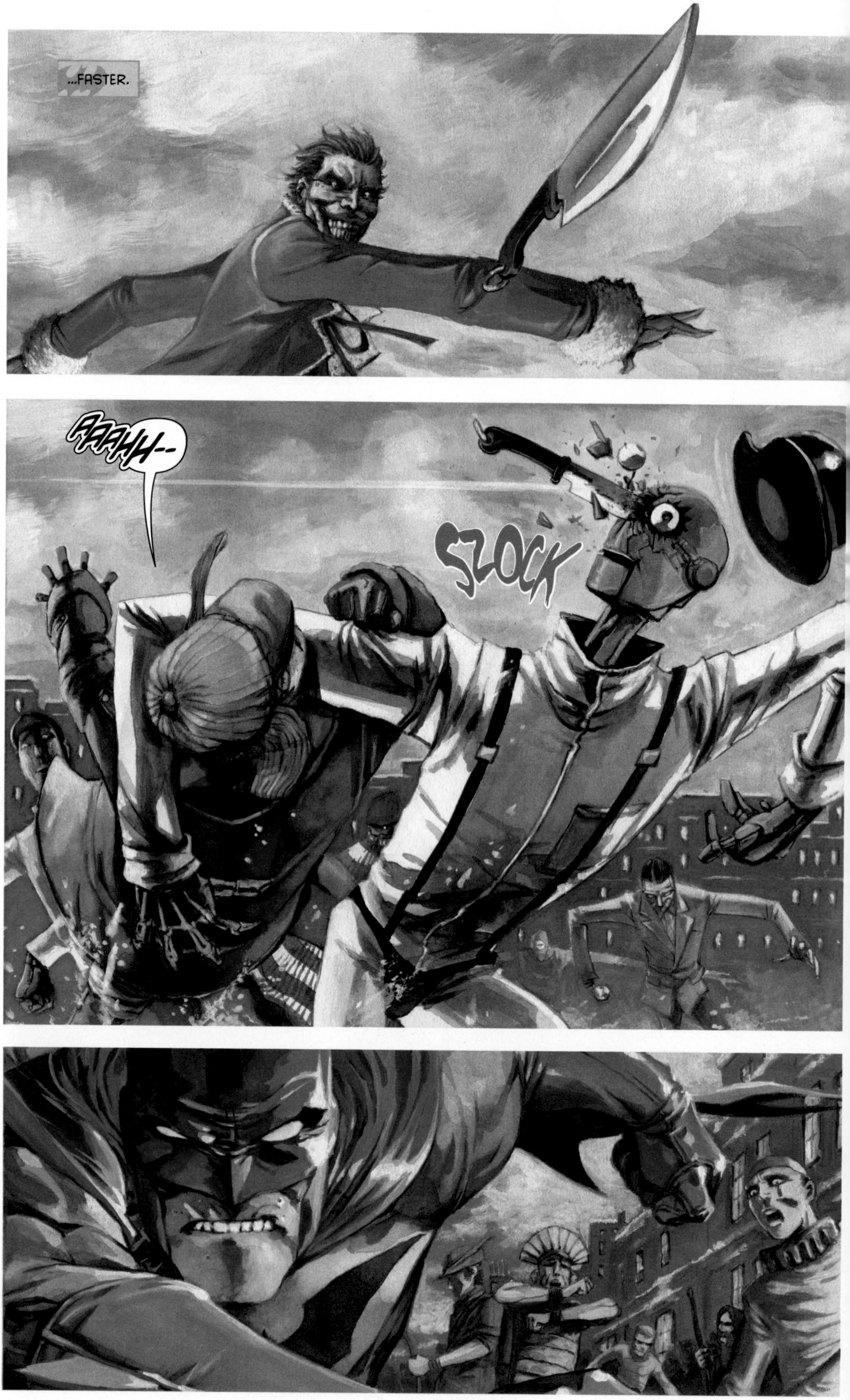
...FASTER.
AAAHH--
SZOCK

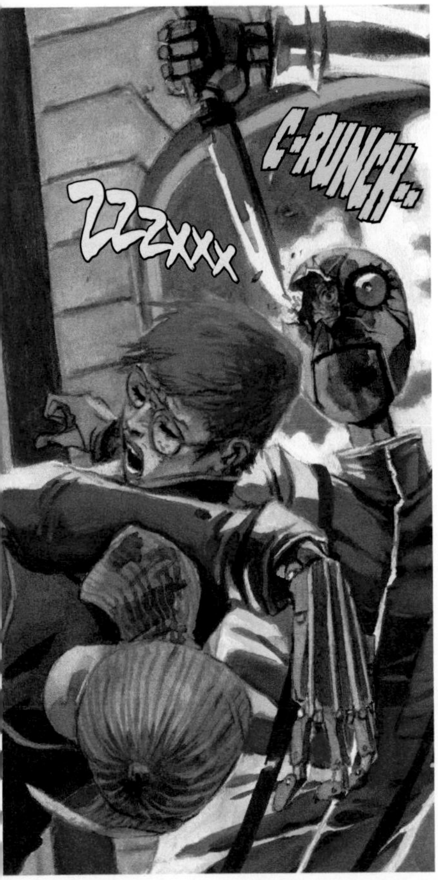
ZZZXXX
C-RUNCH..

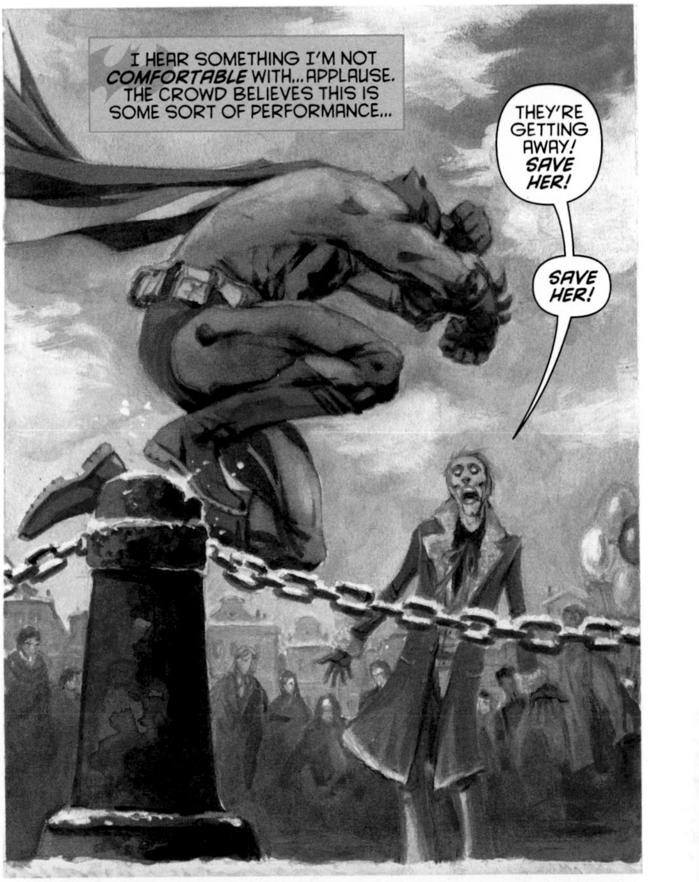
I HEAR SOMETHING I'M NOT *COMFORTABLE* WITH...APPLAUSE. THE CROWD BELIEVES THIS IS SOME SORT OF PERFORMANCE...
THEY'RE GETTING AWAY! *SAVE HER!*
SAVE HER!

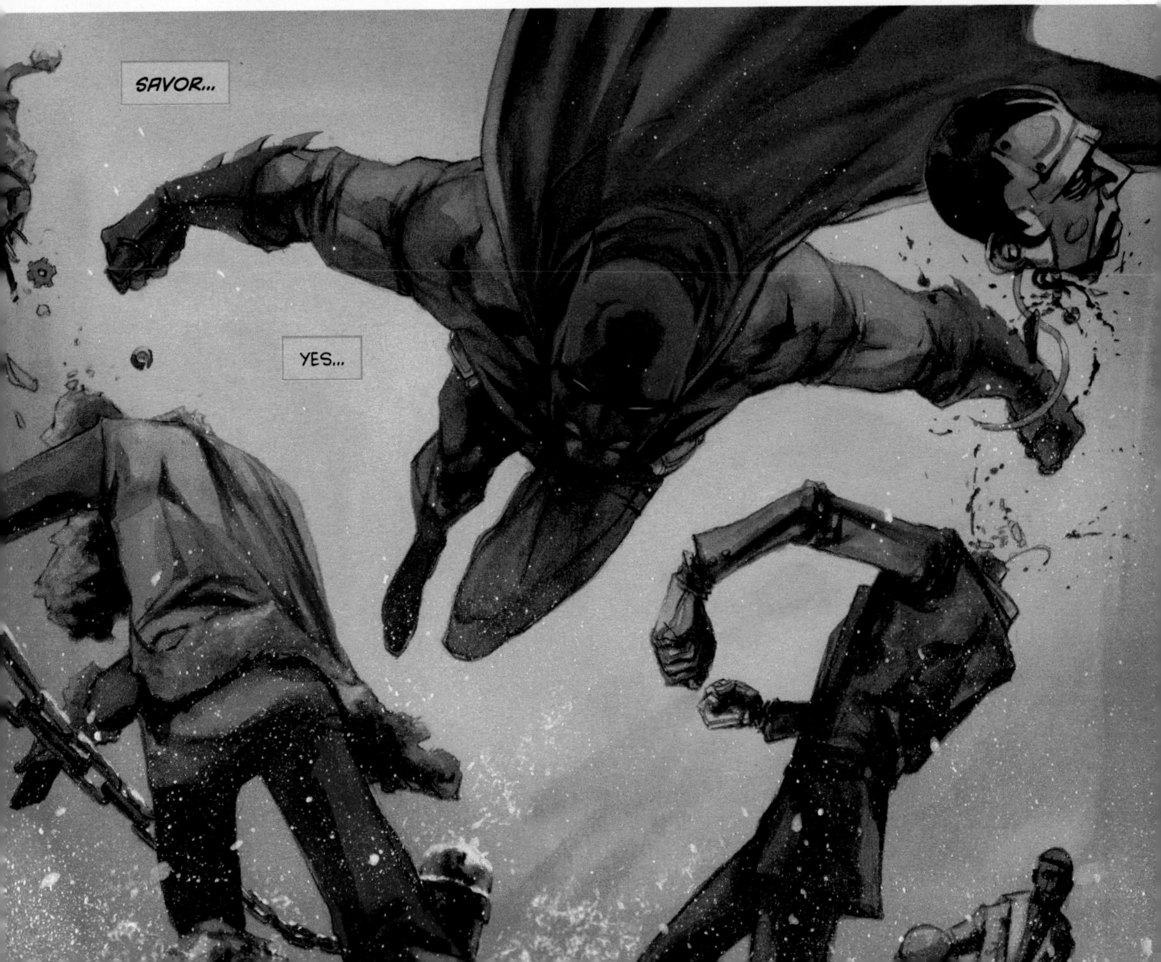
SAVOR...
YES...

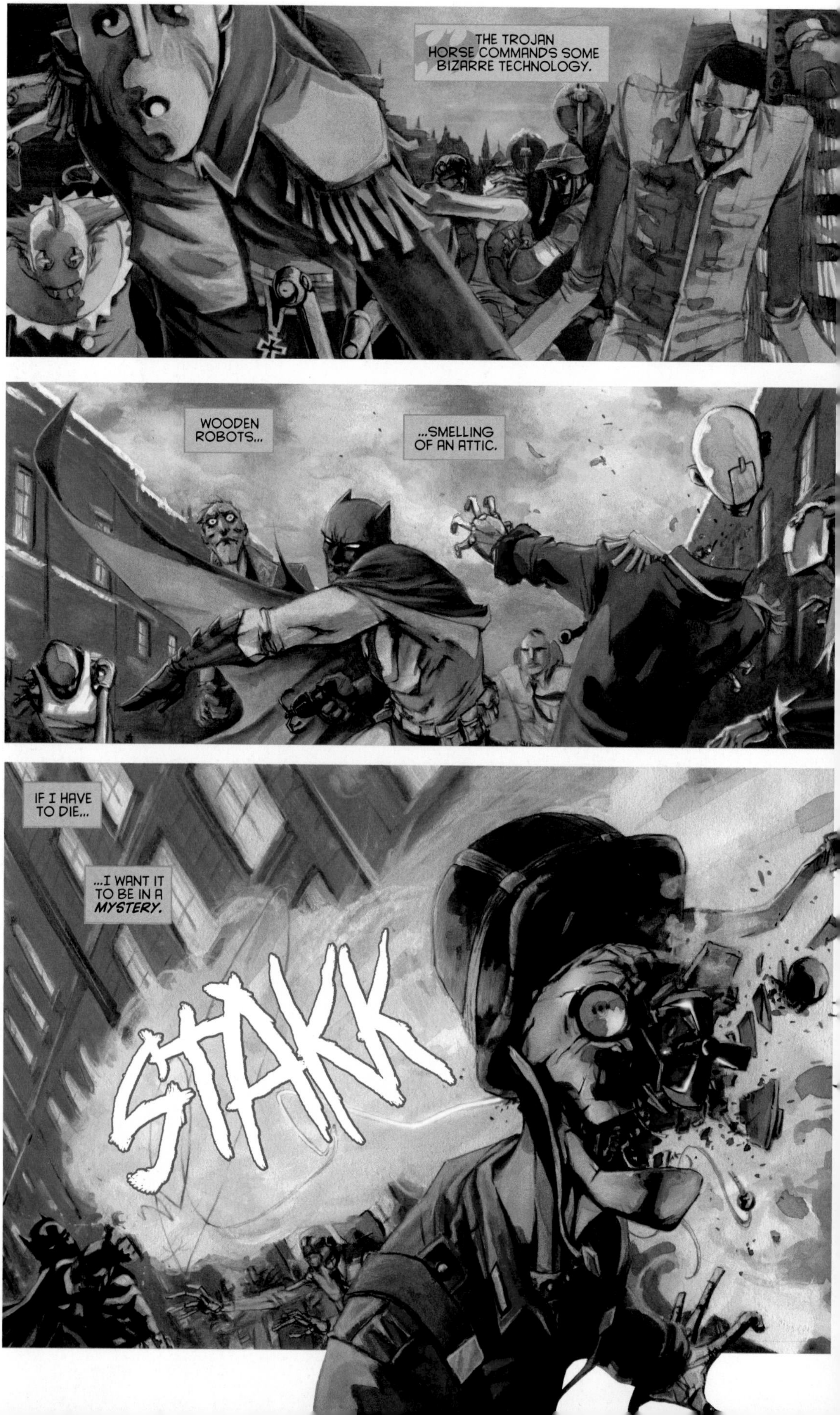
THE TROJAN HORSE COMMANDS SOME BIZARRE TECHNOLOGY.
WOODEN ROBOTS...
...SMELLING OF AN ATTIC.
IF I HAVE TO DIE...
...I WANT IT TO BE IN A *MYSTERY.*
STAKK

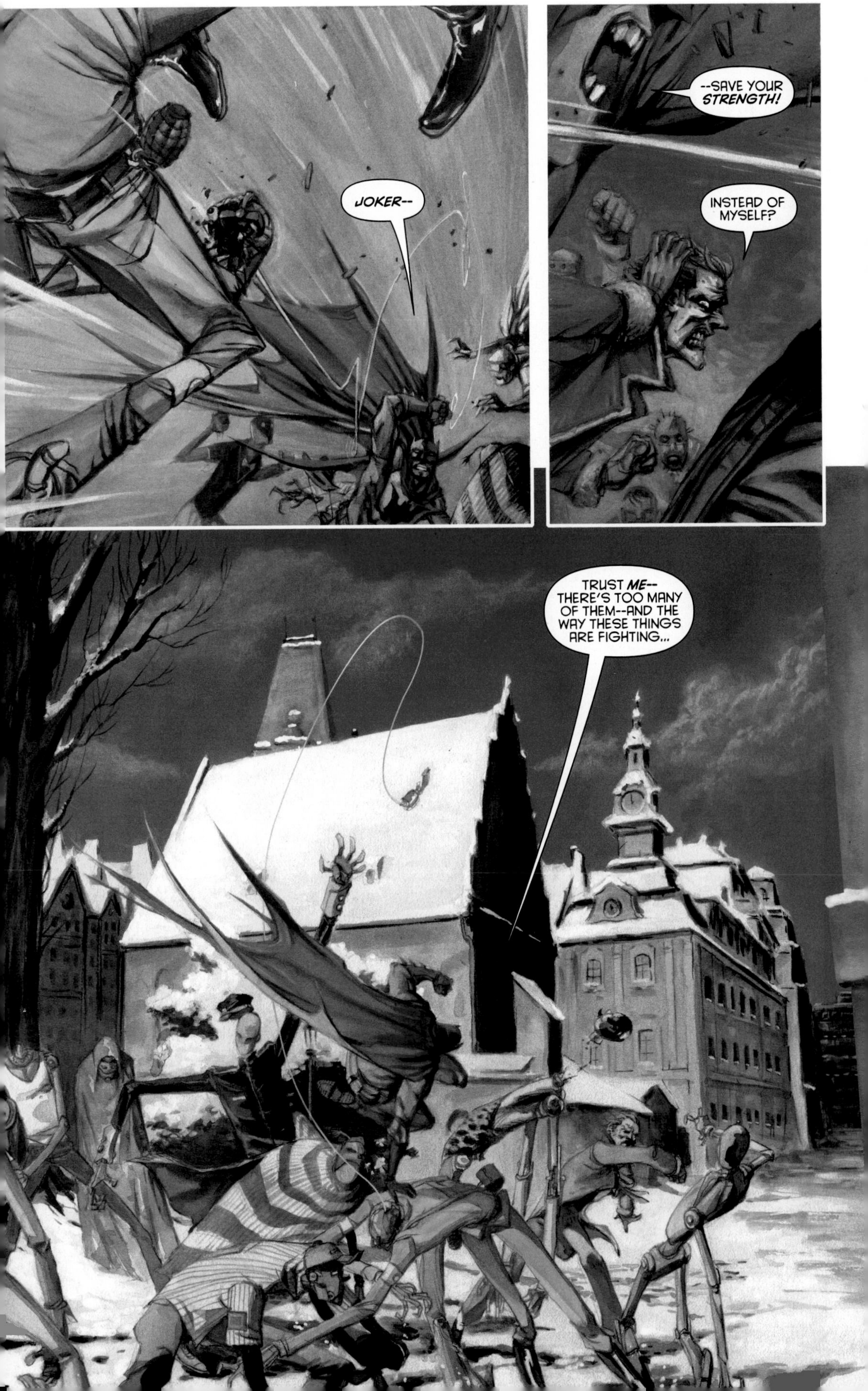
JOKER--
--SAVE YOUR STRENGTH!
INSTEAD OF MYSELF?
TRUST ME--THERE'S TOO MANY OF THEM--AND THE WAY THESE THINGS ARE FIGHTING...

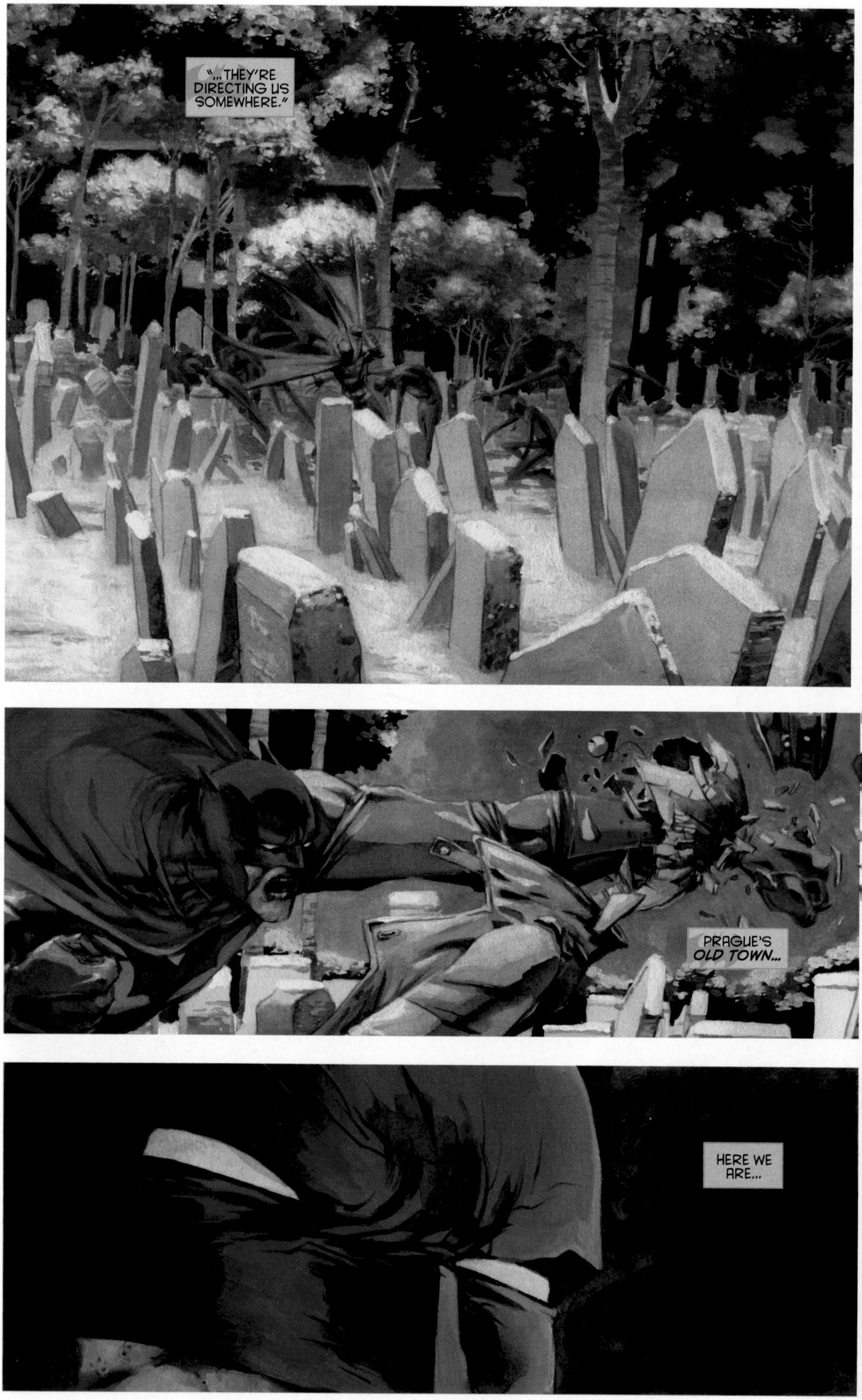
"...THEY'RE DIRECTING US SOMEWHERE."
PRAGUE'S *OLD TOWN*...
HERE WE ARE...

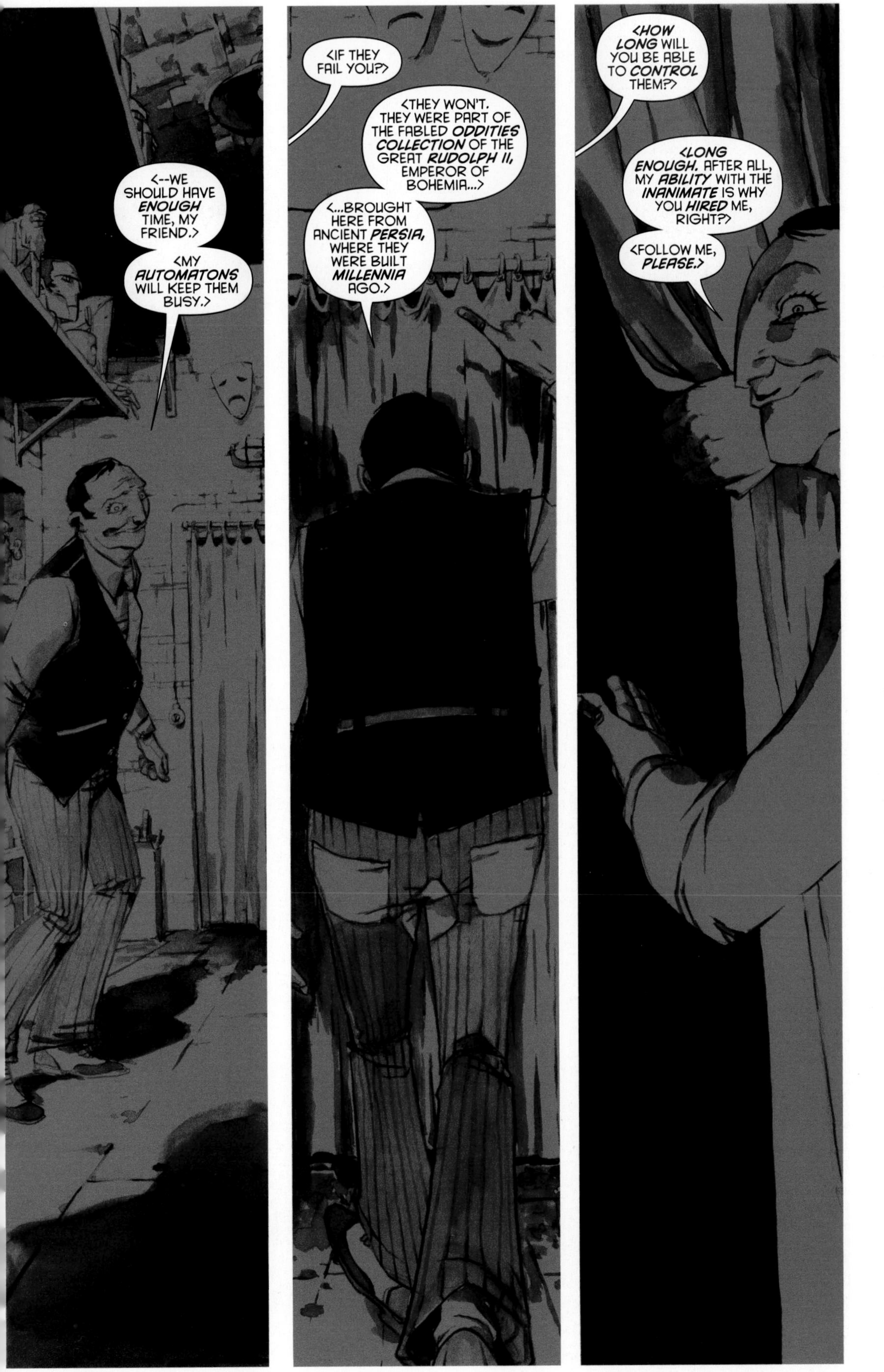

<--WE SHOULD HAVE ENOUGH TIME, MY FRIEND.>
<MY AUTOMATONS WILL KEEP THEM BUSY.>
<IF THEY FAIL YOU?>
<THEY WON'T. THEY WERE PART OF THE FABLED ODDITIES COLLECTION OF THE GREAT RUDOLPH II, EMPEROR OF BOHEMIA...>
<...BROUGHT HERE FROM ANCIENT PERSIA, WHERE THEY WERE BUILT MILLENNIA AGO.>
<HOW LONG WILL YOU BE ABLE TO CONTROL THEM?>
<LONG ENOUGH. AFTER ALL, MY ABILITY WITH THE INANIMATE IS WHY YOU HIRED ME, RIGHT?>
<FOLLOW ME, PLEASE.>

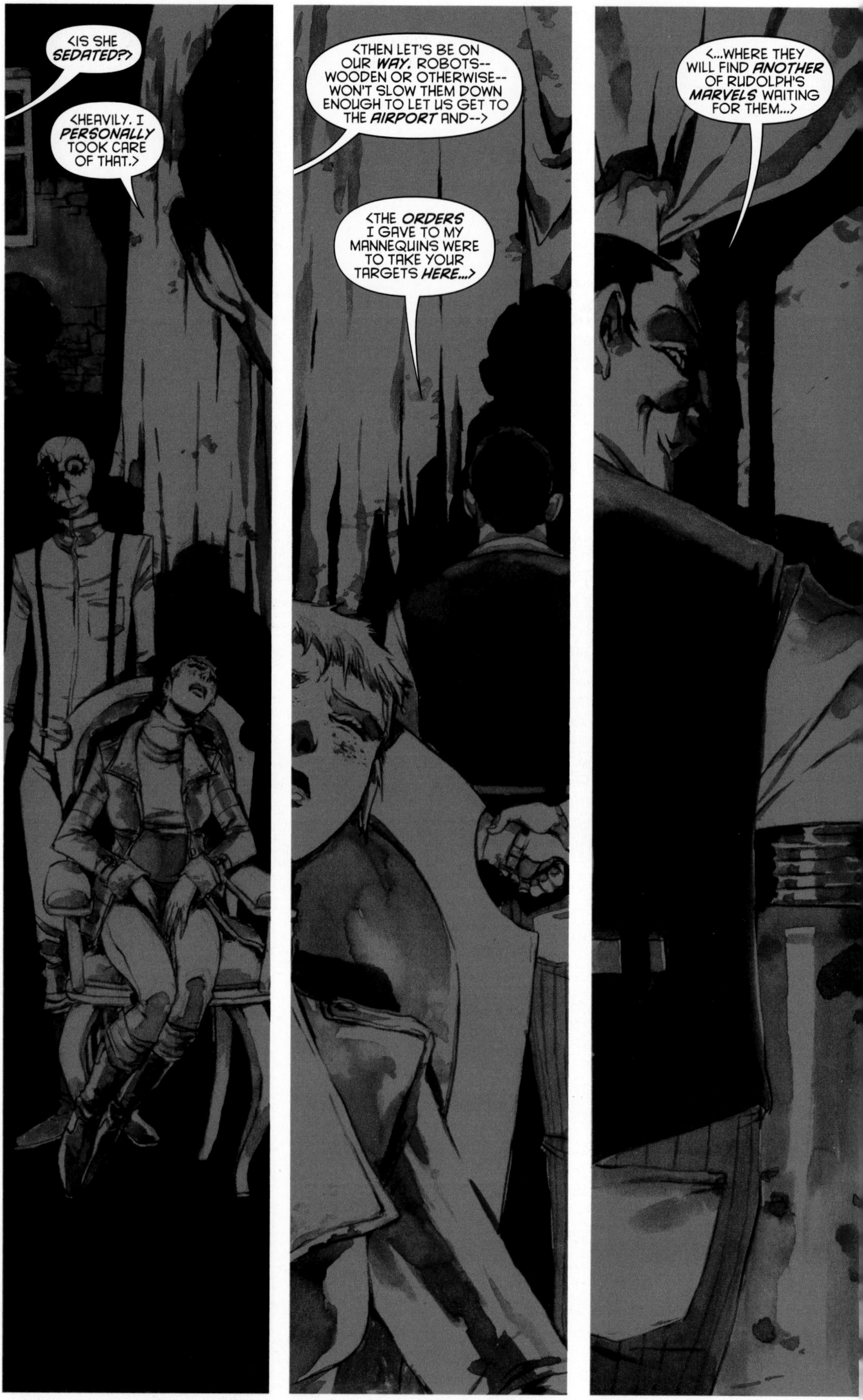
<IS SHE SEDATED?>
<HEAVILY. I PERSONALLY TOOK CARE OF THAT.>
<THEN LET'S BE ON OUR WAY. ROBOTS--WOODEN OR OTHERWISE--WON'T SLOW THEM DOWN ENOUGH TO LET US GET TO THE AIRPORT AND-->
<THE ORDERS I GAVE TO MY MANNEQUINS WERE TO TAKE YOUR TARGETS HERE...>
<...WHERE THEY WILL FIND ANOTHER OF RUDOLPH'S MARVELS WAITING FOR THEM...>

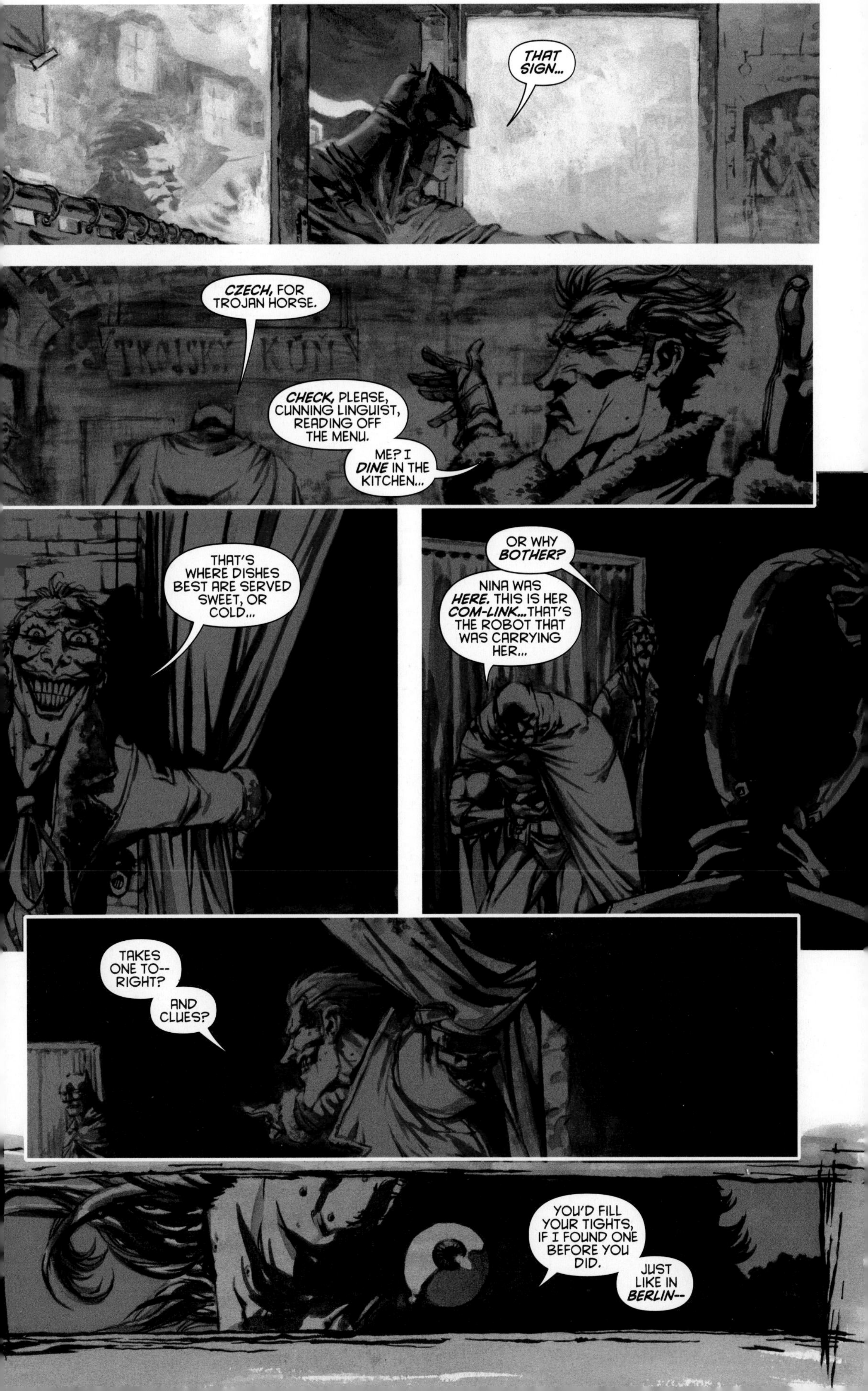
THAT SIGN...
CZECH, FOR TROJAN HORSE.
TROJSKÝ KŮŇ
CHECK, PLEASE, CUNNING LINGUIST, READING OFF THE MENU.
ME? I DINE IN THE KITCHEN...
THAT'S WHERE DISHES BEST ARE SERVED SWEET, OR COLD...
OR WHY BOTHER?
NINA WAS HERE. THIS IS HER COM-LINK...THAT'S THE ROBOT THAT WAS CARRYING HER...
TAKES ONE TO--RIGHT?
AND CLUES?
YOU'D FILL YOUR TIGHTS, IF I FOUND ONE BEFORE YOU DID.
JUST LIKE IN BERLIN--

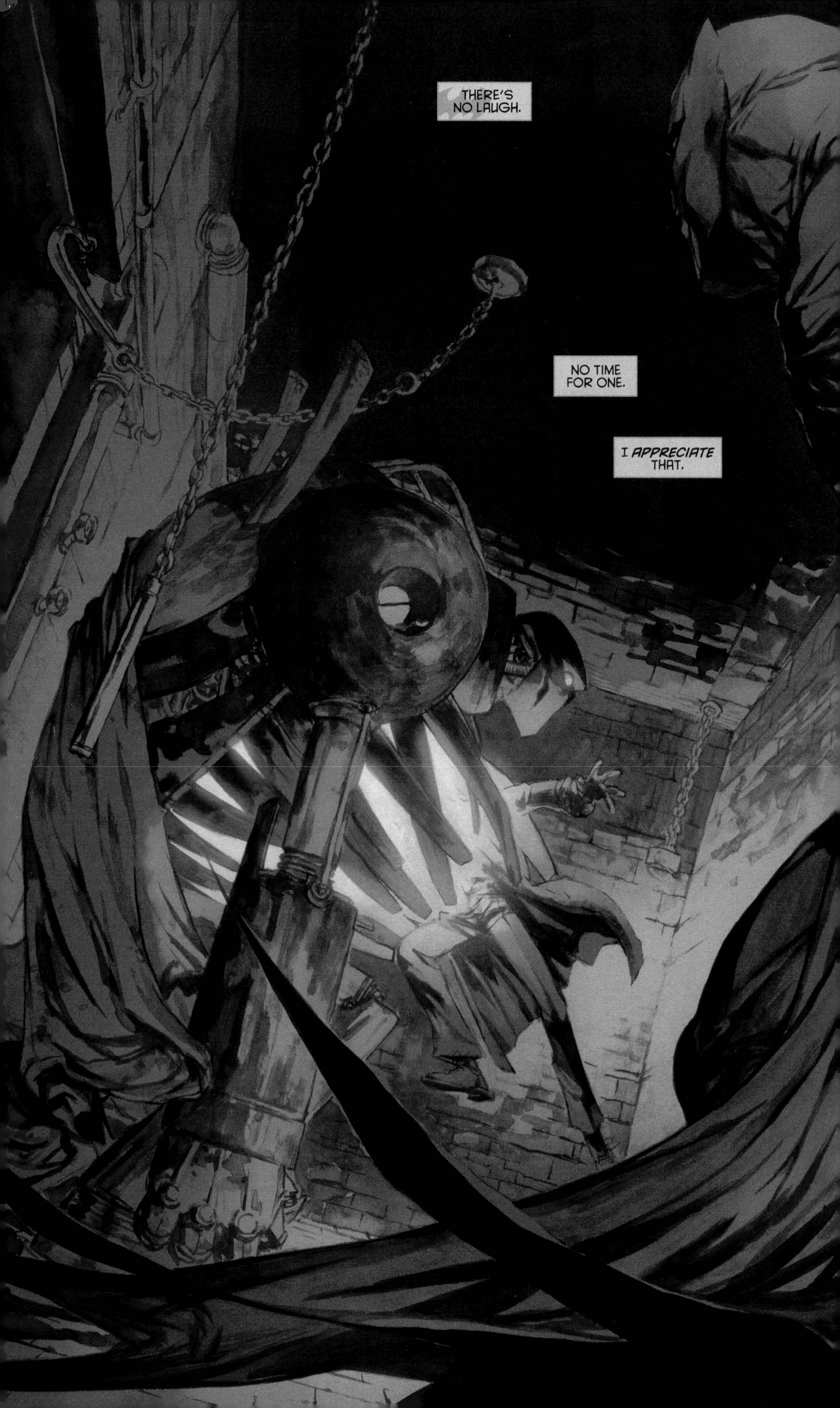
THERE'S NO LAUGH.
NO TIME FOR ONE.
I *APPRECIATE* THAT.

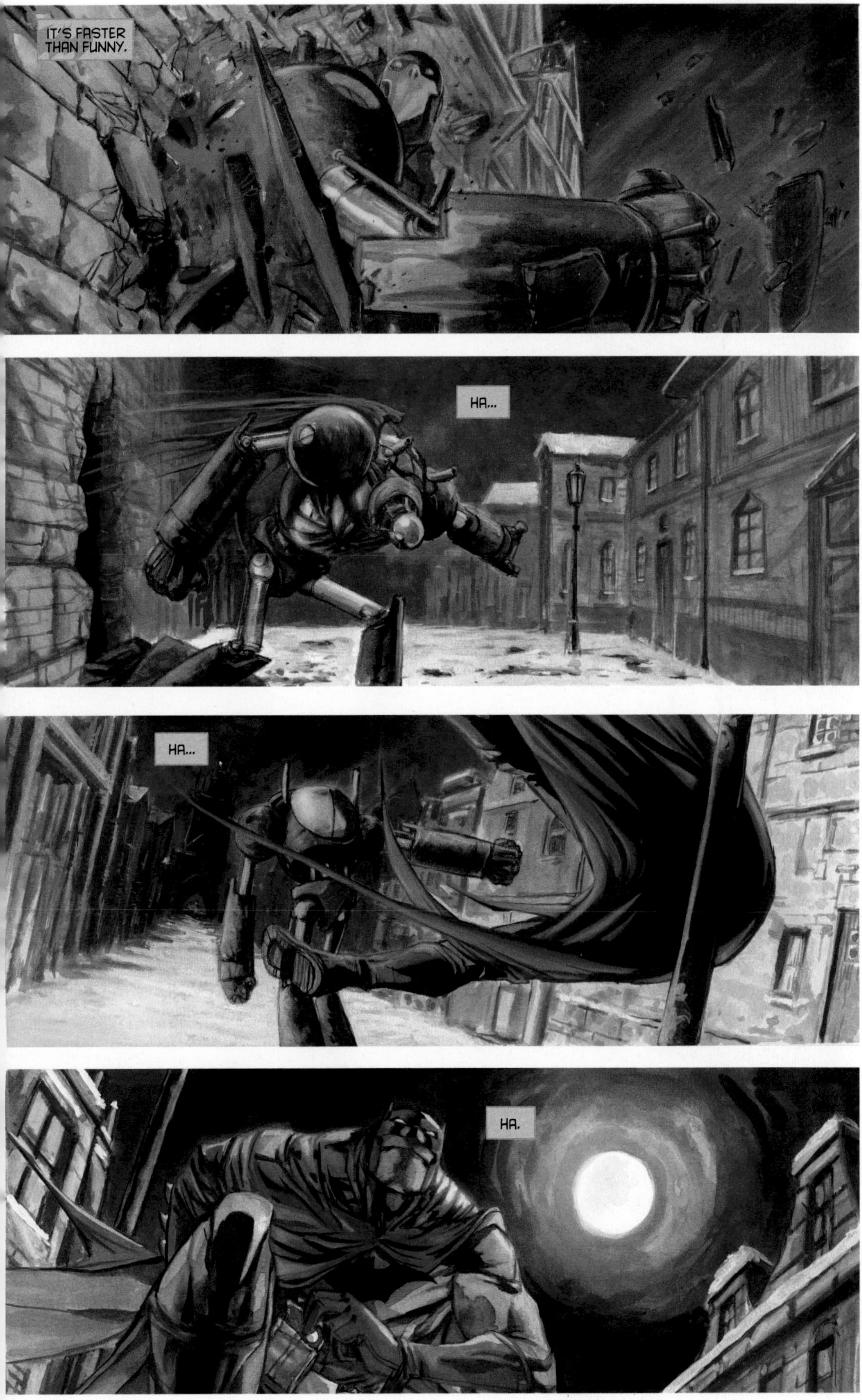
IT'S FASTER THAN FUNNY.
HA...
HA...
HA.

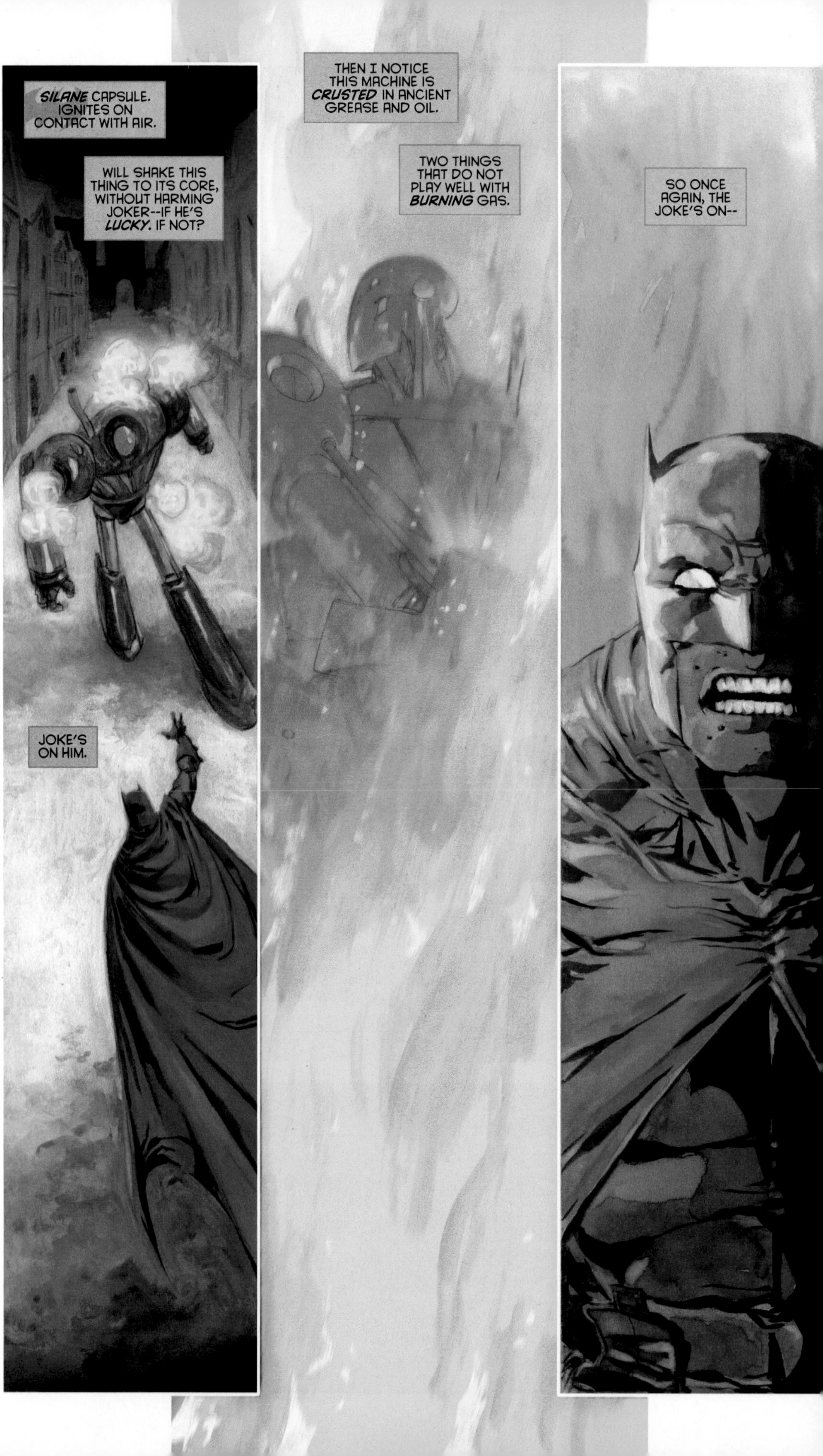
SILANE CAPSULE. IGNITES ON CONTACT WITH AIR.
WILL SHAKE THIS THING TO ITS CORE, WITHOUT HARMING JOKER--IF HE'S LUCKY. IF NOT?
JOKE'S ON HIM.
THEN I NOTICE THIS MACHINE IS CRUSTED IN ANCIENT GREASE AND OIL.
TWO THINGS THAT DO NOT PLAY WELL WITH BURNING GAS.
SO ONCE AGAIN, THE JOKE'S ON--

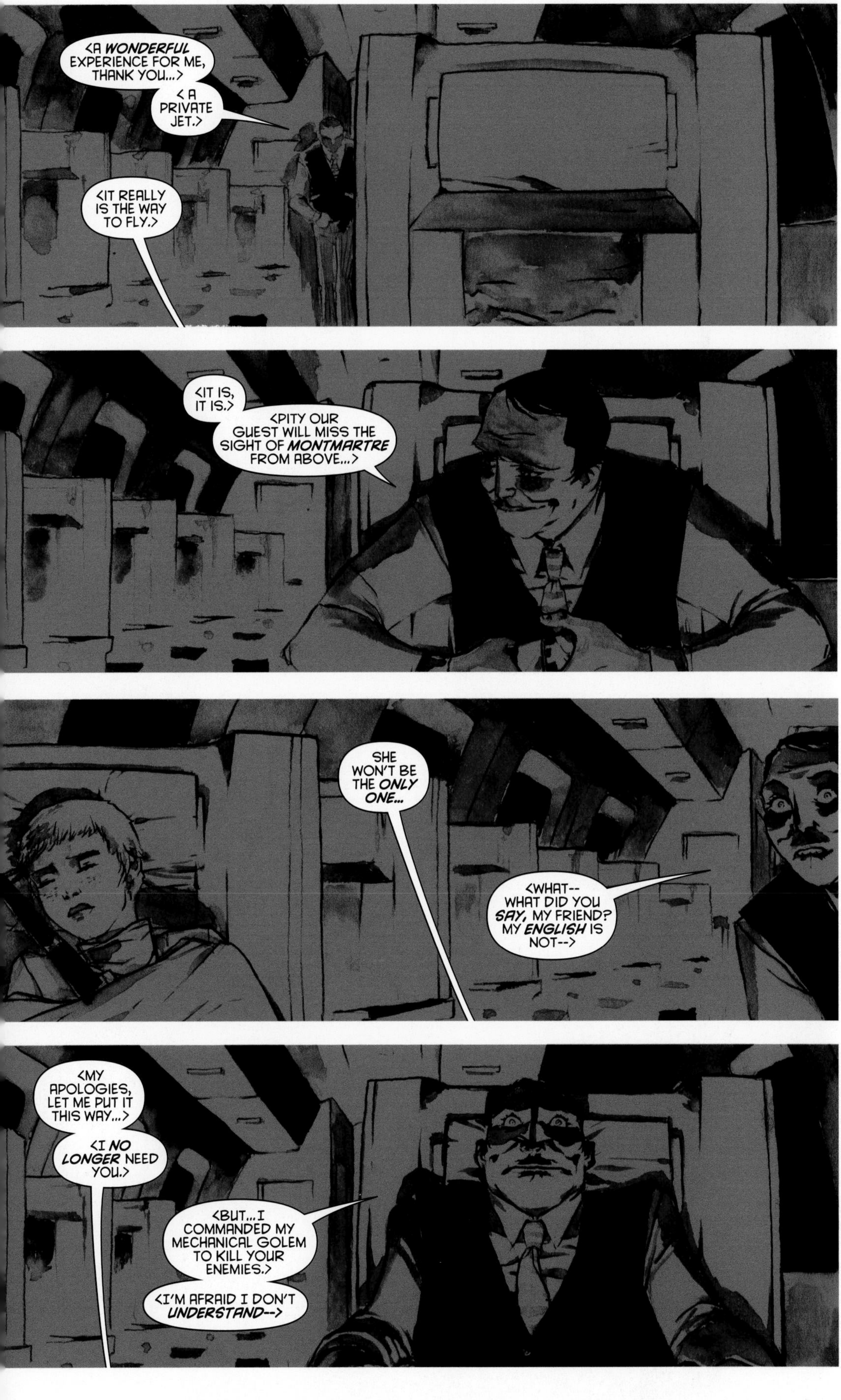
<A WONDERFUL EXPERIENCE FOR ME, THANK YOU...>
<A PRIVATE JET.>
<IT REALLY IS THE WAY TO FLY.>
<IT IS, IT IS.>
<PITY OUR GUEST WILL MISS THE SIGHT OF MONTMARTRE FROM ABOVE...>
SHE WON'T BE THE ONLY ONE...
<WHAT-- WHAT DID YOU SAY, MY FRIEND? MY ENGLISH IS NOT-->
<MY APOLOGIES, LET ME PUT IT THIS WAY...>
<I NO LONGER NEED YOU.>
<BUT...I COMMANDED MY MECHANICAL GOLEM TO KILL YOUR ENEMIES.>
<I'M AFRAID I DON'T UNDERSTAND-->

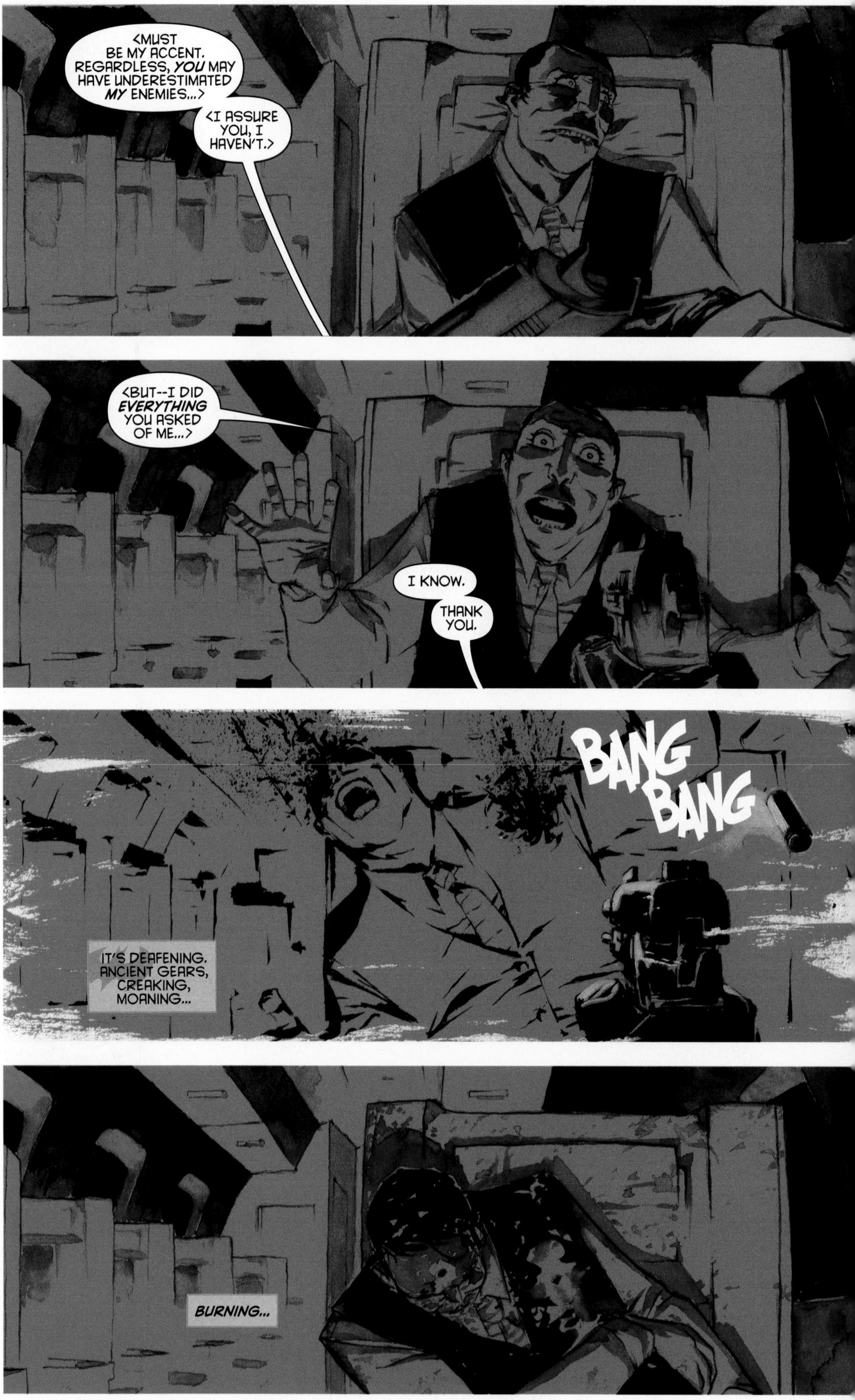
<MUST BE MY ACCENT. REGARDLESS, *YOU* MAY HAVE UNDERESTIMATED *MY* ENEMIES...>
<I ASSURE YOU, I HAVEN'T.>
<BUT--I DID *EVERYTHING* YOU ASKED OF ME...>
I KNOW.
THANK YOU.
BANG
BANG
IT'S DEAFENING. ANCIENT GEARS, CREAKING, MOANING...
BURNING...

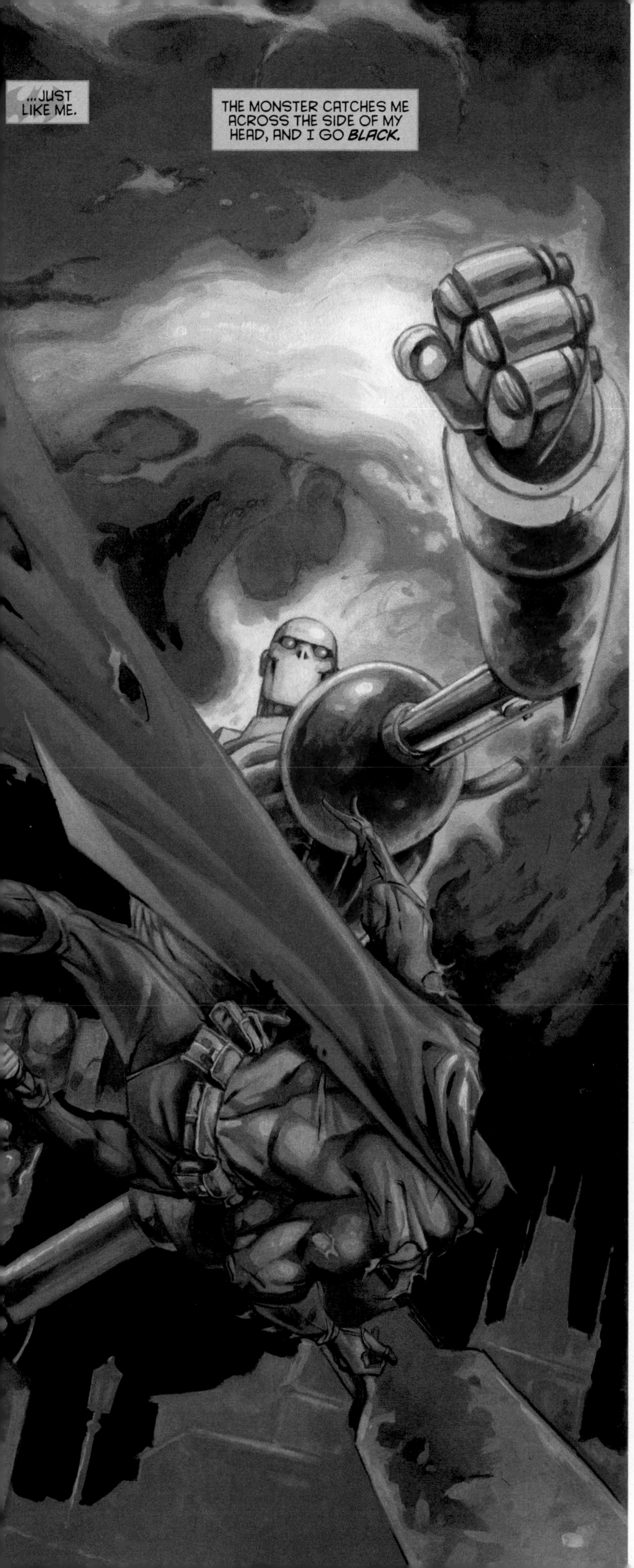
...JUST LIKE ME.
THE MONSTER CATCHES ME ACROSS THE SIDE OF MY HEAD, AND I GO BLACK.

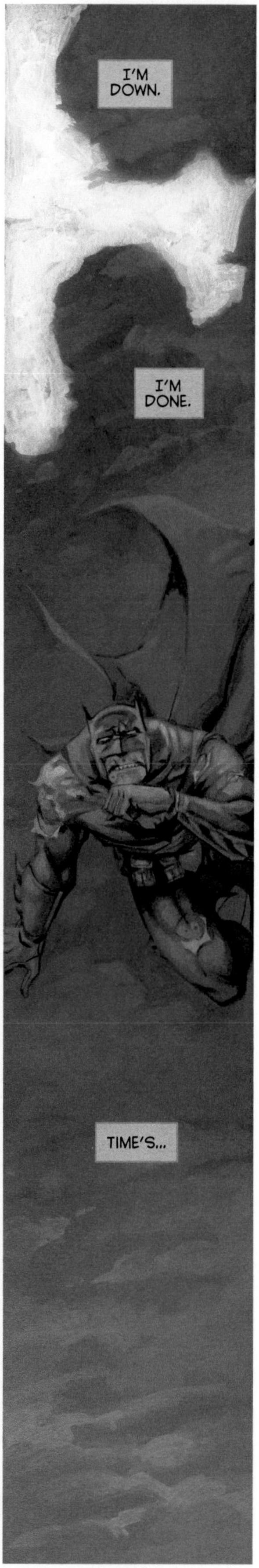
I'M DOWN.
I'M DONE.
TIME'S...

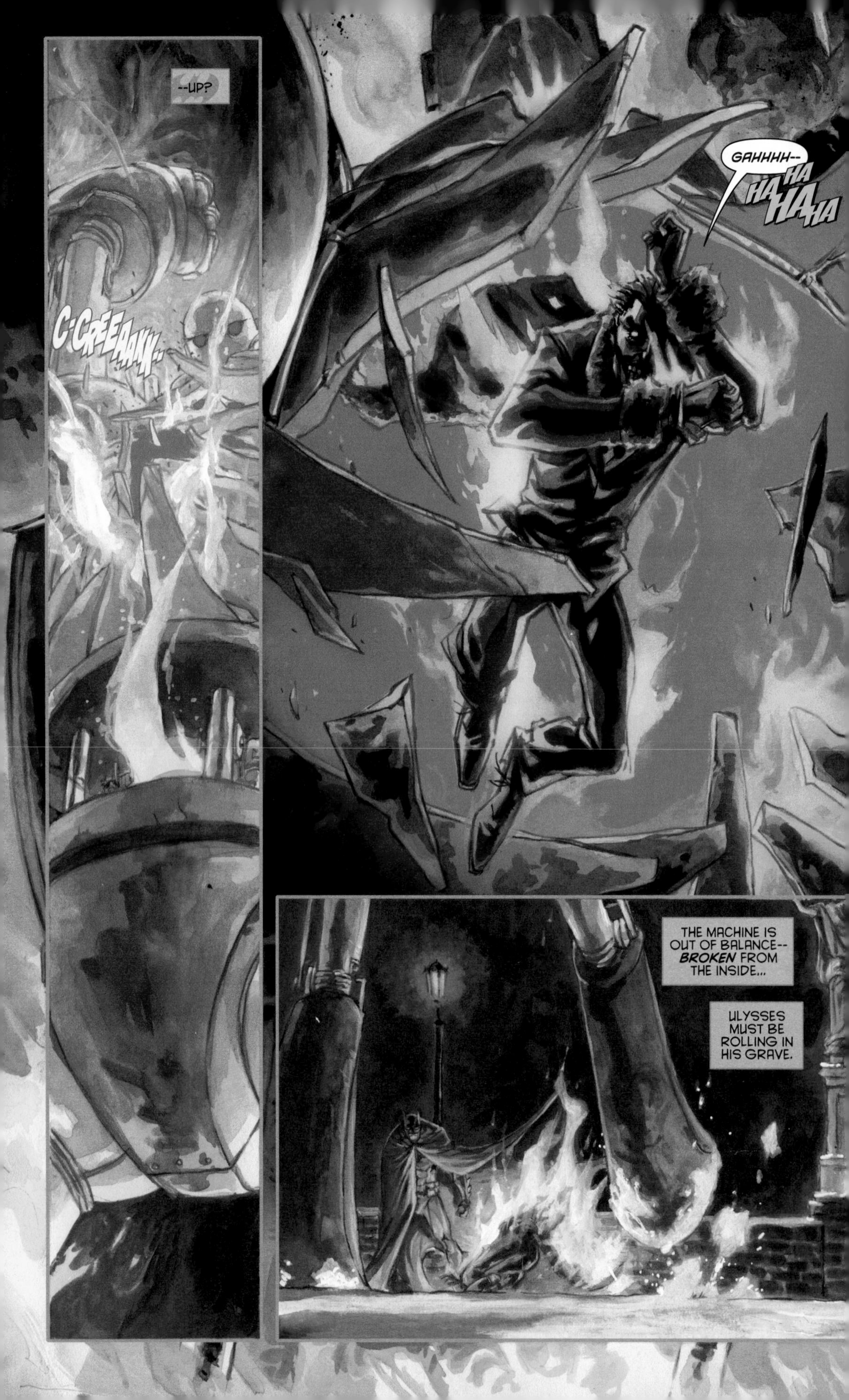

--UP?
C-CREEAAKK--
GAHHHH--
HA HA HA HA
THE MACHINE IS OUT OF BALANCE-- BROKEN FROM THE INSIDE...
ULYSSES MUST BE ROLLING IN HIS GRAVE.

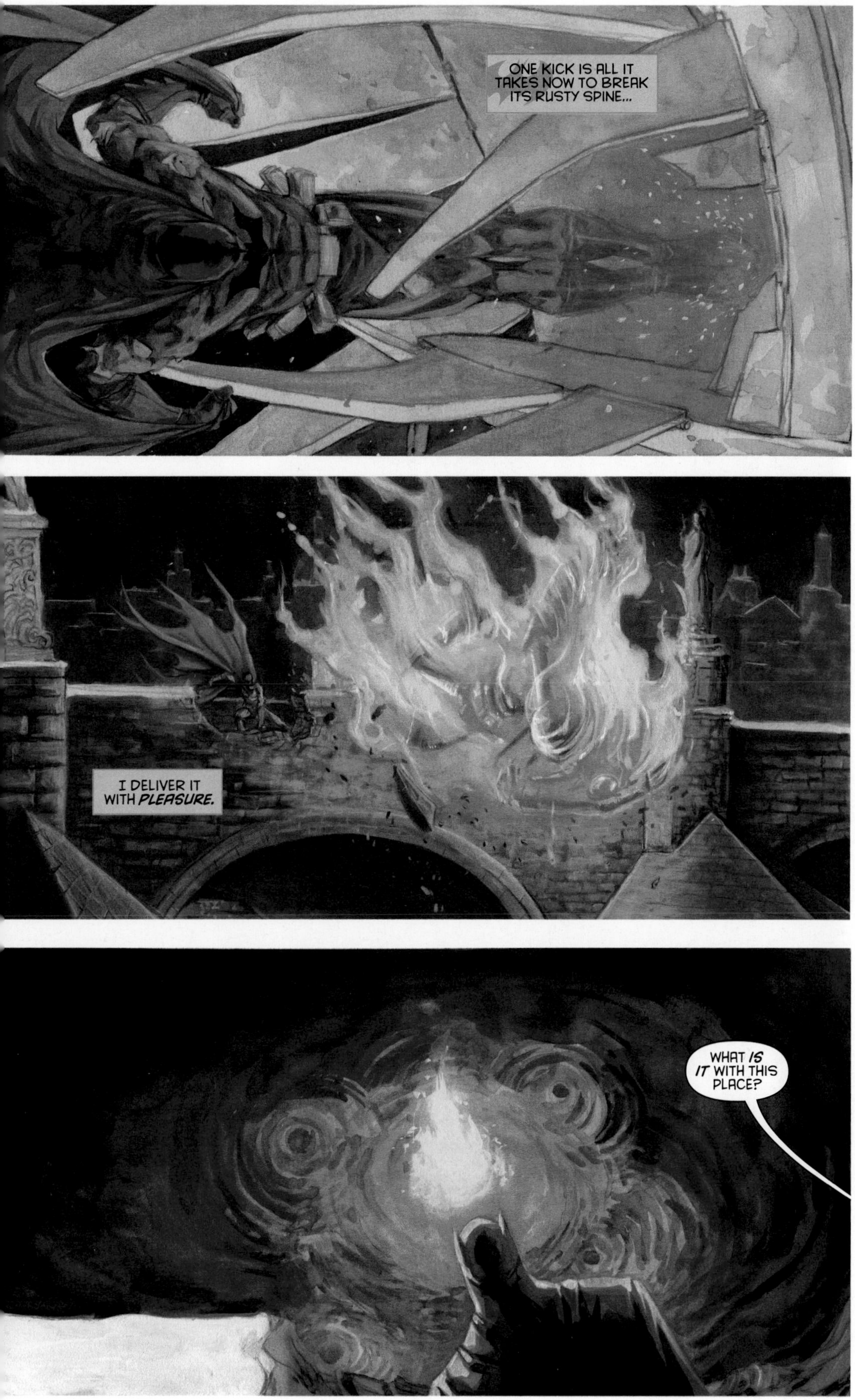
ONE KICK IS ALL IT TAKES NOW TO BREAK ITS RUSTY SPINE...
I DELIVER IT WITH *PLEASURE.*
WHAT *IS IT* WITH THIS PLACE?

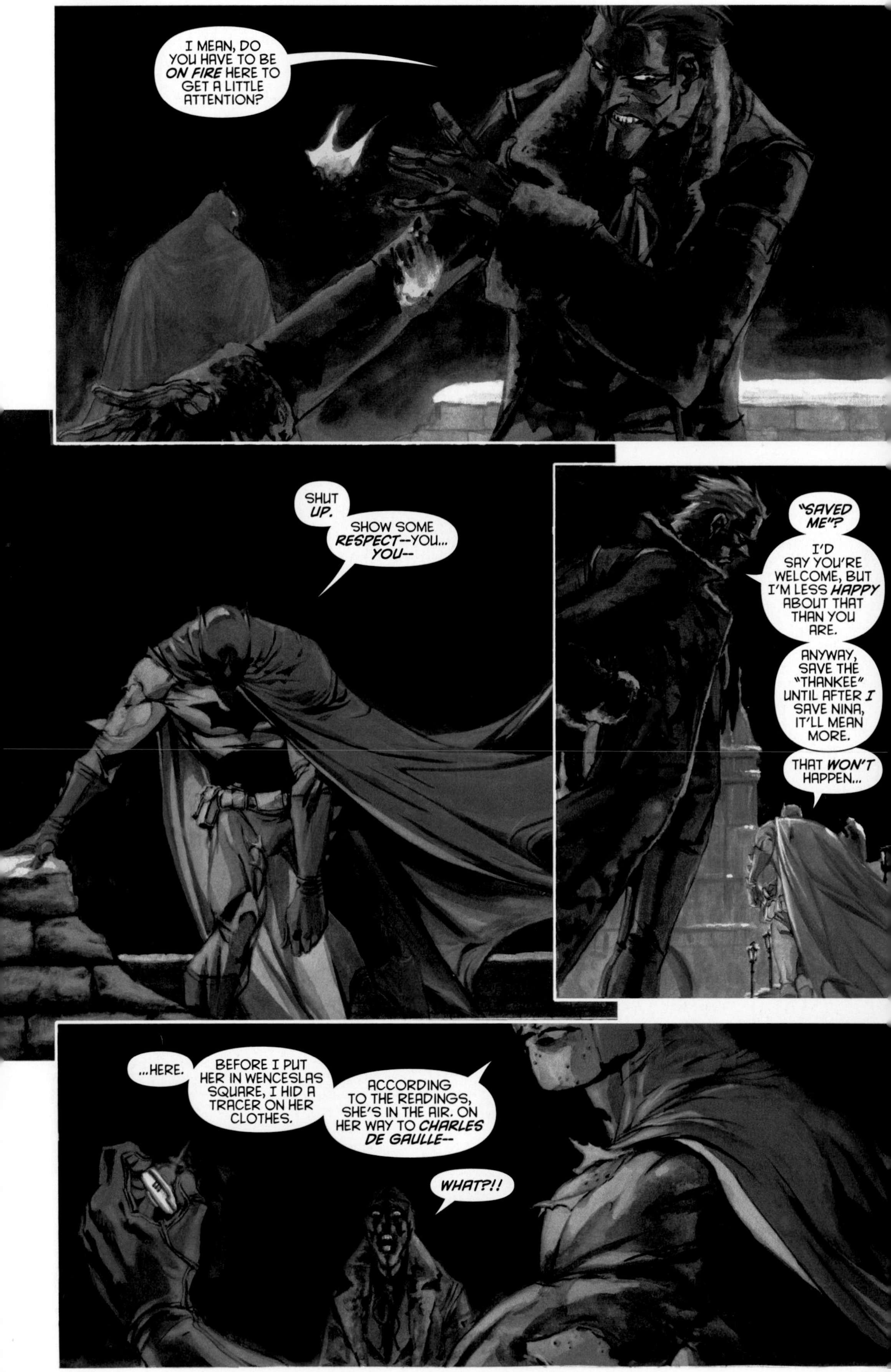

I MEAN, DO YOU HAVE TO BE *ON FIRE* HERE TO GET A LITTLE ATTENTION?
SHUT *UP.*
SHOW SOME *RESPECT*--YOU... *YOU*--
"SAVED ME"?
I'D SAY YOU'RE WELCOME, BUT I'M LESS *HAPPY* ABOUT THAT THAN YOU ARE.
ANYWAY, SAVE THE "THANKEE" UNTIL AFTER *I* SAVE NINA, IT'LL MEAN MORE.
THAT *WON'T* HAPPEN...
...HERE.
BEFORE I PUT HER IN WENCESLAS SQUARE, I HID A TRACER ON HER CLOTHES.
ACCORDING TO THE READINGS, SHE'S IN THE AIR. ON HER WAY TO *CHARLES DE GAULLE*--
WHAT?!!

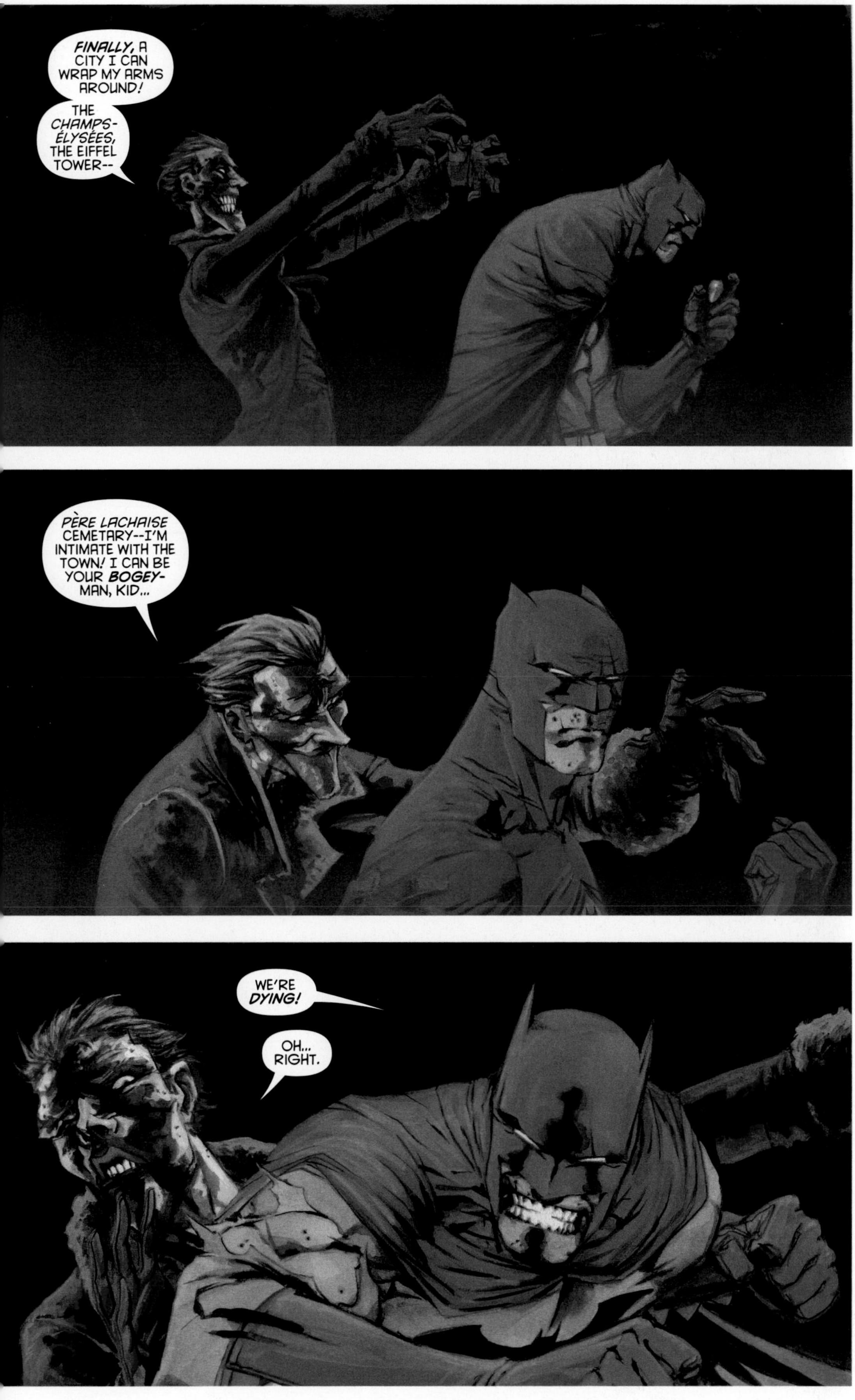
FINALLY, A CITY I CAN WRAP MY ARMS AROUND!
THE CHAMPS-ÉLYSÉES, THE EIFFEL TOWER--
PÈRE LACHAISE CEMETARY--I'M INTIMATE WITH THE TOWN! I CAN BE YOUR BOGEY-MAN, KID...
WE'RE DYING!
OH... RIGHT.

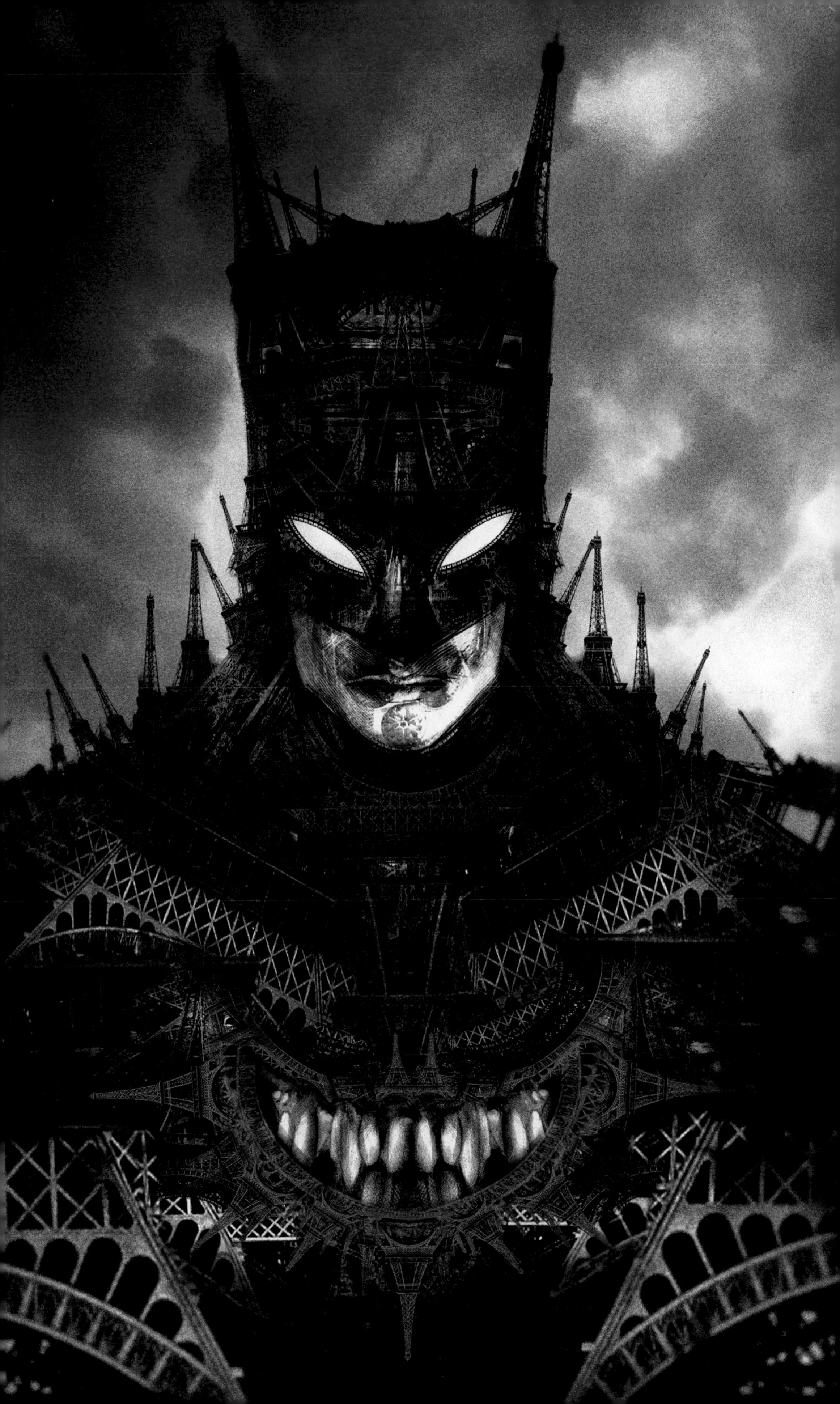

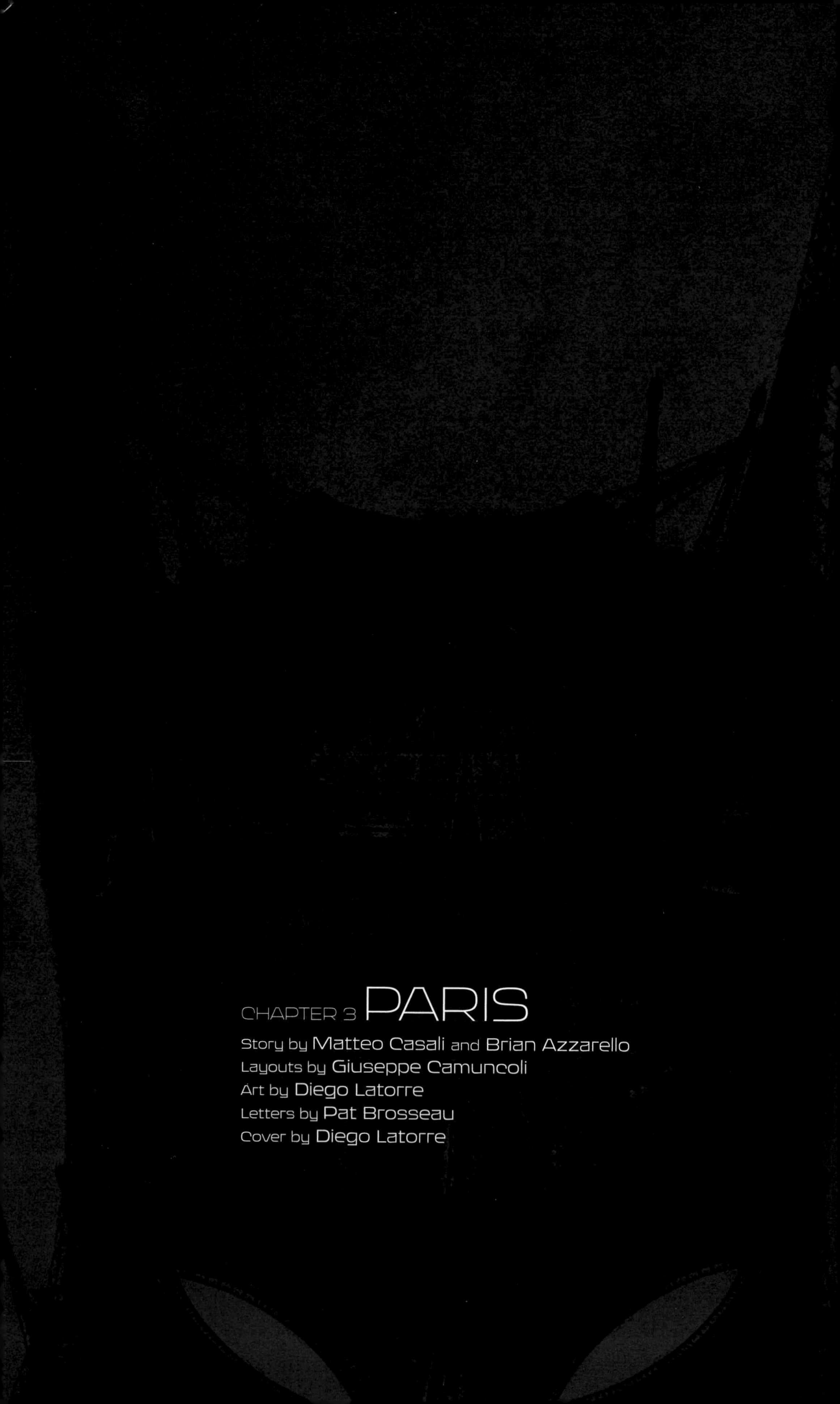

CHAPTER 3 PARIS

Story by Matteo Casali and Brian Azzarello
Layouts by Giuseppe Camuncoli
Art by Diego Latorre
Letters by Pat Brosseau
Cover by Diego Latorre

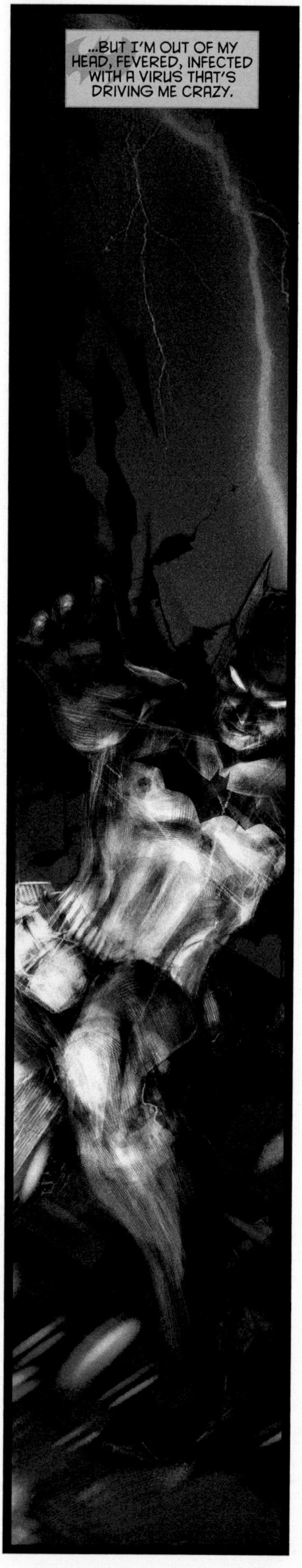
...BUT I'M OUT OF MY HEAD, FEVERED, INFECTED WITH A VIRUS THAT'S DRIVING ME CRAZY.

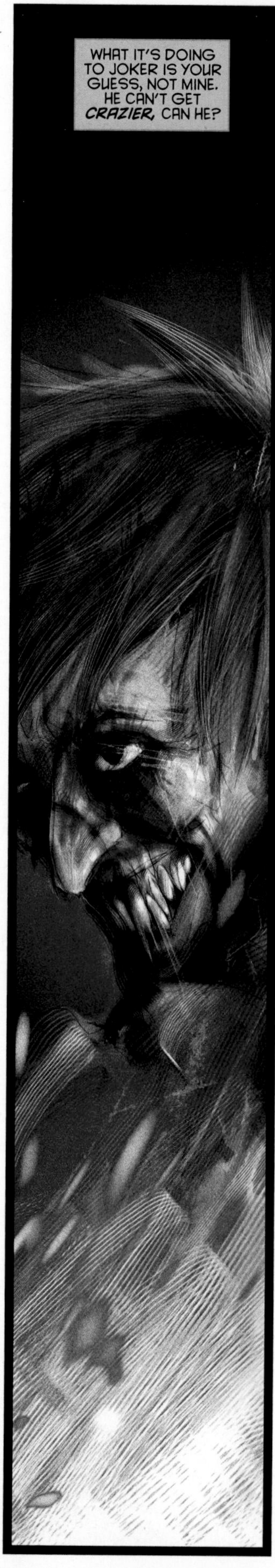
WHAT IT'S DOING TO JOKER IS YOUR GUESS, NOT MINE. HE CAN'T GET *CRAZIER,* CAN HE?

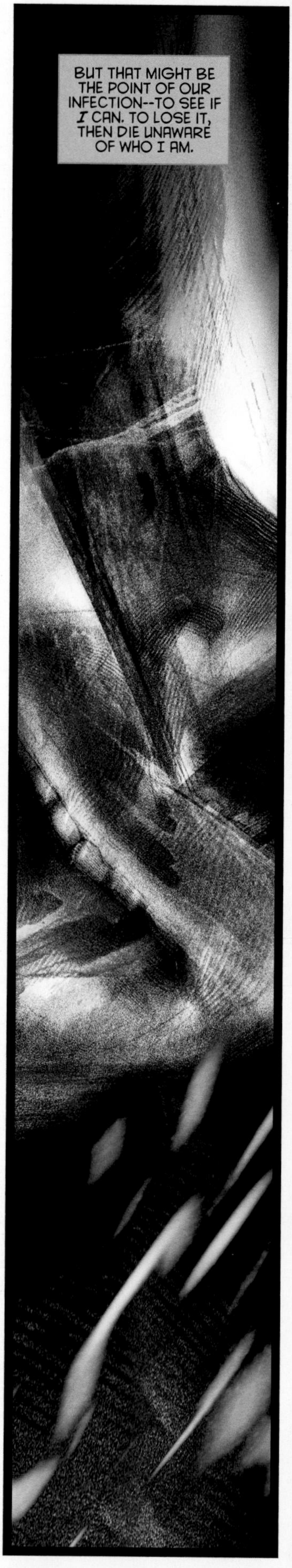
BUT THAT MIGHT BE THE POINT OF OUR INFECTION--TO SEE IF *I* CAN. TO LOSE IT, THEN DIE UNAWARE OF WHO I AM.

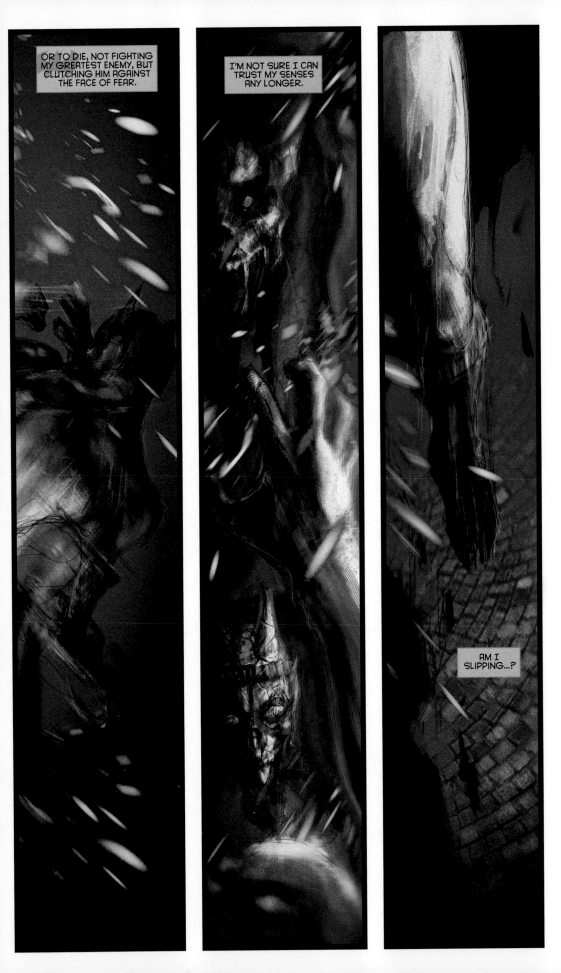

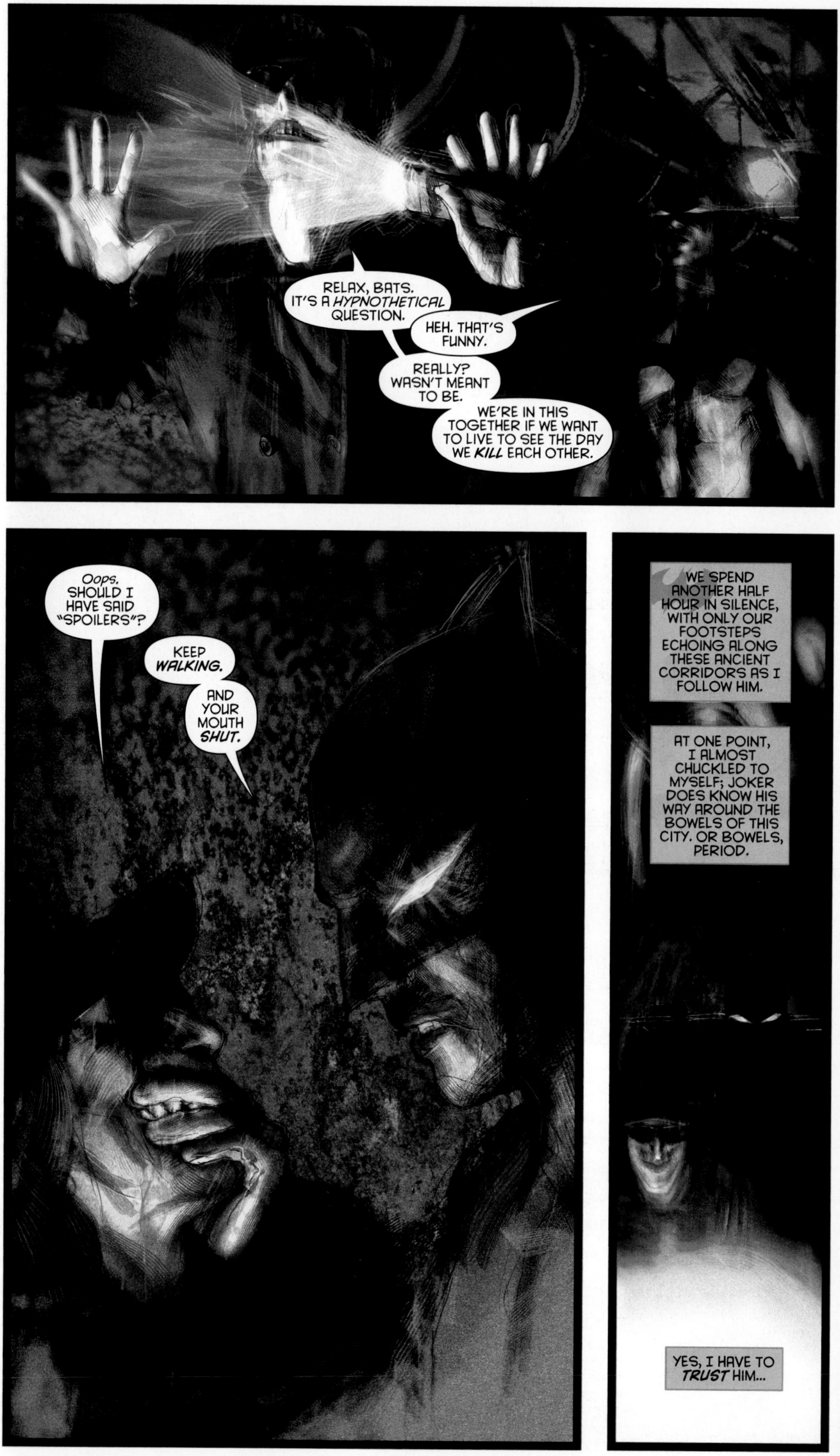
RELAX, BATS. IT'S A HYPNOTHETICAL QUESTION.
HEH. THAT'S FUNNY.
REALLY? WASN'T MEANT TO BE.
WE'RE IN THIS TOGETHER IF WE WANT TO LIVE TO SEE THE DAY WE KILL EACH OTHER.
Oops. SHOULD I HAVE SAID "SPOILERS"?
KEEP WALKING.
AND YOUR MOUTH SHUT.
WE SPEND ANOTHER HALF HOUR IN SILENCE, WITH ONLY OUR FOOTSTEPS ECHOING ALONG THESE ANCIENT CORRIDORS AS I FOLLOW HIM.
AT ONE POINT, I ALMOST CHUCKLED TO MYSELF; JOKER DOES KNOW HIS WAY AROUND THE BOWELS OF THIS CITY. OR BOWELS, PERIOD.
YES, I HAVE TO TRUST HIM...

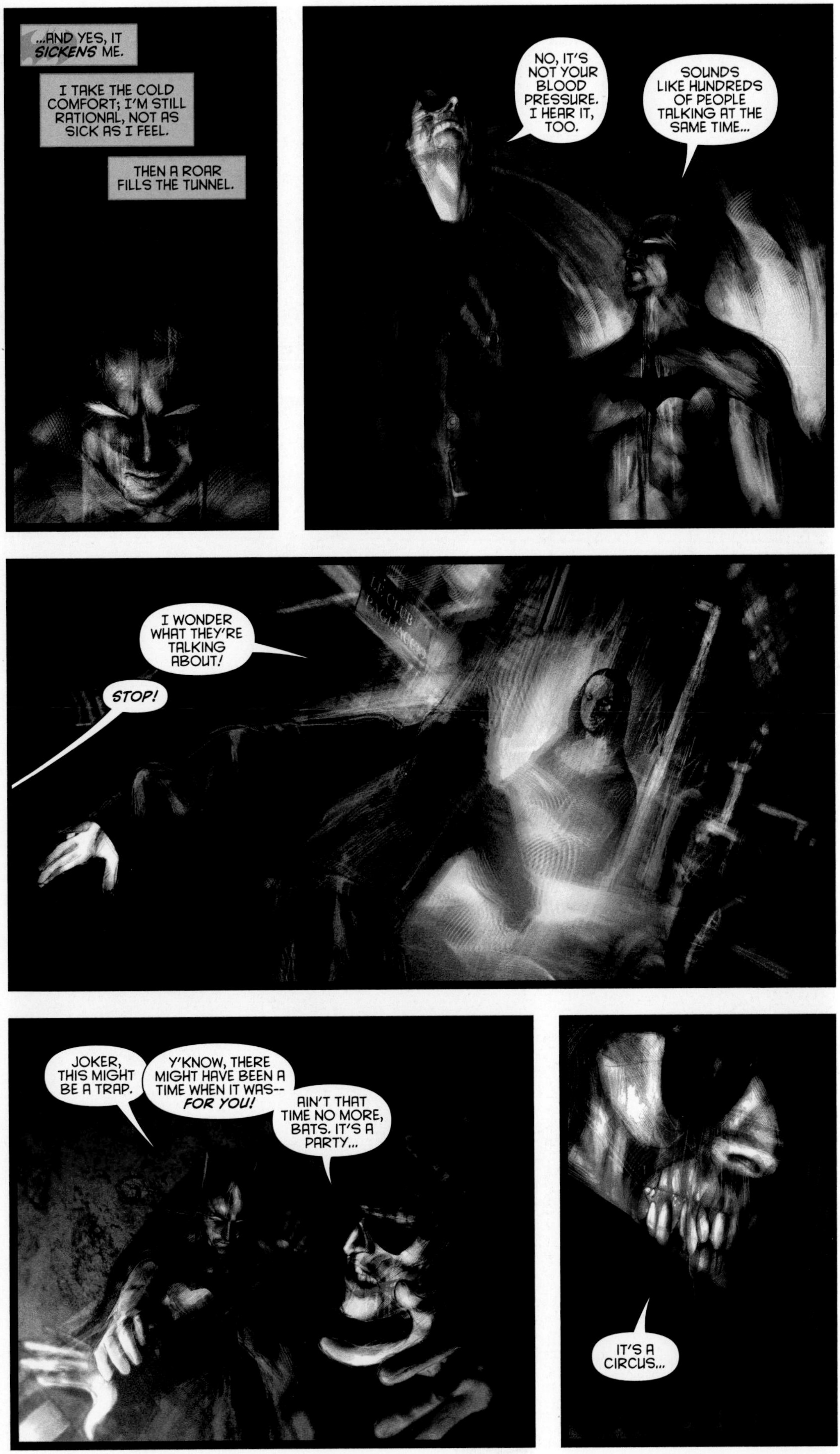
...AND YES, IT SICKENS ME.
I TAKE THE COLD COMFORT; I'M STILL RATIONAL, NOT AS SICK AS I FEEL.
THEN A ROAR FILLS THE TUNNEL.
NO, IT'S NOT YOUR BLOOD PRESSURE. I HEAR IT, TOO.
SOUNDS LIKE HUNDREDS OF PEOPLE TALKING AT THE SAME TIME...
I WONDER WHAT THEY'RE TALKING ABOUT!
STOP!
JOKER, THIS MIGHT BE A TRAP.
Y'KNOW, THERE MIGHT HAVE BEEN A TIME WHEN IT WAS-- FOR YOU!
AIN'T THAT TIME NO MORE, BATS. IT'S A PARTY...
IT'S A CIRCUS...

LE CIRQUE DU ROI DES CLOWNS.

IF I WEREN'T BURNING UP WITH A FEVER, THE SIGHT WOULD HAVE CHILLED ME TO MY CORE.

THOUGH THEY LOOKED IT, THESE PEOPLE WEREN'T VICTIMS OF JOKER'S LAUGHING GAS.

THEY WERE VICTIMS OF HIS *CHARM.*

AND WHILE FATAL, I REALIZED THE VIRUS I WAS INFECTED WITH WAS *PREFERABLE.*

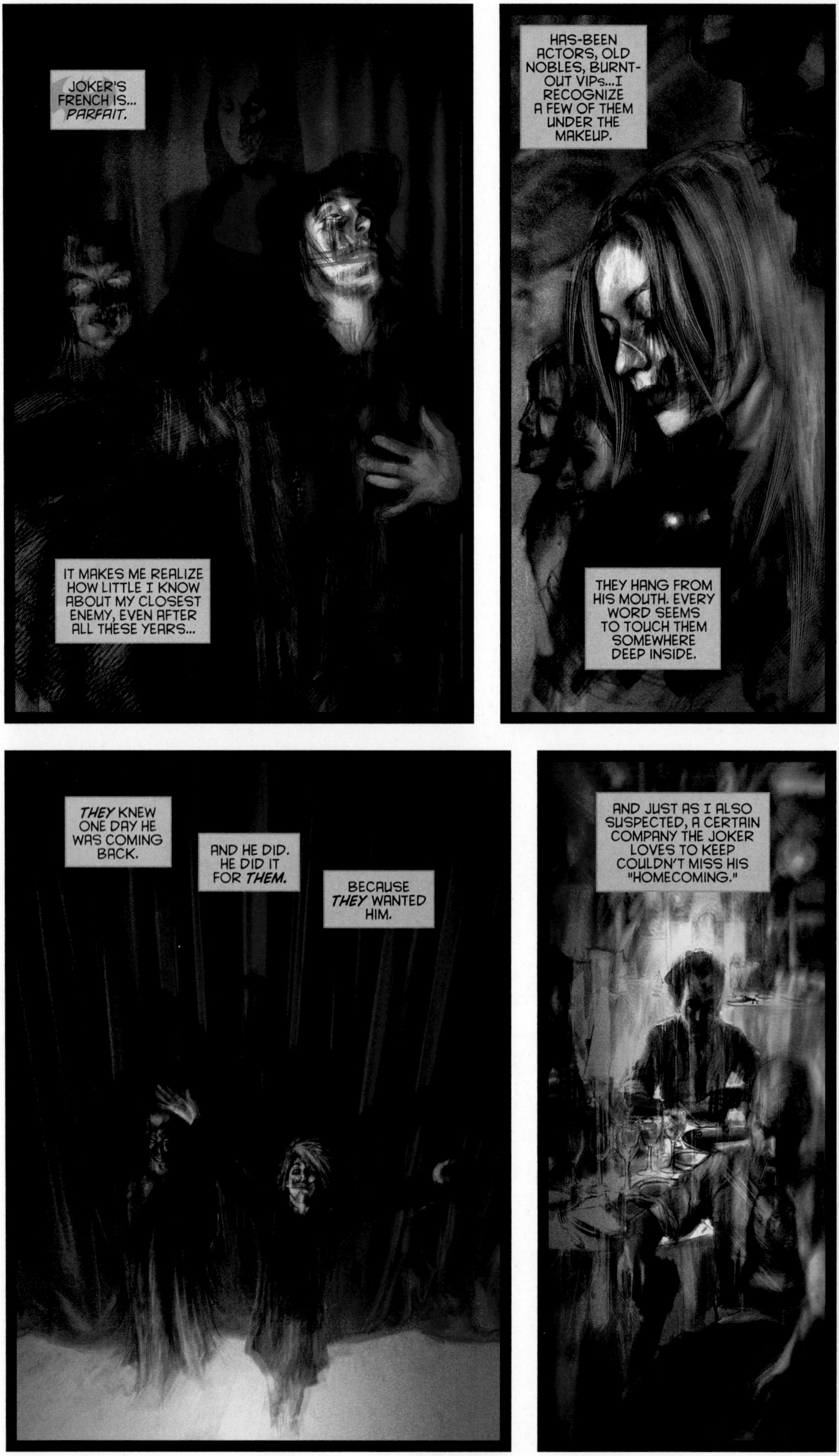
JOKER'S FRENCH IS... *PARFAIT.*
IT MAKES ME REALIZE HOW LITTLE I KNOW ABOUT MY CLOSEST ENEMY, EVEN AFTER ALL THESE YEARS...
HAS-BEEN ACTORS, OLD NOBLES, BURNT-OUT VIPs...I RECOGNIZE A FEW OF THEM UNDER THE MAKEUP.
THEY HANG FROM HIS MOUTH. EVERY WORD SEEMS TO TOUCH THEM SOMEWHERE DEEP INSIDE.
THEY KNEW ONE DAY HE WAS COMING BACK.
AND HE DID. HE DID IT FOR *THEM.*
BECAUSE *THEY* WANTED HIM.
AND JUST AS I ALSO SUSPECTED, A CERTAIN COMPANY THE JOKER LOVES TO KEEP COULDN'T MISS HIS "HOMECOMING."

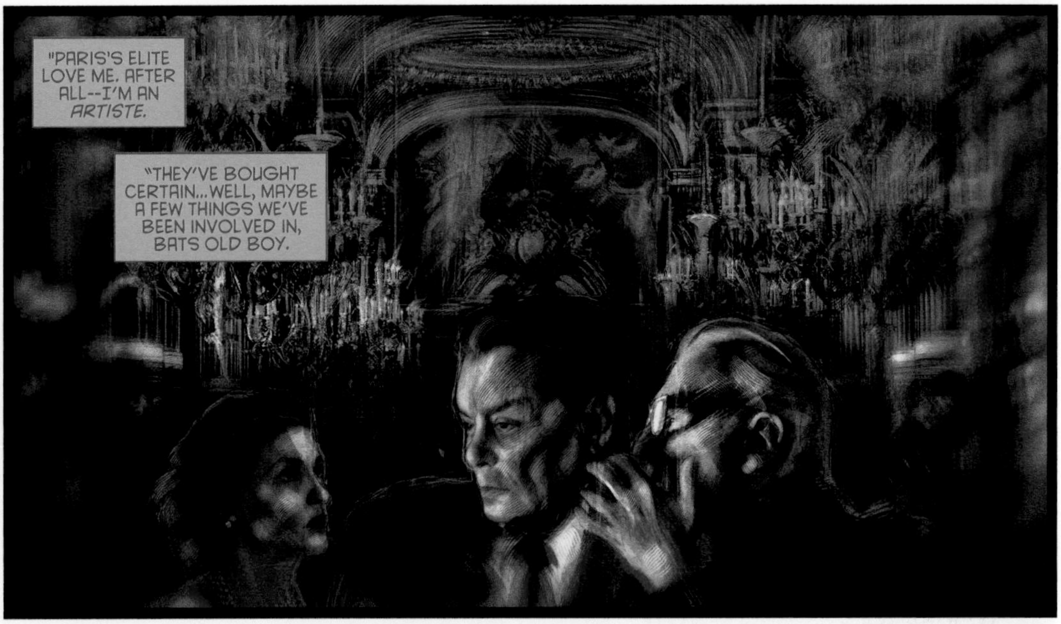
"PARIS'S ELITE LOVE ME. AFTER ALL--I'M AN *ARTISTE.*
"THEY'VE BOUGHT CERTAIN...WELL, MAYBE A FEW THINGS WE'VE BEEN INVOLVED IN, BATS OLD BOY.

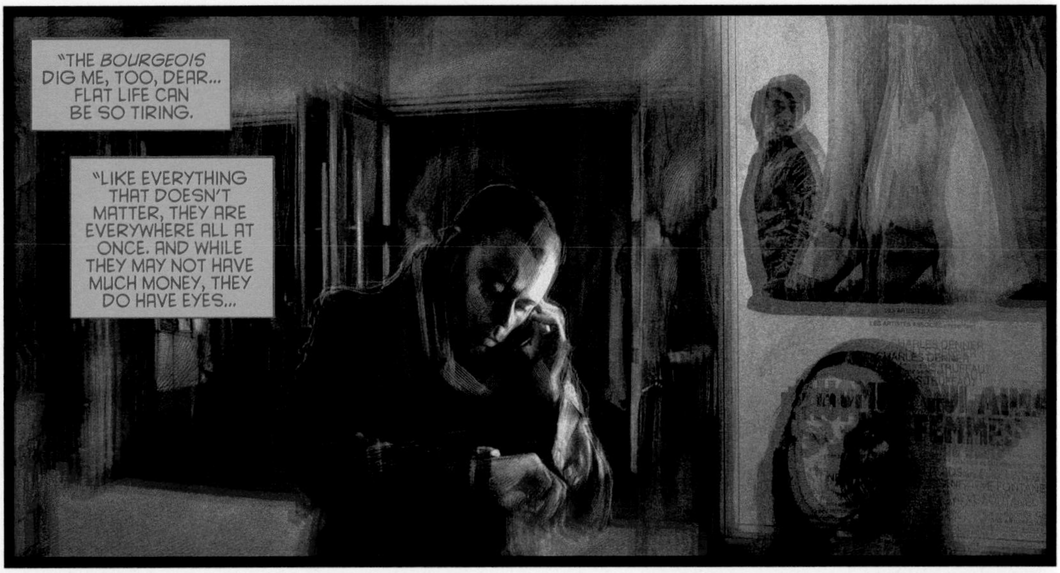
"THE *BOURGEOIS* DIG ME, TOO, DEAR... FLAT LIFE CAN BE SO TIRING.
"LIKE EVERYTHING THAT DOESN'T MATTER, THEY ARE EVERYWHERE ALL AT ONCE. AND WHILE THEY MAY NOT HAVE MUCH MONEY, THEY DO HAVE EYES...

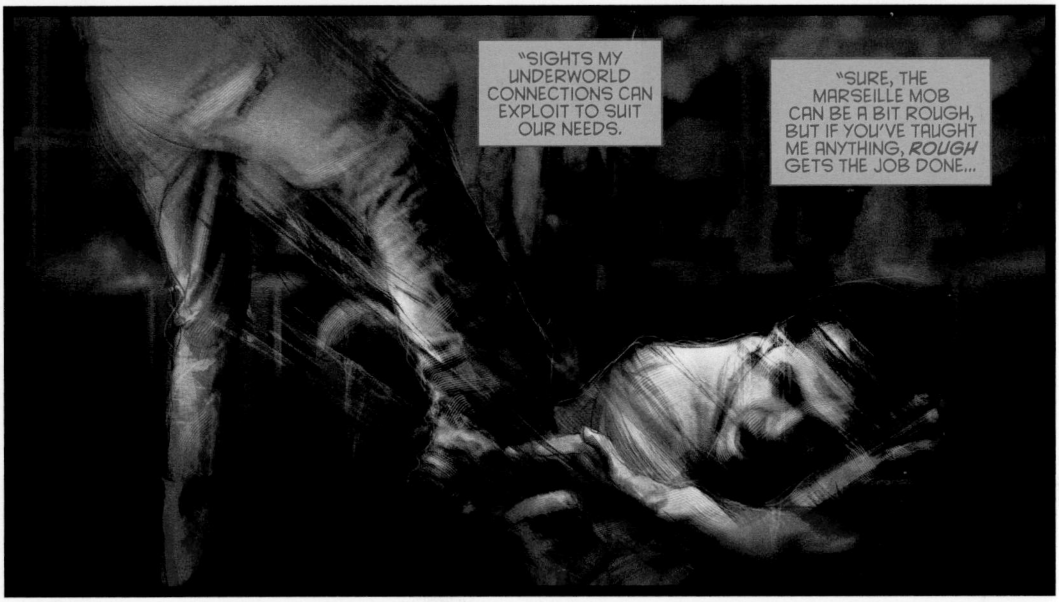
"SIGHTS MY UNDERWORLD CONNECTIONS CAN EXPLOIT TO SUIT OUR NEEDS.
"SURE, THE MARSEILLE MOB CAN BE A BIT ROUGH, BUT IF YOU'VE TAUGHT ME ANYTHING, *ROUGH* GETS THE JOB DONE...

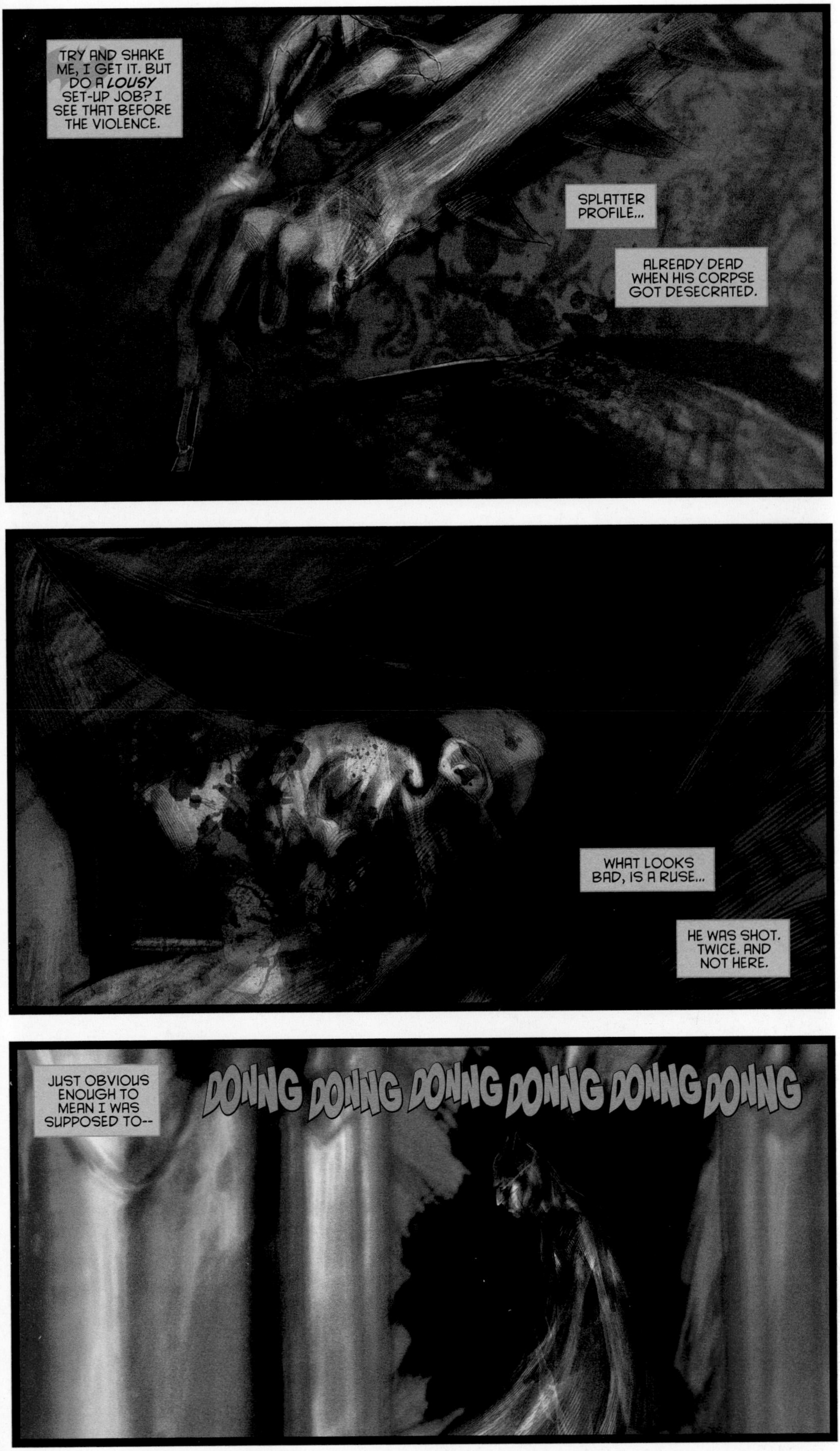
TRY AND SHAKE ME, I GET IT. BUT DO A *LOUSY* SET-UP JOB? I SEE THAT BEFORE THE VIOLENCE.
SPLATTER PROFILE...
ALREADY DEAD WHEN HIS CORPSE GOT DESECRATED.
WHAT LOOKS BAD, IS A RUSE...
HE WAS SHOT. TWICE. AND NOT HERE.
JUST OBVIOUS ENOUGH TO MEAN I WAS SUPPOSED TO--
DONNG DONNG DONNG DONNG DONNG DONNG

GETTING TO THE ROOF WAS HARDER THAN IT SHOULD HAVE BEEN.

BUT THEN, I HAVE MY MONKEY ON MY BACK.

HEH.

DONNG
DONNG
DONNG
DONNG
DONNG
DONNG

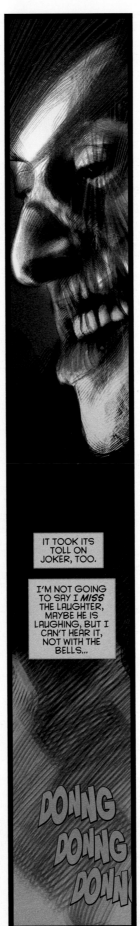

IT TOOK ITS TOLL ON JOKER, TOO.

I'M NOT GOING TO SAY I *MISS* THE LAUGHTER, MAYBE HE IS LAUGHING, BUT I CAN'T HEAR IT, NOT WITH THE BELLS...

DONNG
DONNG
DONN

...OR THE NIGHTMARE.

YOU MADE IT?! *BRAVO!* HOW FORTUNATE THAT THE VIRUS HAS NOT FINISHED YOU YET.

THOUGH I CONFESS, I THOUGHT ONE OF YOU WOULD BE DEAD BY NOW.

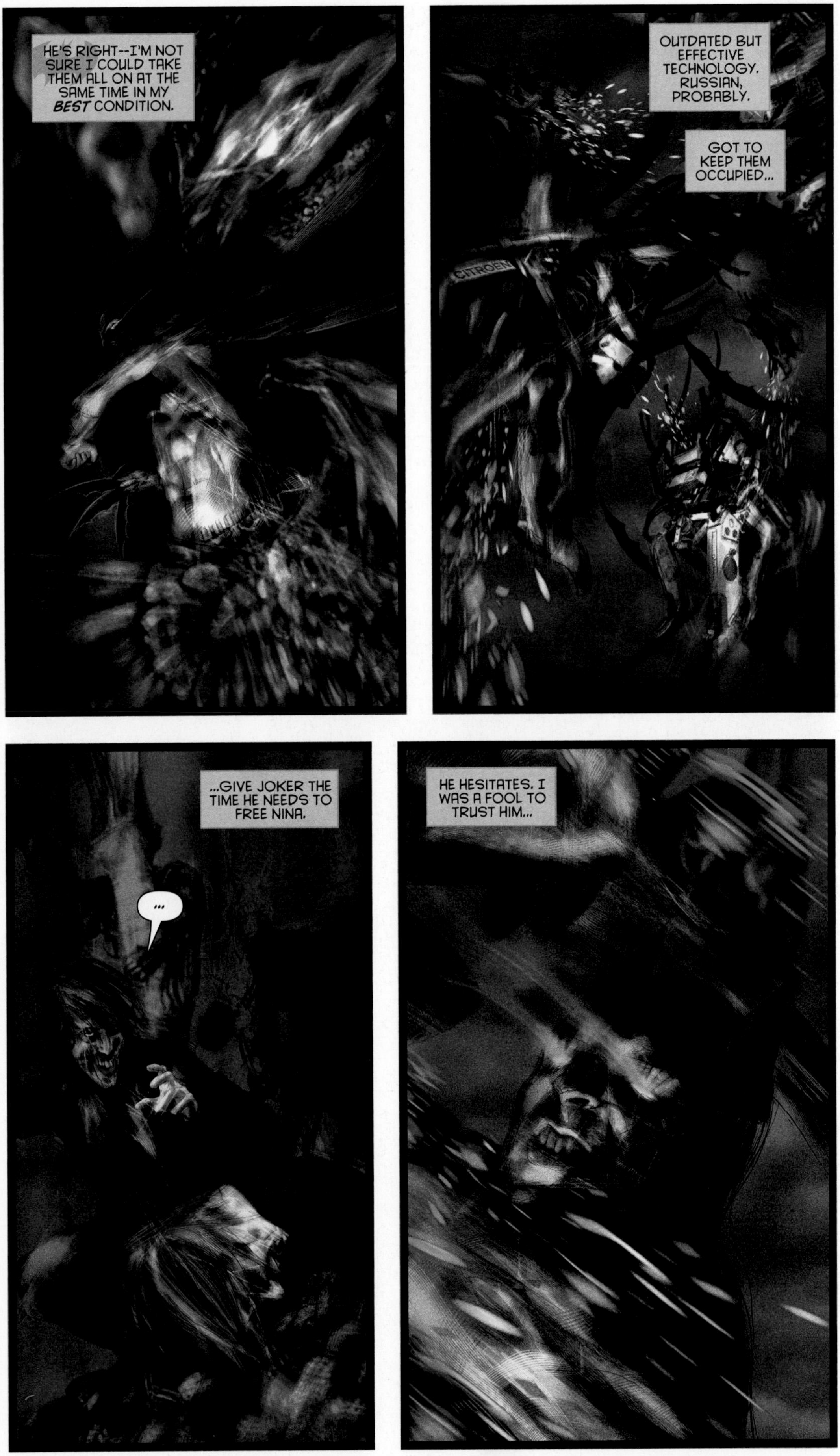
HE'S RIGHT--I'M NOT SURE I COULD TAKE THEM ALL ON AT THE SAME TIME IN MY *BEST* CONDITION.
OUTDATED BUT EFFECTIVE TECHNOLOGY. RUSSIAN, PROBABLY.
GOT TO KEEP THEM OCCUPIED...
CITROEN
...GIVE JOKER THE TIME HE NEEDS TO FREE NINA.
...
HE HESITATES. I WAS A FOOL TO TRUST HIM...

AM I SLIPPING... OR LETTING GO?

CLUTCHING MADNESS OR STRAWS IN THE FACE OF FEAR?

I CAN FEEL THE BELLS TOLL, BUT I CAN'T HEAR THEM.

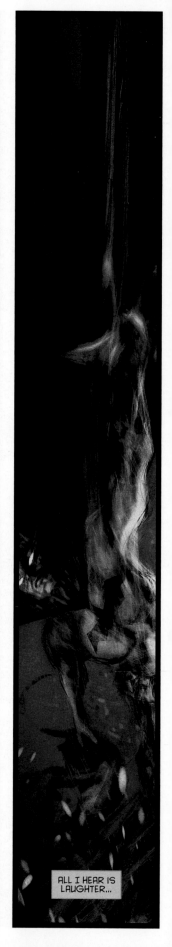

ALL I HEAR IS LAUGHTER...

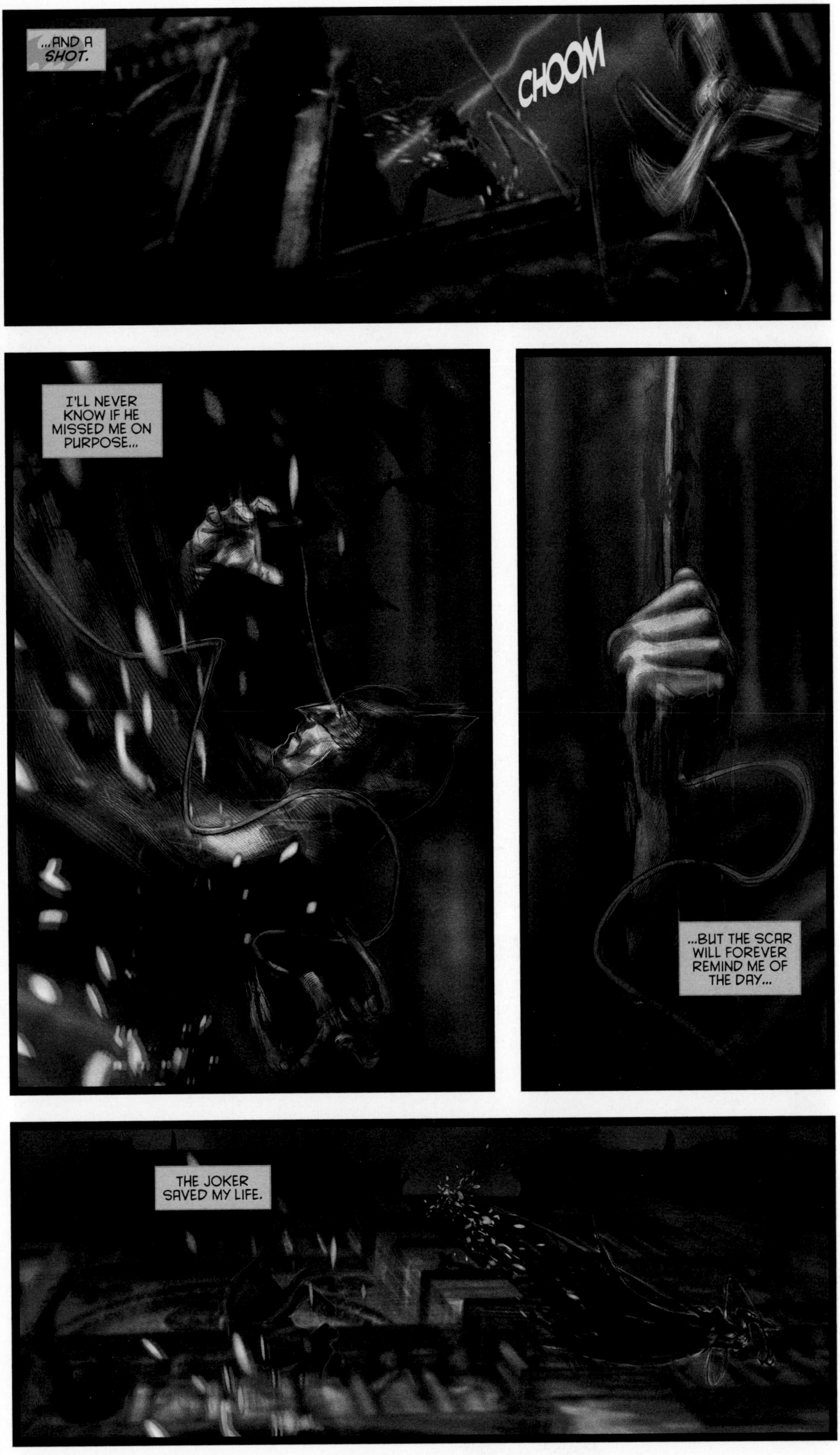
...AND A SHOT.
CHOOM
I'LL NEVER KNOW IF HE MISSED ME ON PURPOSE...
...BUT THE SCAR WILL FOREVER REMIND ME OF THE DAY...
THE JOKER SAVED MY LIFE.

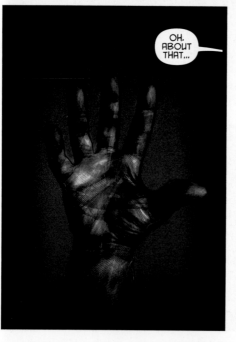

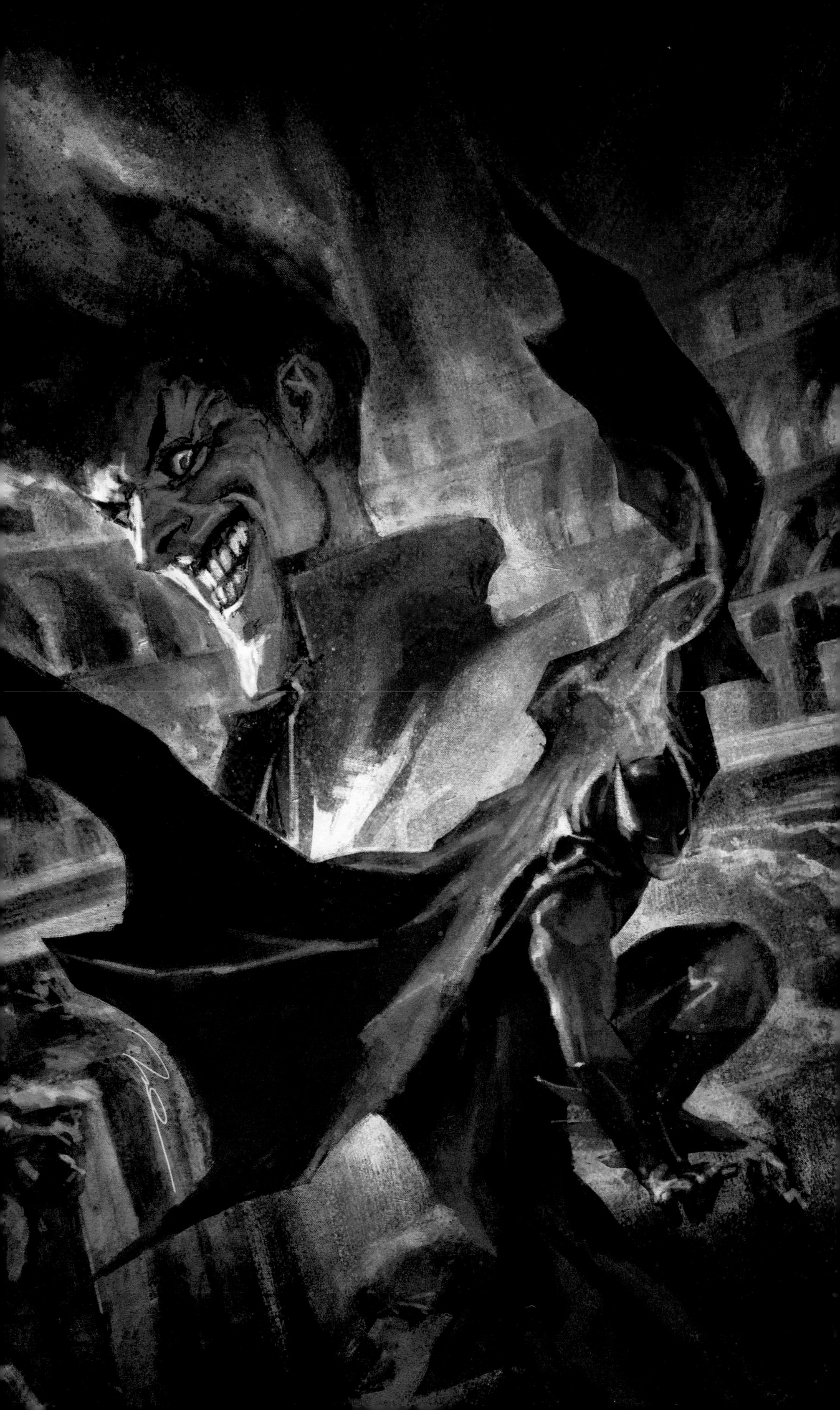

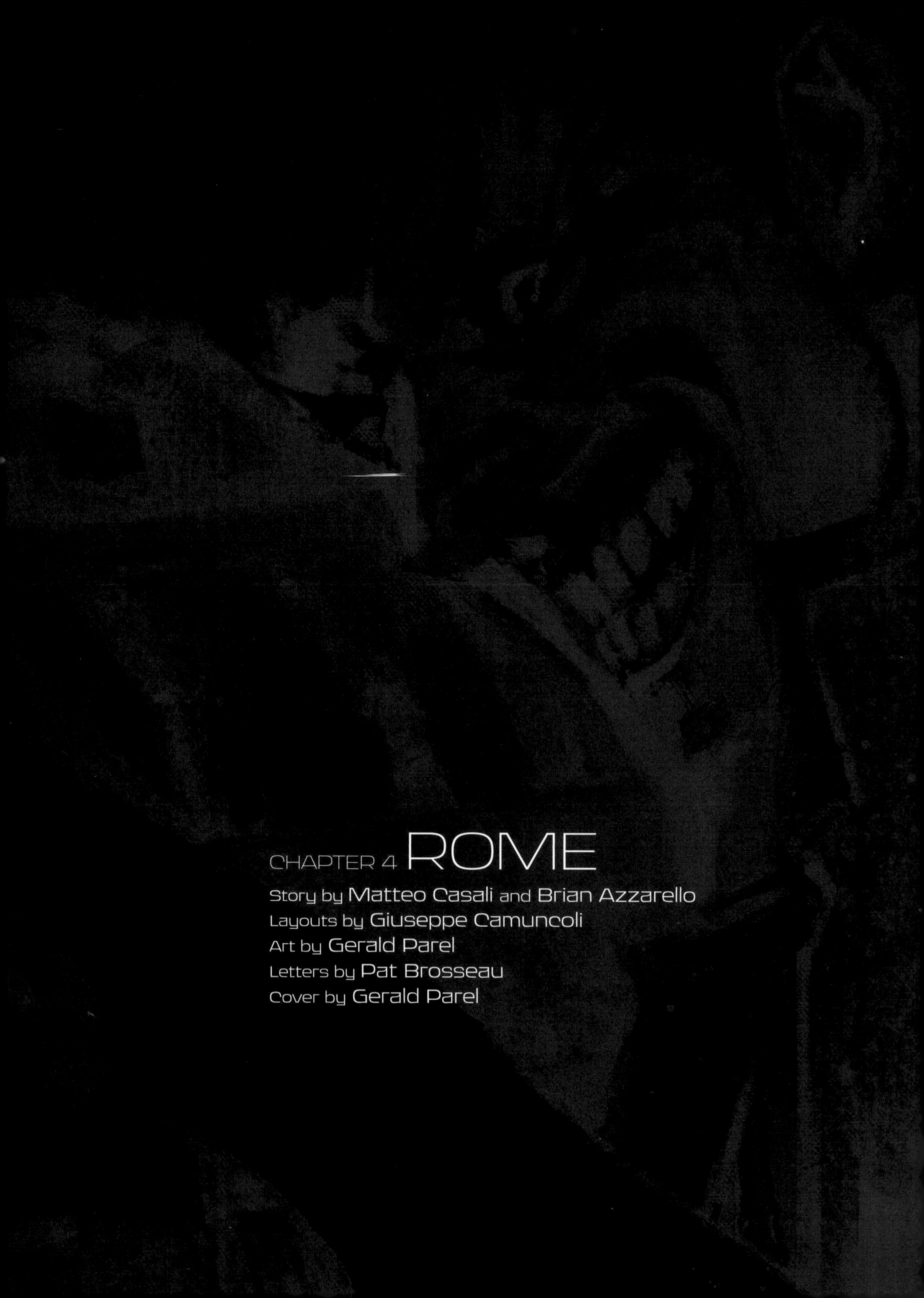

CHAPTER 4 ROME

Story by Matteo Casali and Brian Azzarello
Layouts by Giuseppe Camuncoli
Art by Gerald Parel
Letters by Pat Brosseau
Cover by Gerald Parel

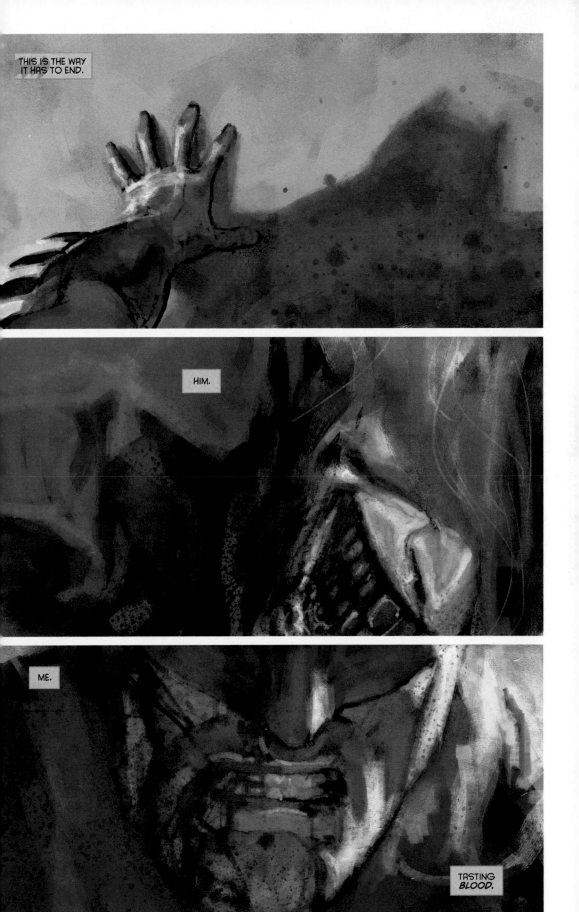

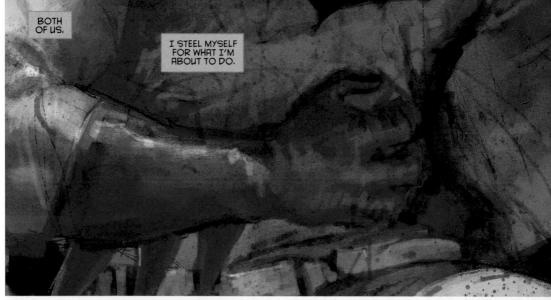

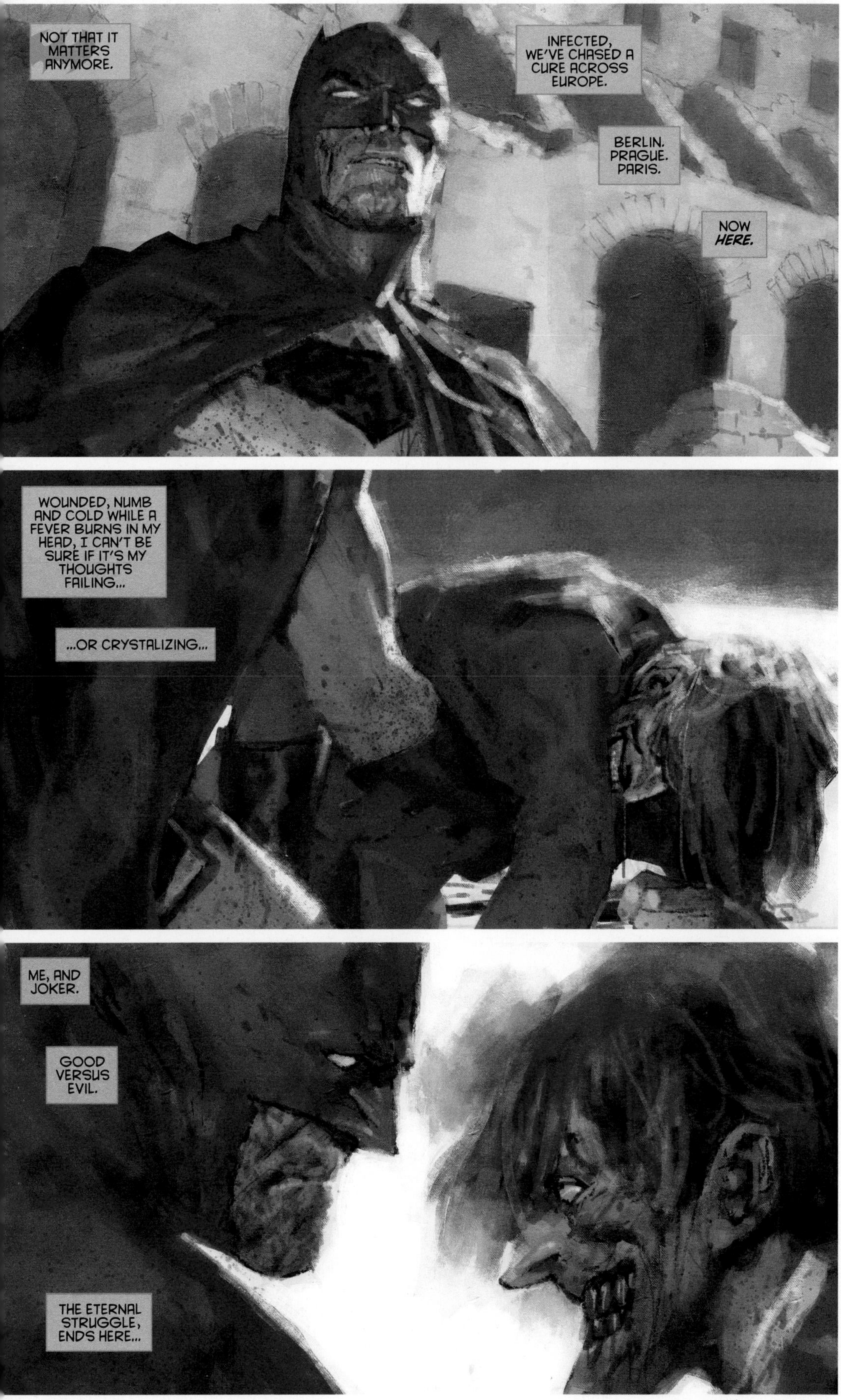
NOT THAT IT MATTERS ANYMORE.
INFECTED, WE'VE CHASED A CURE ACROSS EUROPE.
BERLIN. PRAGUE. PARIS.
NOW *HERE.*
WOUNDED, NUMB AND COLD WHILE A FEVER BURNS IN MY HEAD, I CAN'T BE SURE IF IT'S MY THOUGHTS FAILING...
...OR CRYSTALIZING...
ME, AND JOKER.
GOOD VERSUS EVIL.
THE ETERNAL STRUGGLE, ENDS HERE...

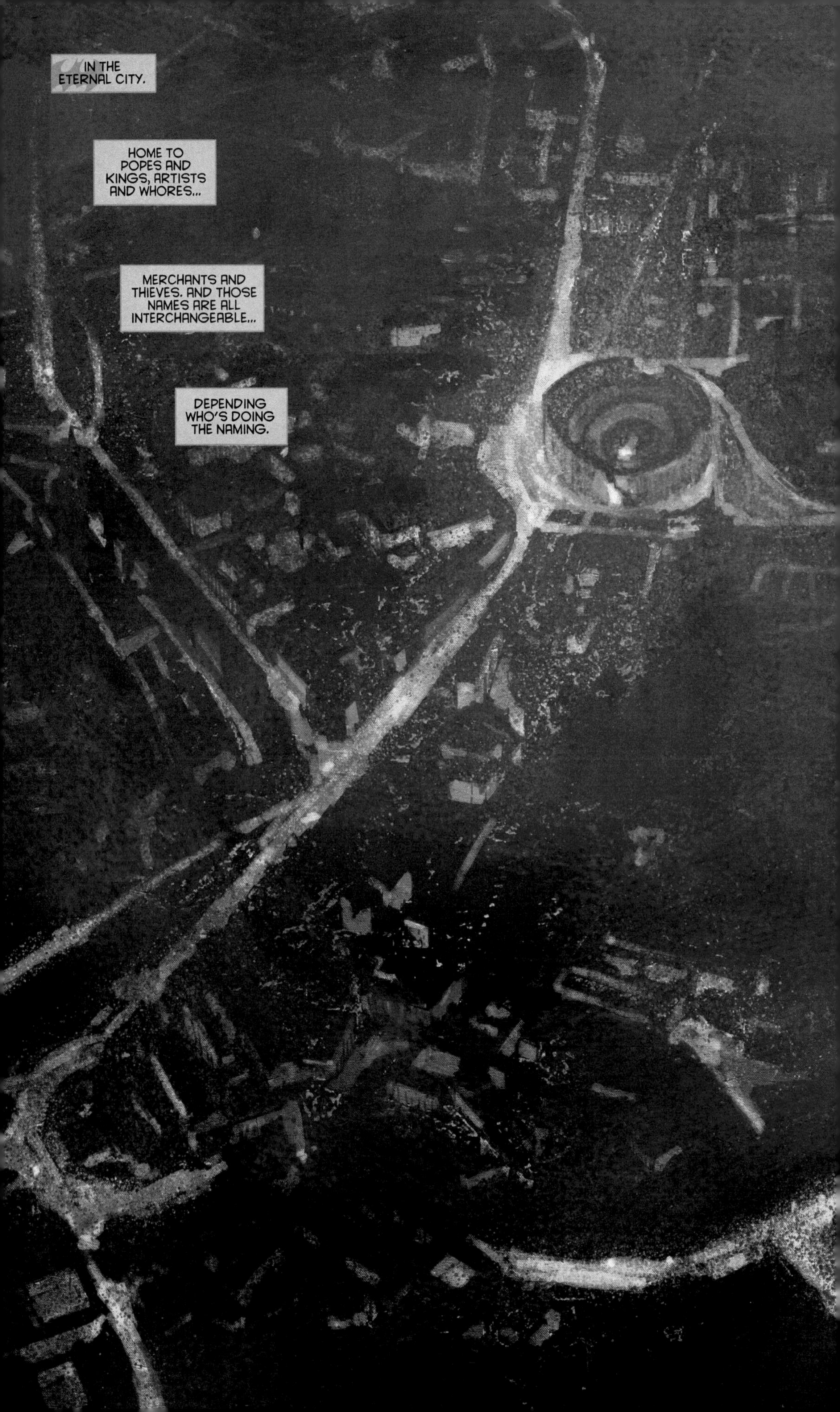
IN THE ETERNAL CITY.
HOME TO POPES AND KINGS, ARTISTS AND WHORES...
MERCHANTS AND THIEVES. AND THOSE NAMES ARE ALL INTERCHANGEABLE...
DEPENDING WHO'S DOING THE NAMING.

THIS IS THE CITY THAT *NERO* TORCHED TO THE GROUND...THAT *CALIGULA* USED FOR THE TIME OF HIS LIFE BEFORE HE WAS MURDERED FOR IT!

FROM *CARAVAGGIO* TO *MACHO-LINI,* THEY WERE *ALL*--

NAME'S *MUSSOLINI.*

OH, I *KNOW.* AND I KNOW YOU KNOW... OH, DO I KNOW!

IT'S *NOT* JUST A *HISTORY CHANNEL* THING YOU HAVE FOR HIM, HUH?

HA HA HA HA

BASTA!

WE'RE HERE.

HMMM... JUDGING BY THE SHAPE OF SECURITY, I'D SAY THERE'S A NEW EMPEROR IN TOWN.

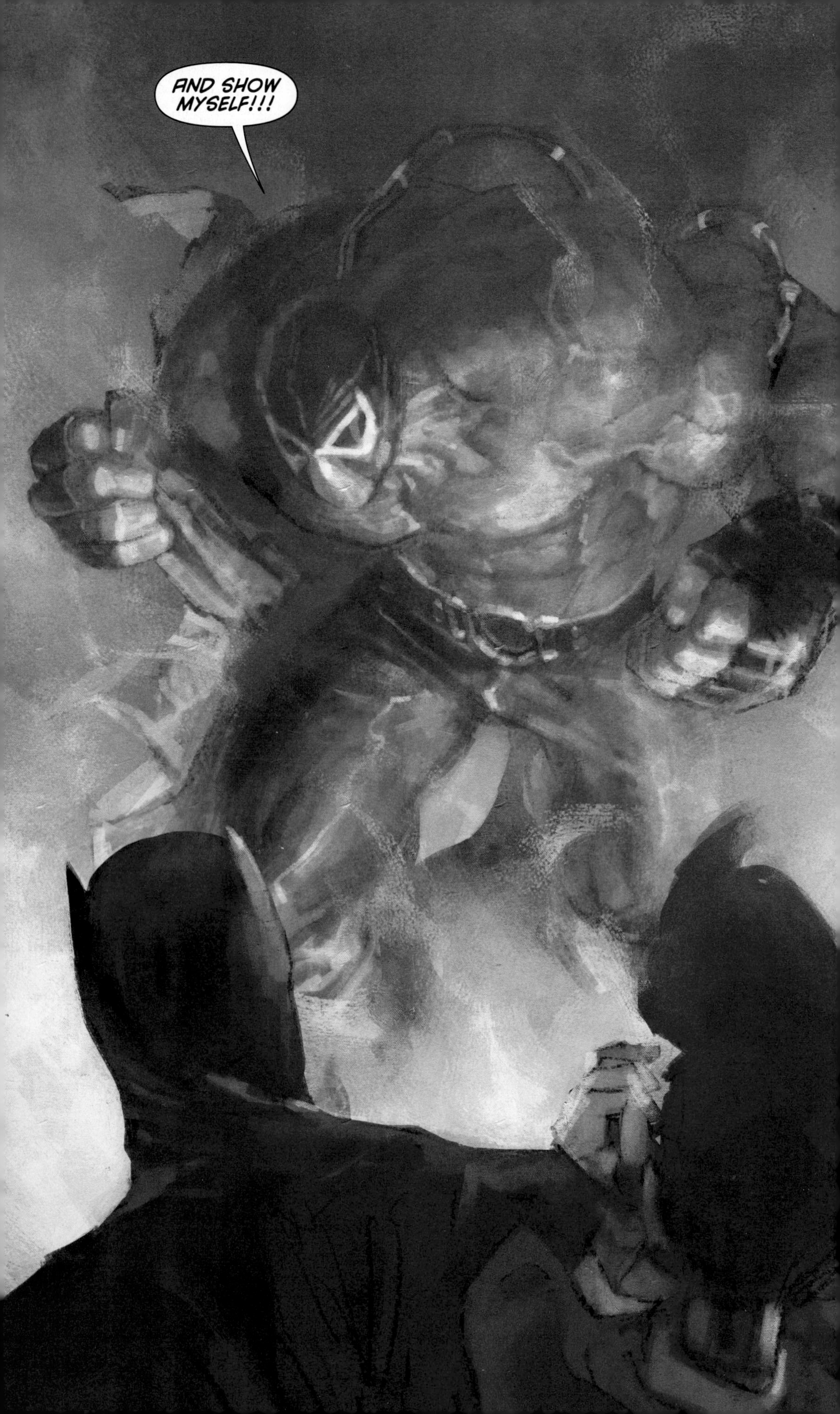
AND SHOW MYSELF!!!

BANE.

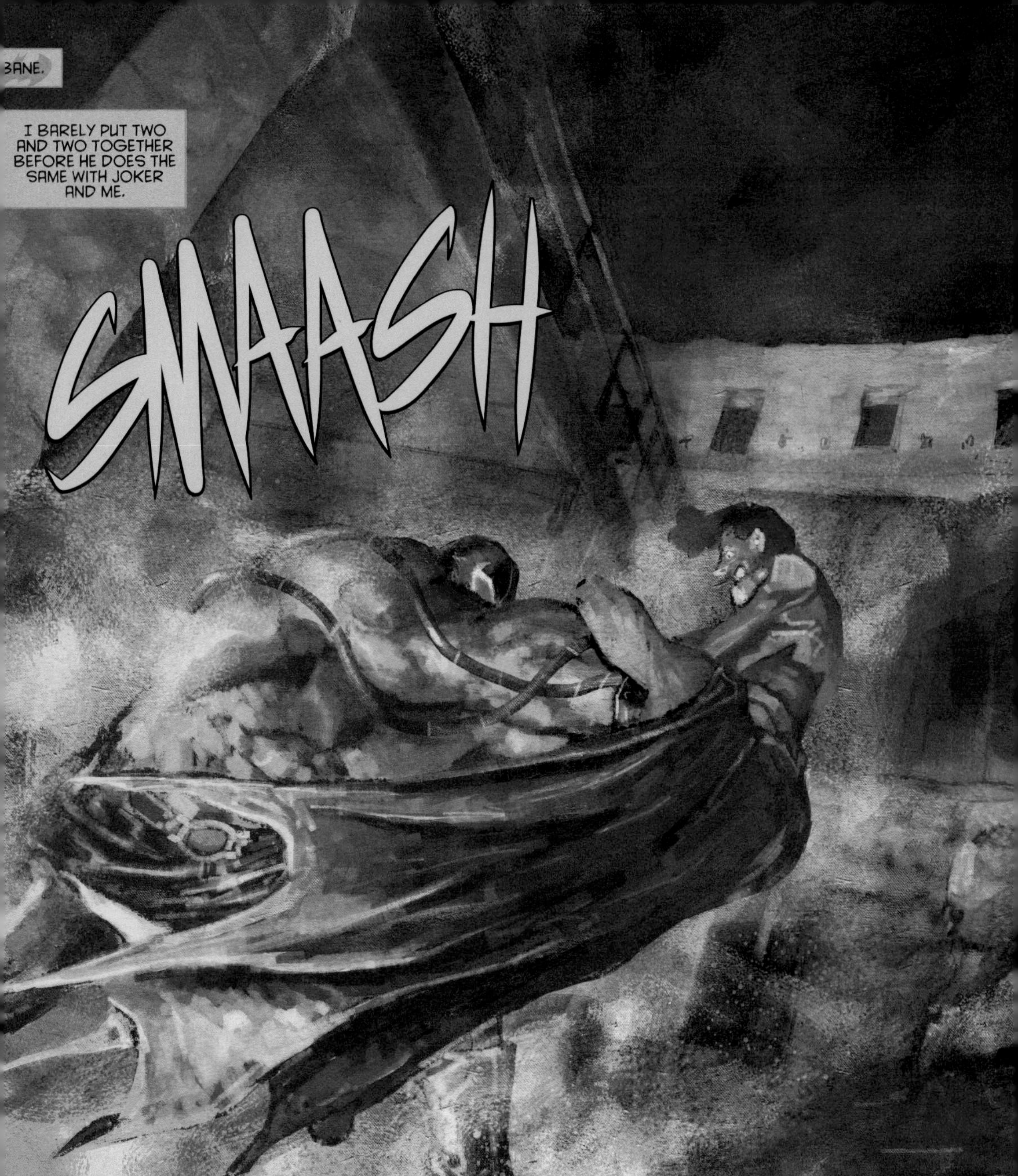

I BARELY PUT TWO AND TWO TOGETHER BEFORE HE DOES THE SAME WITH JOKER AND ME.

SMAASH

CRUNCHYH

UGH--!

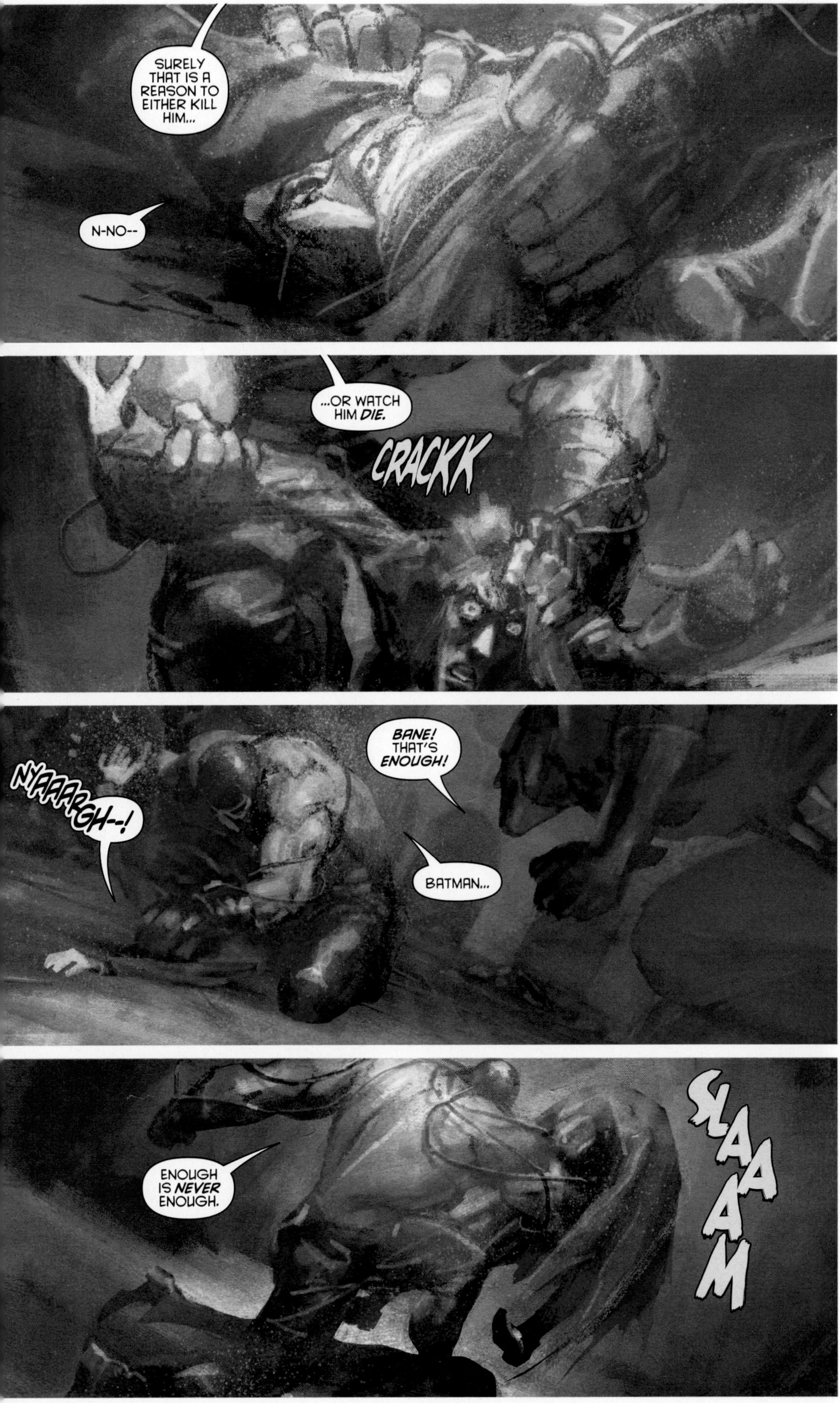

SURELY THAT IS A REASON TO EITHER KILL HIM...
N-NO--
...OR WATCH HIM DIE.
CRACKK
NYAAARGH--!
BANE! THAT'S ENOUGH!
BATMAN...
ENOUGH IS NEVER ENOUGH.
SLAAAAM

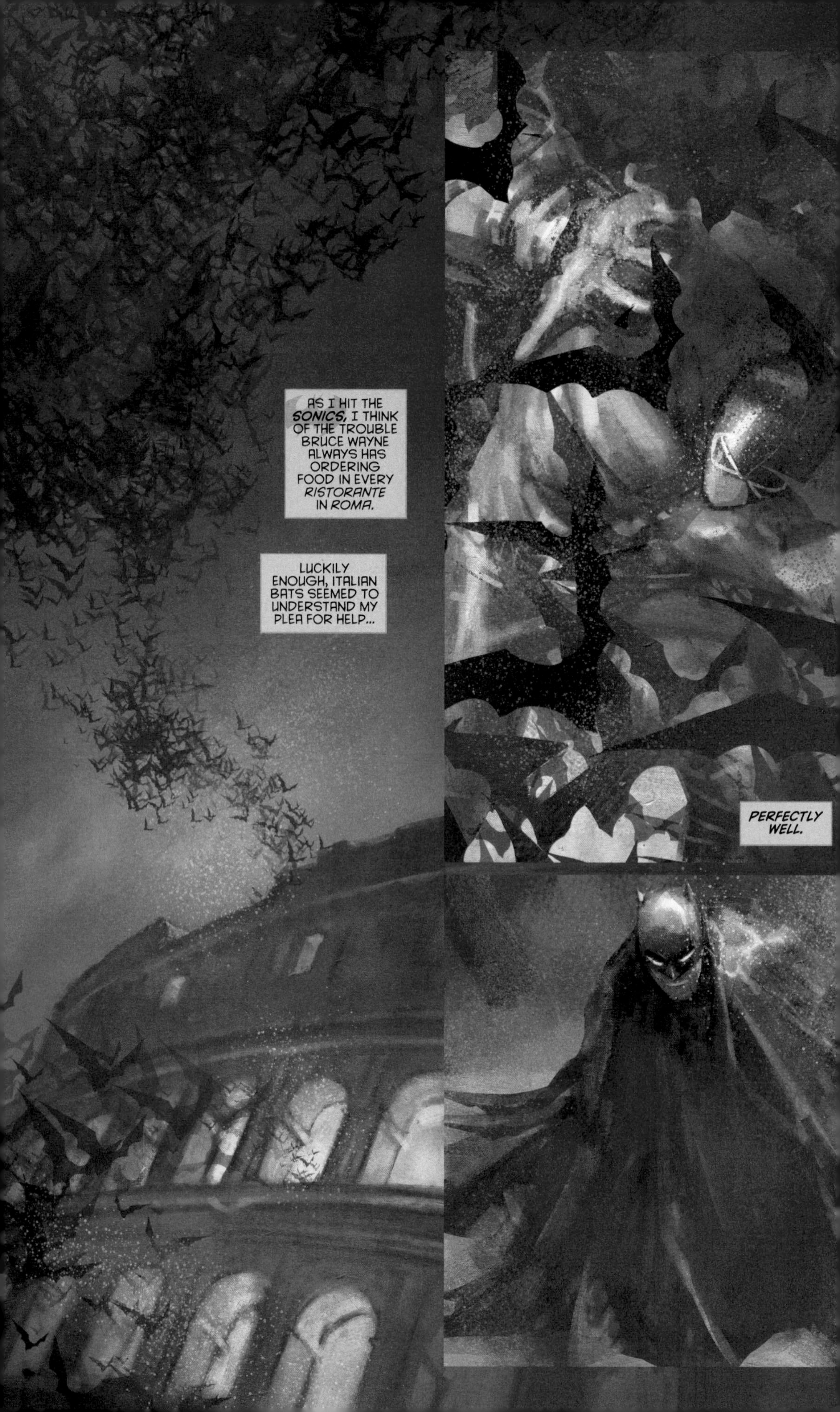
AS I HIT THE *SONICS,* I THINK OF THE TROUBLE BRUCE WAYNE ALWAYS HAS ORDERING FOOD IN EVERY *RISTORANTE* IN *ROMA.*
LUCKILY ENOUGH, ITALIAN BATS SEEMED TO UNDERSTAND MY PLEA FOR HELP...
PERFECTLY WELL.

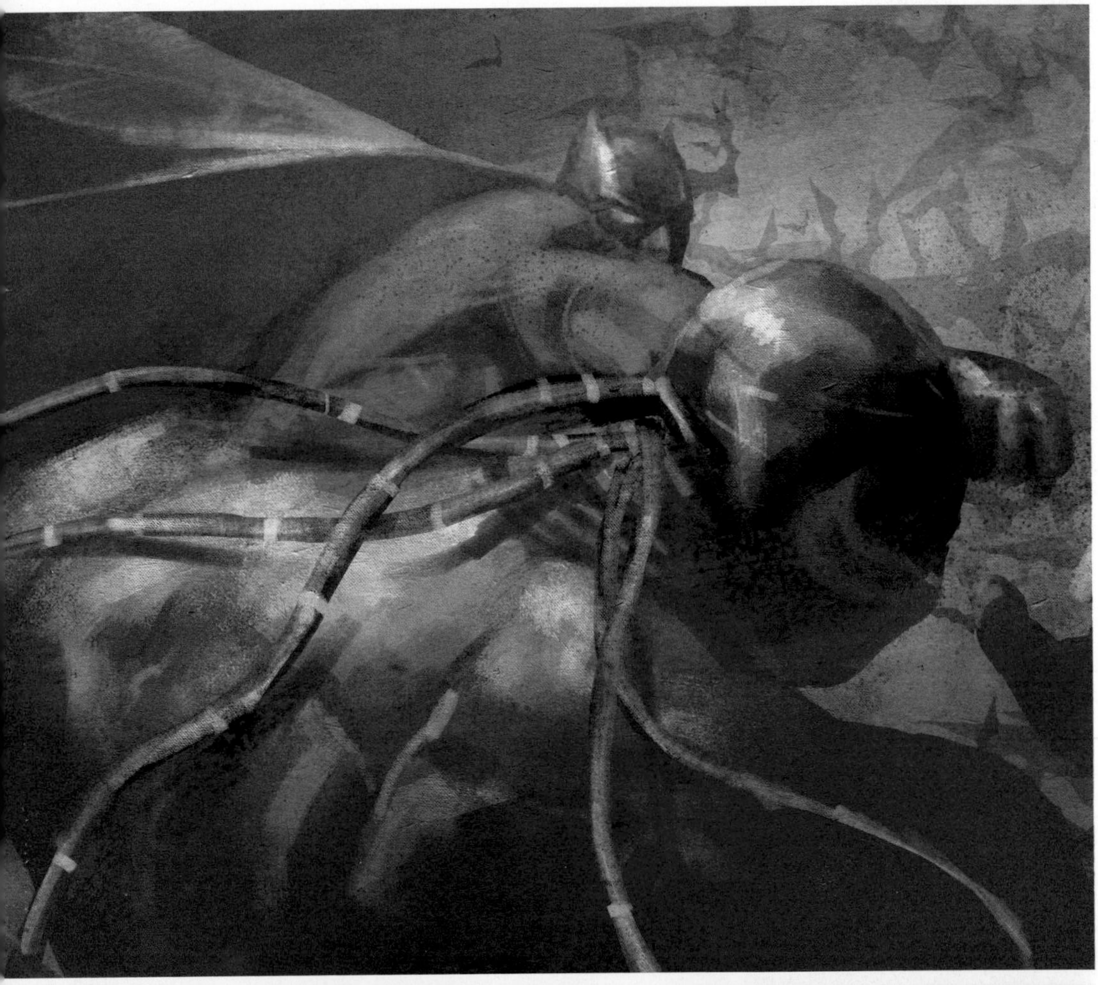

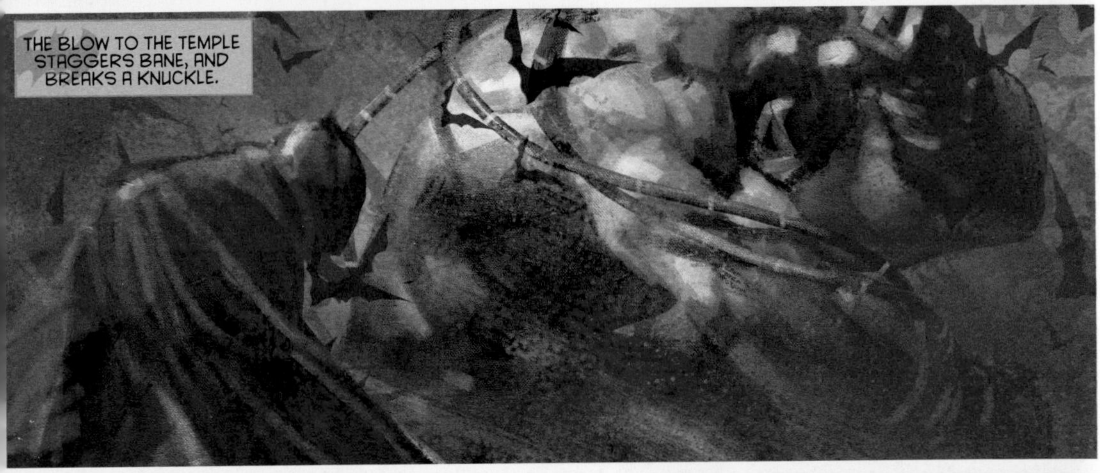
THE BLOW TO THE TEMPLE STAGGERS BANE, AND BREAKS A KNUCKLE.

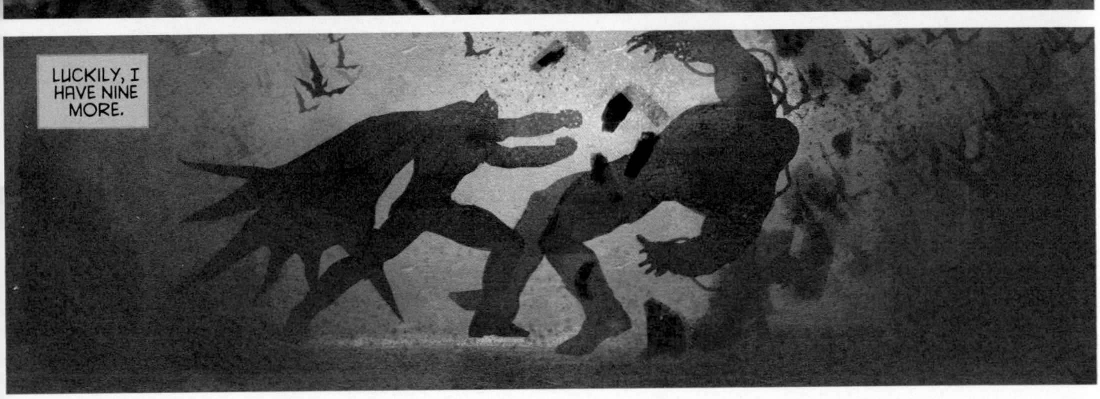
LUCKILY, I HAVE NINE MORE.

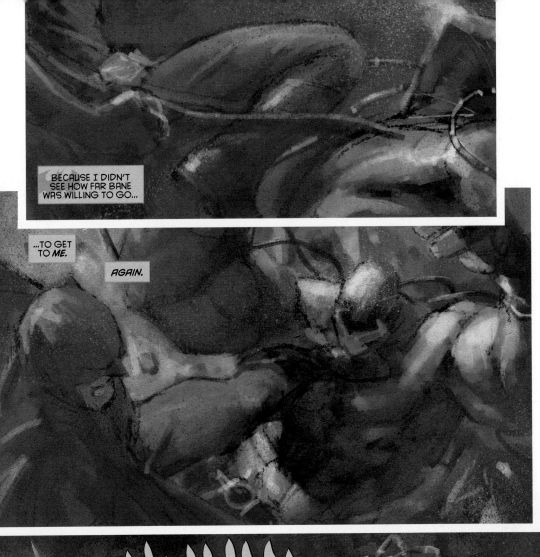

BECAUSE I DIDN'T SEE HOW FAR BANE WAS WILLING TO GO...

...TO GET TO *ME.*

AGAIN.

WHUMP

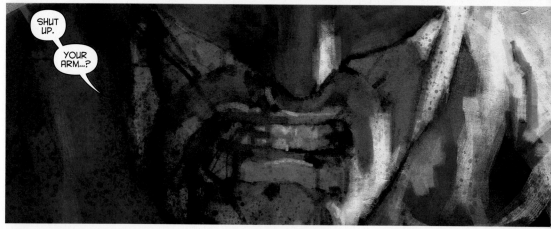

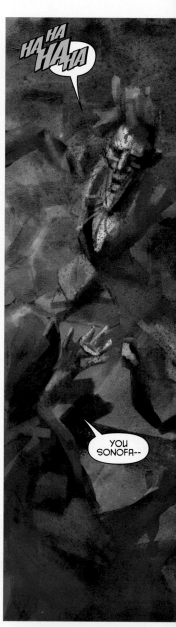

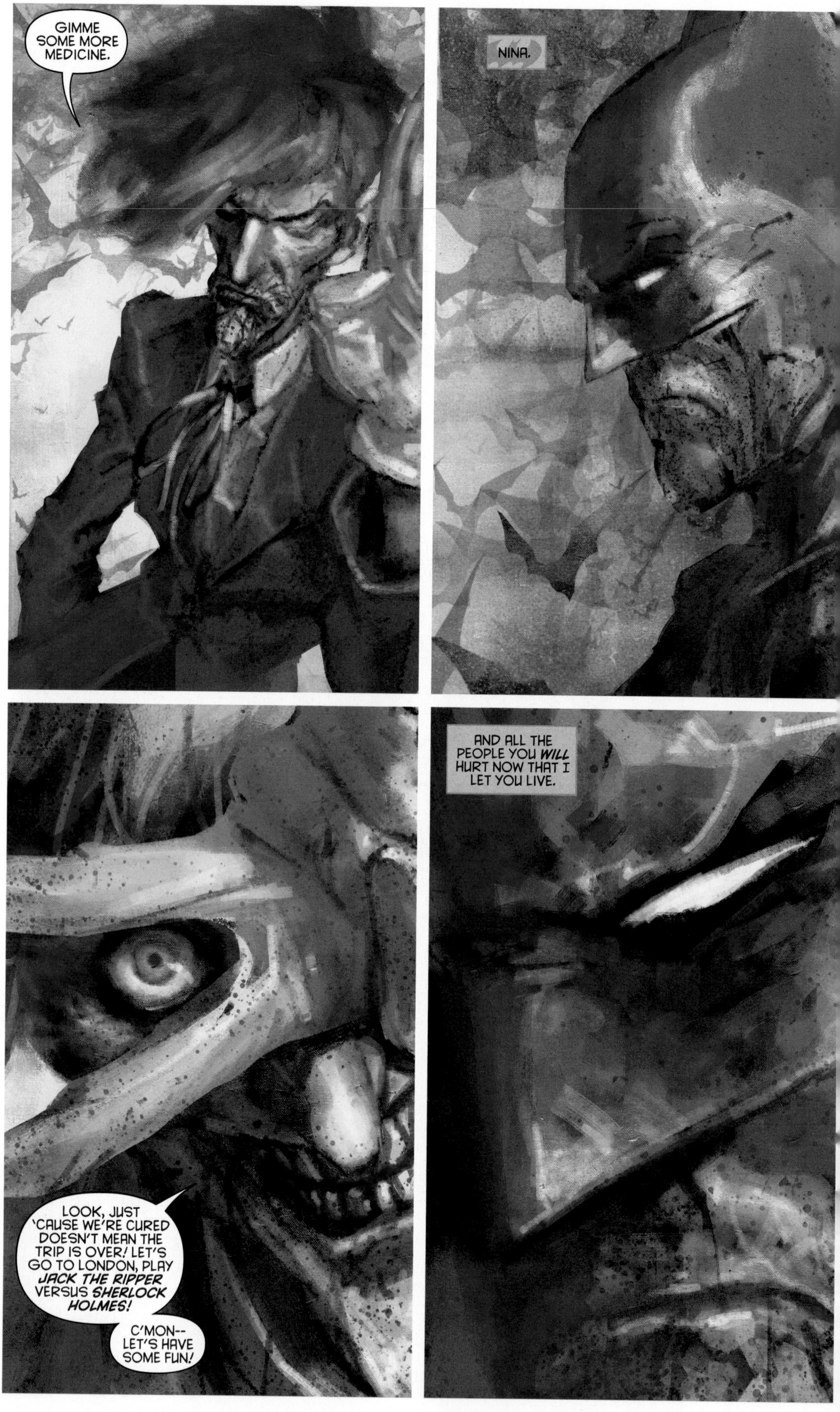
GIMME SOME MORE MEDICINE.
NINA.
LOOK, JUST 'CAUSE WE'RE CURED DOESN'T MEAN THE TRIP IS OVER! LET'S GO TO LONDON, PLAY JACK THE RIPPER VERSUS SHERLOCK HOLMES!
C'MON-- LET'S HAVE SOME FUN!
AND ALL THE PEOPLE YOU WILL HURT NOW THAT I LET YOU LIVE.

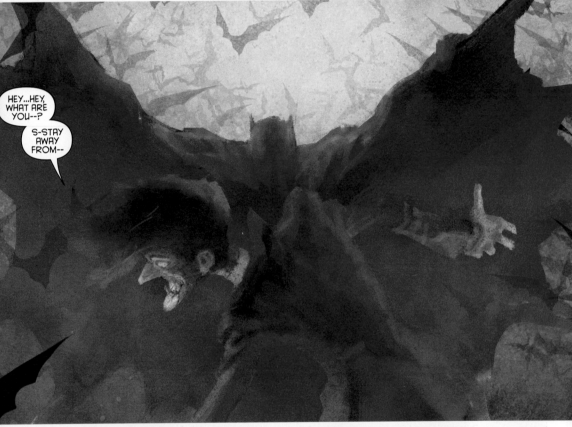

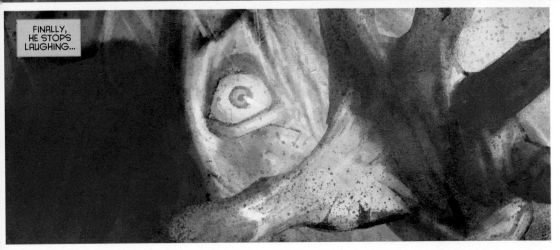

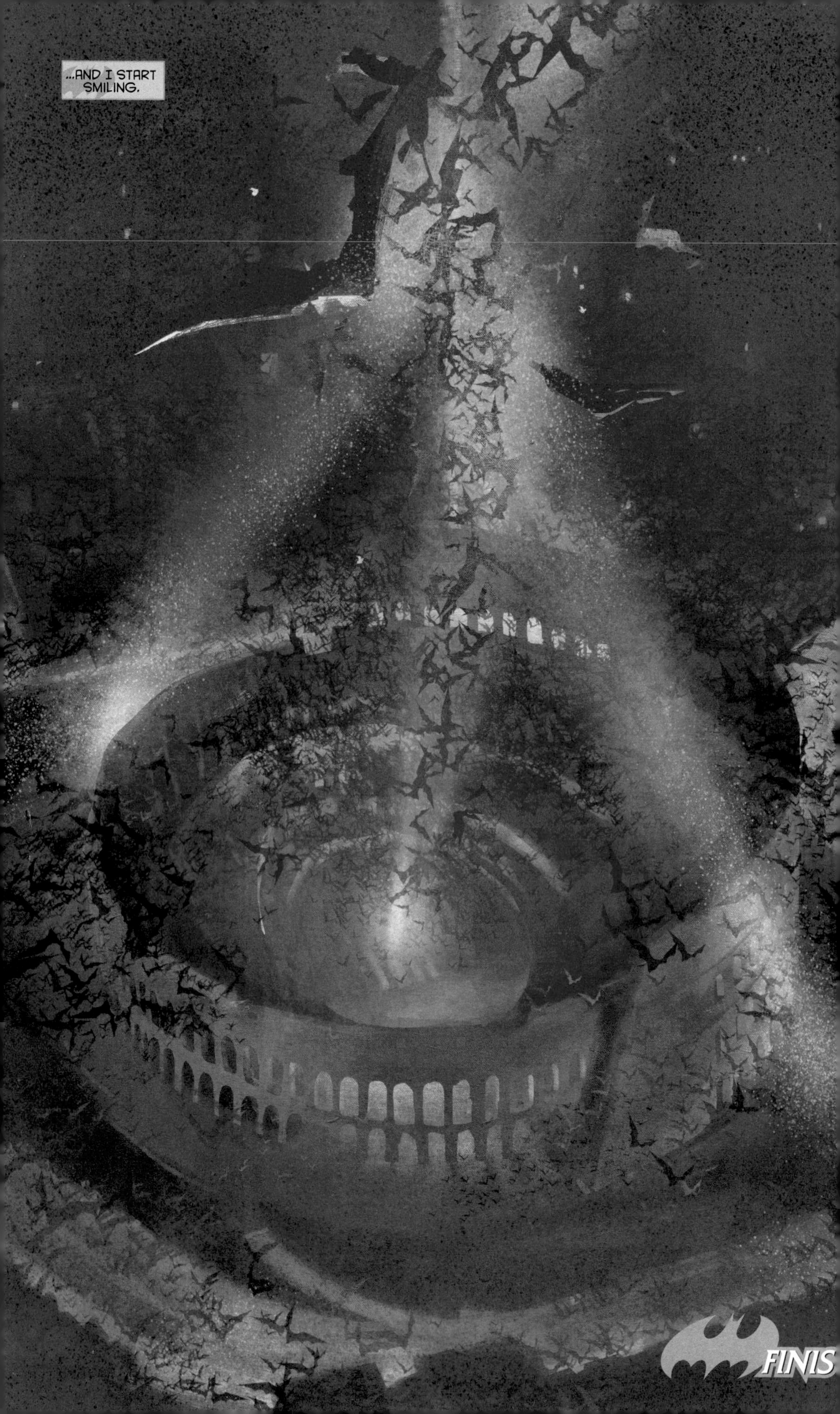

...AND I START SMILING.
FINIS

VARIANT COVER GALLERY

BATMAN: EUROPA #1 Variant by Lee Bermejo
BATMAN: EUROPA #2 Variant by Massimo Carnevale
BATMAN: EUROPA #3 Variant by Francesco Mattina
BATMAN: EUROPA #4 Variant by Jock
BATMAN: EUROPA #1 Sketch variant by Jim Lee
BATMAN: EUROPA #2 Sketch variant by Giuseppe Camuncoli
BATMAN: EUROPA #3 Sketch variant by Diego Latorre
BATMAN: EUROPA #4 Sketch variant by Gerald Parel

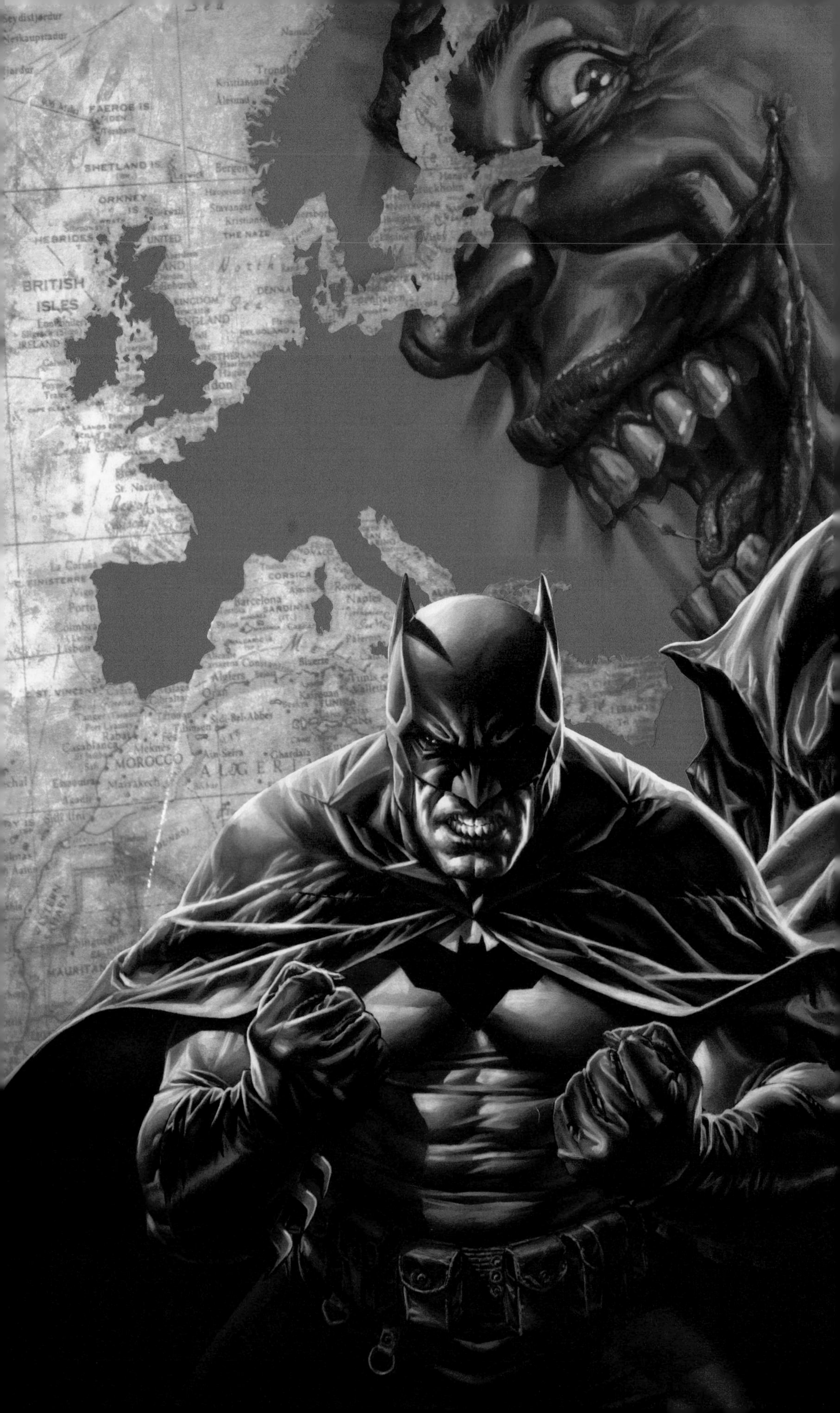

FAEROE IS.
SHETLAND IS.
ORKNEY
HEBRIDES
BRITISH
ISLES
Bergen
Stavanger
THE NAZE
CORSICA
SARDINIA
Barcelona
Naples
Algiers
MOROCCO
A L G E R I A

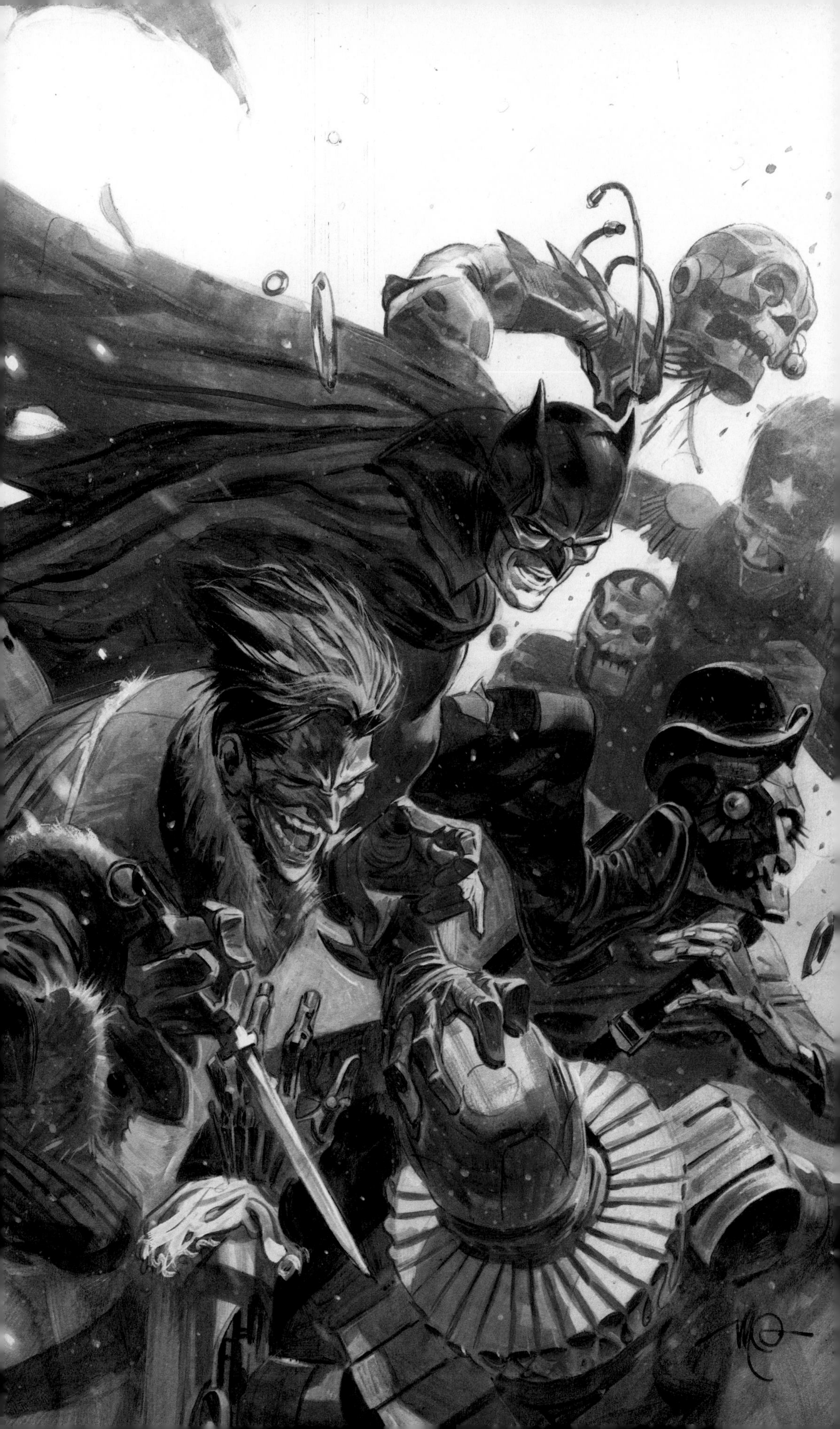

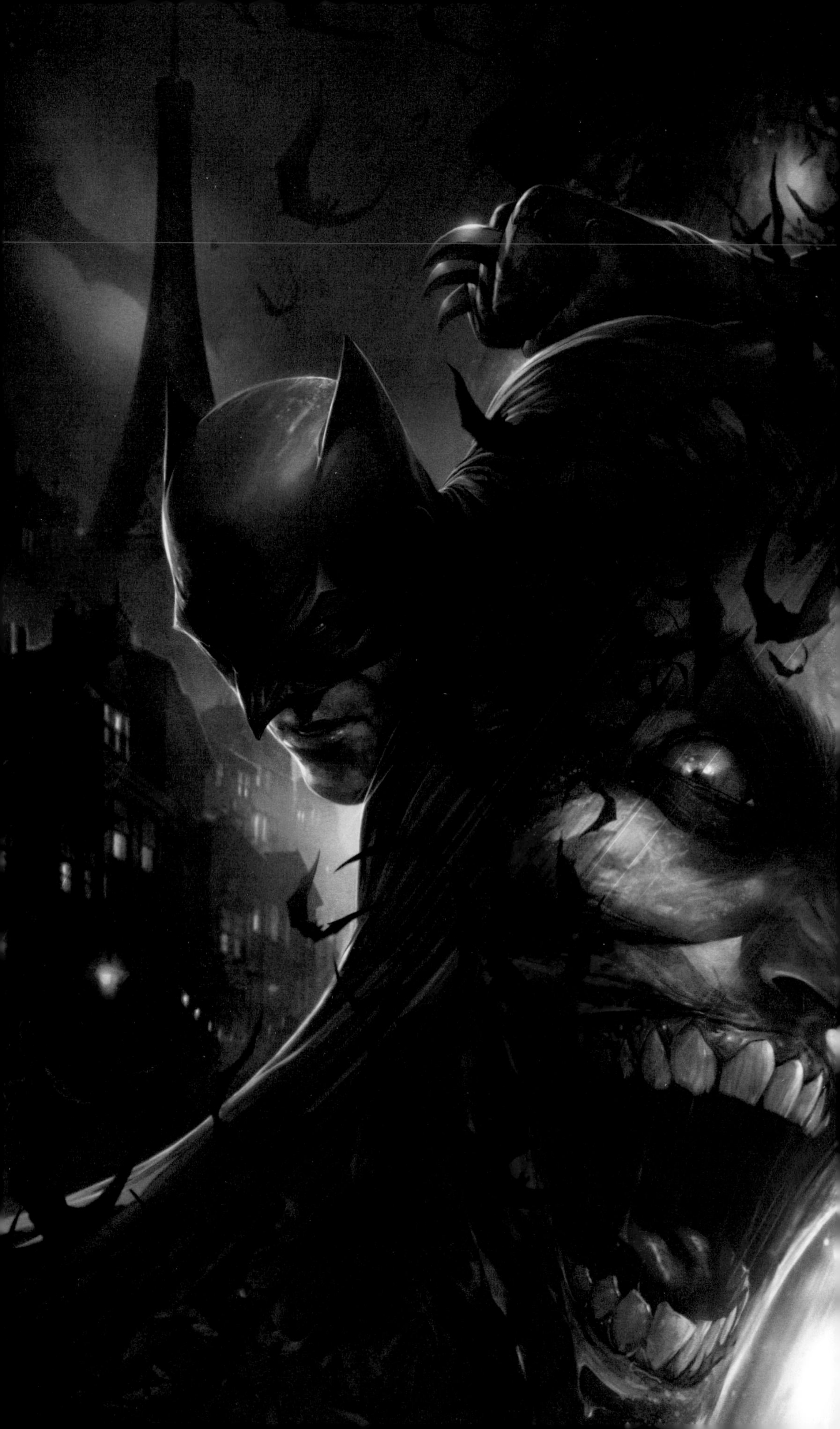

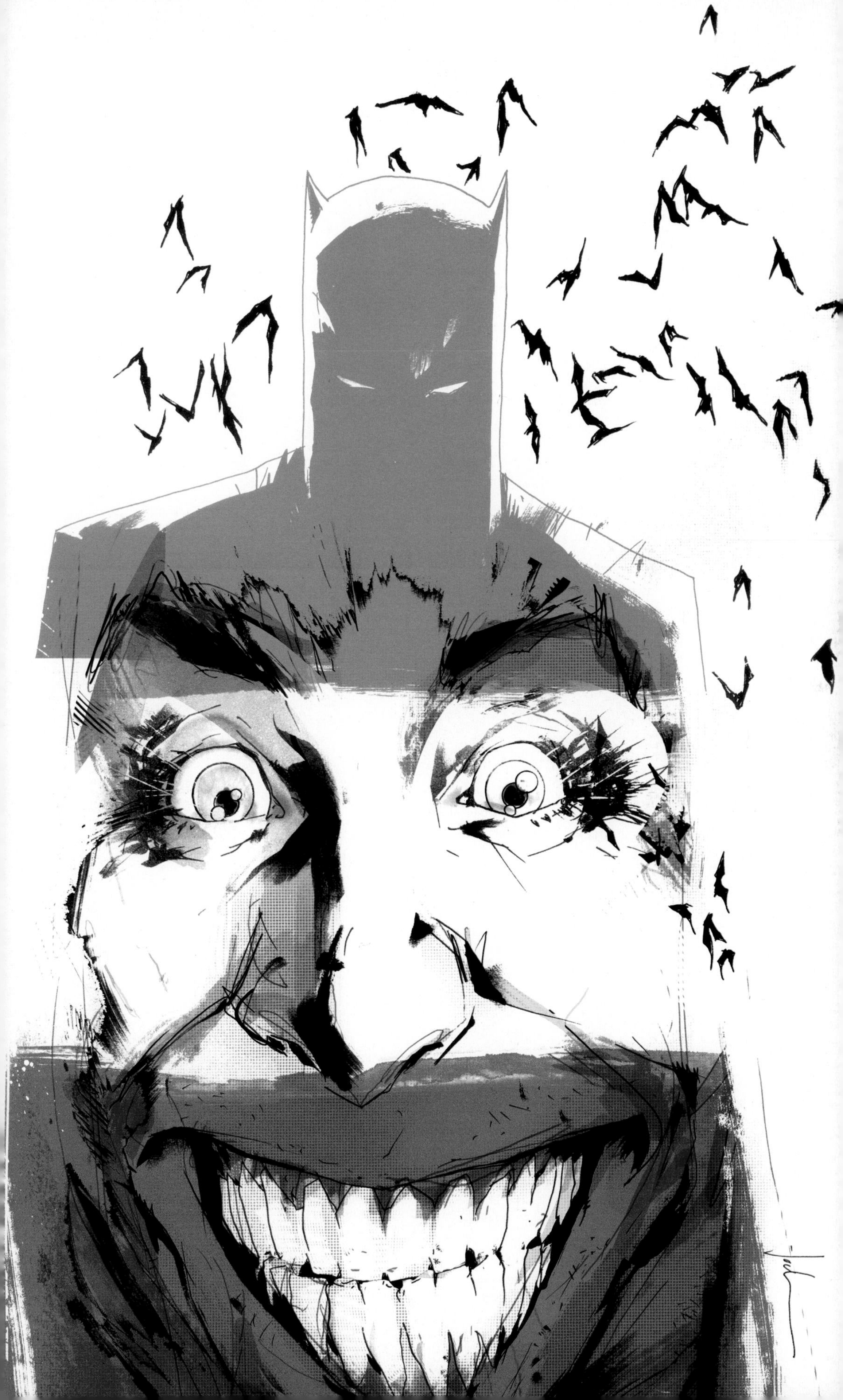

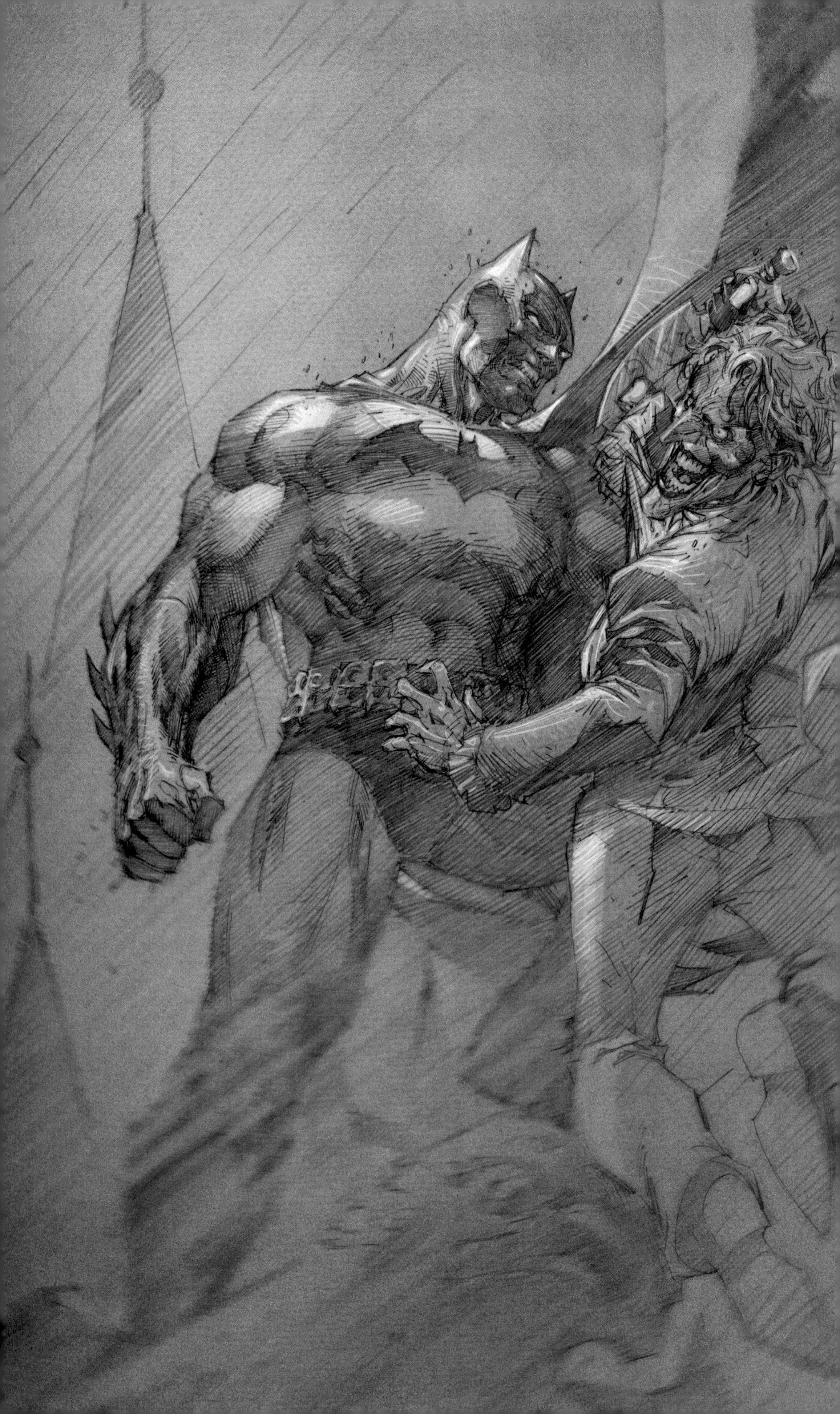

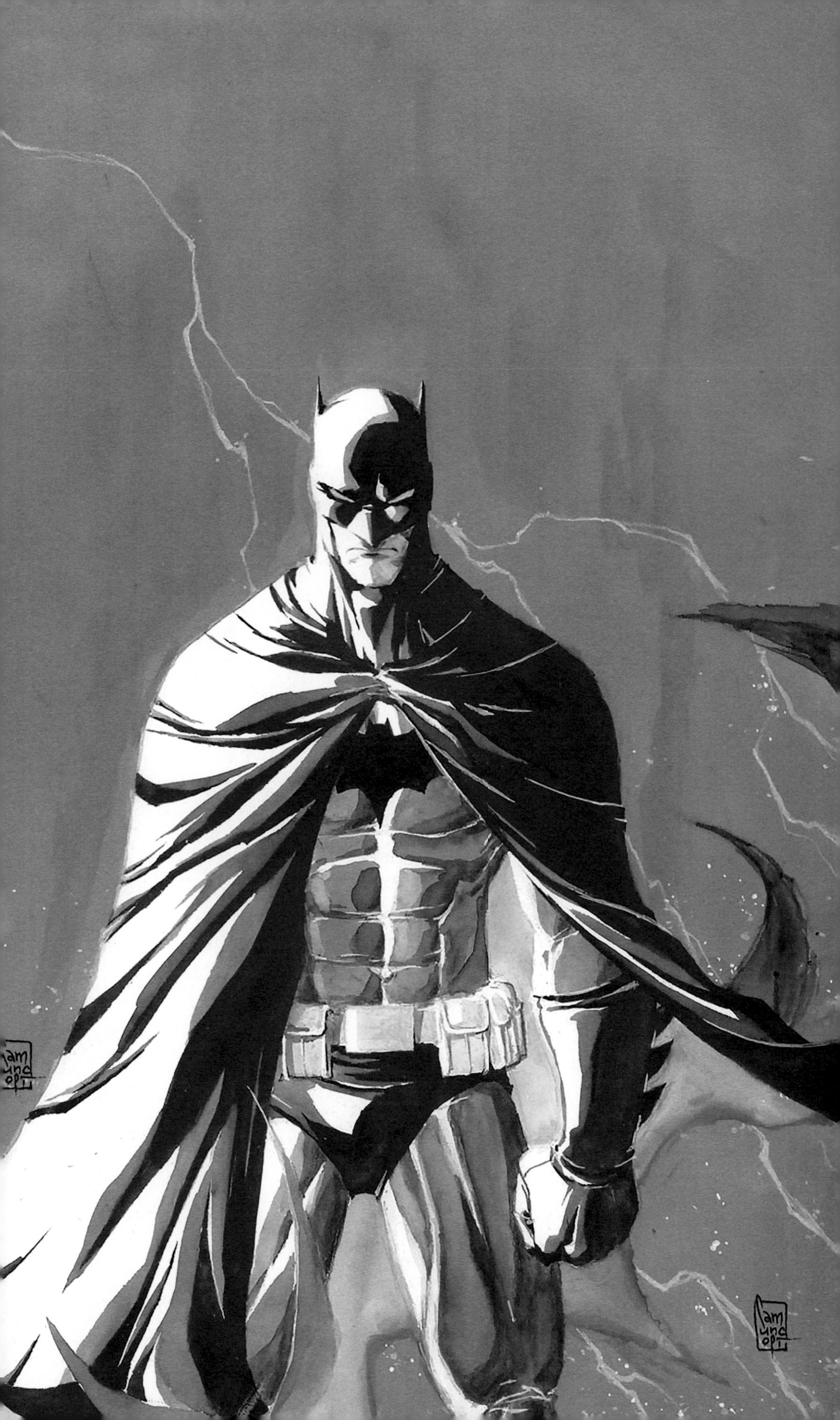

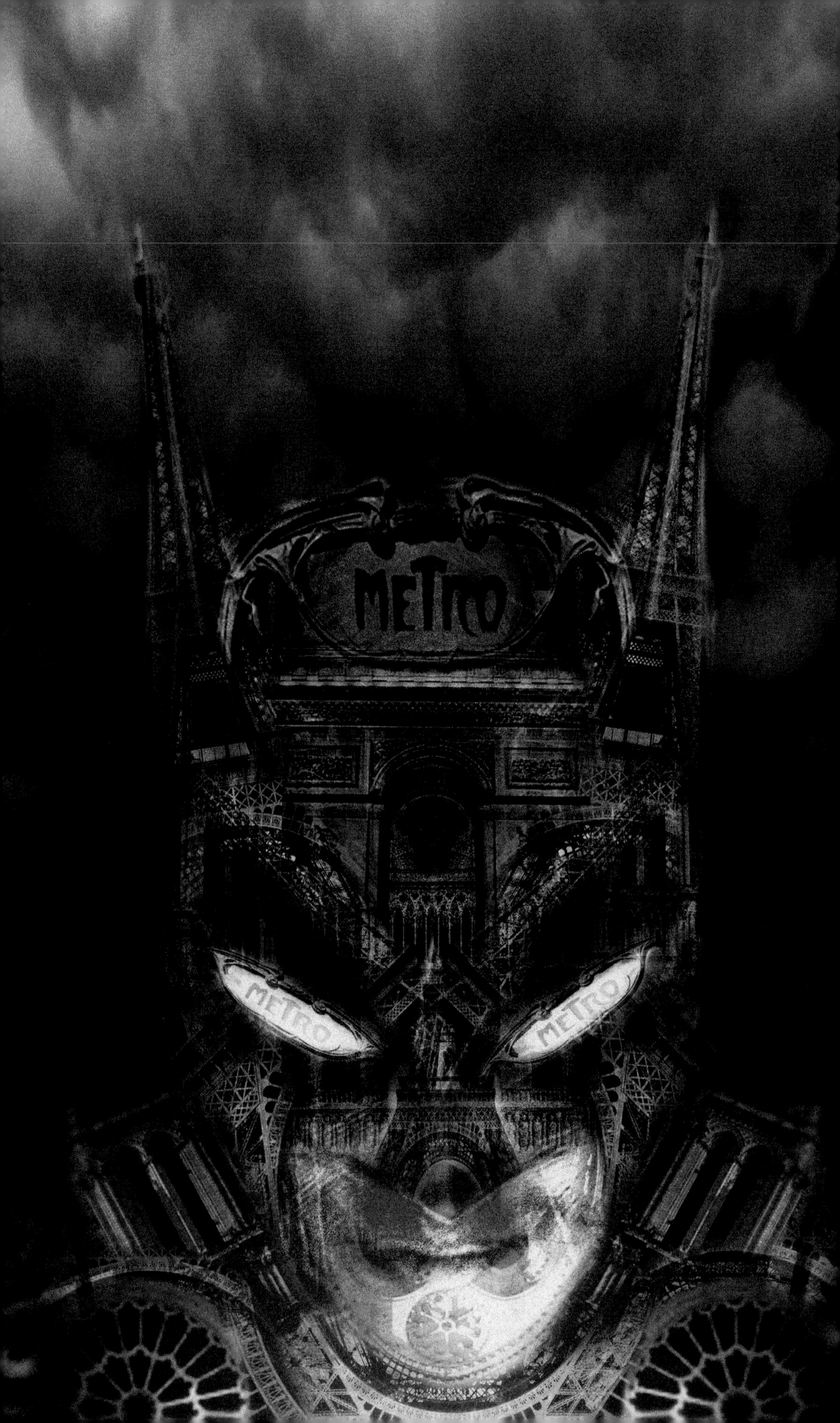

METRO
METRO
METRO

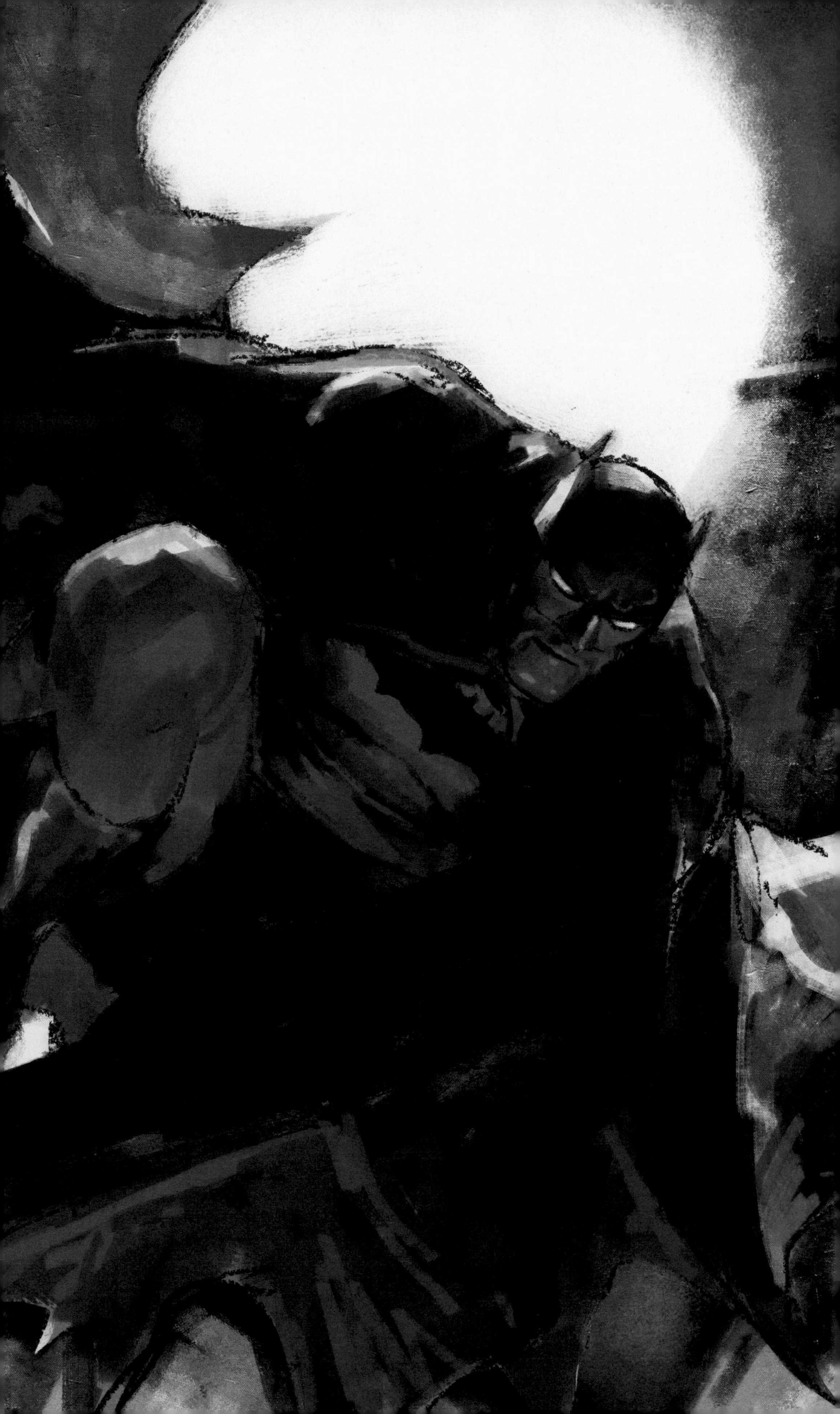

MATTEO CASALI hails from Italy, where he started writing comics, such as *Bonerest* and *Quebrada*, that took him around well, Europa first—and then farther away. He has worked for various "old-world" publishers and is the only Italian writer to have worked for Image Comics, Marvel Comics and DC Comics, where he wrote stories for CATWOMAN, JUSTICE LEAGUE UNLIMITED and the graphic novel 99 DAYS, winner of the 2012 Spinetingler Award for best crime comic. He lives in Reggio Emilia, Italy, and teaches scriptwriting and storytelling classes at the International School of Comics, where he acts as creative co-director, along with his longtime friend and colleague Giuseppe Camuncoli.

BRIAN AZZARELLO has been writing comics professionally since the mid-1990s. He is the author of SPACEMAN, BATMAN: BROKEN CITY and the Harvey and Eisner Award-winning 100 BULLETS, all created in collaboration with artist Eduardo Risso. The *New York Times* best-selling author's other work for DC Comics includes the titles HELLBLAZER and LOVELESS (both with Marcelo Frusin), SUPERMAN: FOR TOMORROW (with Jim Lee), JOKER, LUTHOR and BEFORE WATCHMEN: RORSCHACH (with Lee Bermejo), BEFORE WATCHMEN: COMEDIAN (with J.G. Jones), SGT. ROCK: BETWEEN HELL AND A HARD PLACE (with Joe Kubert) and WONDER WOMAN (with Cliff Chiang). Azzarello lives in Chicago and twitters @brianazzarello only when he has something to say.

JIM LEE is a renowned comic book artist and the Co-Publisher of DC Entertainment. Prior to his current position, Lee served as DC's Editorial Director, where he oversaw WildStorm Studios and provided art for many of DC Comics' best-selling comic books and graphic novels, including ALL-STAR BATMAN AND ROBIN, THE BOY WONDER, BATMAN: HUSH and SUPERMAN: FOR TOMORROW. He has drawn JUSTICE LEAGUE and SUPERMAN UNCHAINED as part of DC Comics: The New 52. A veritable legend in the industry, he has received numerous accolades for his work, including the Harvey Special Award for New Talent in 1990, the Inkpot Award in 1992 and the Wizard Fan Award in 1996, 2002 and 2003.

Italian artist **GIUSEPPE CAMUNCOLI** first broke onto the American comics scene in 2001 with Vertigo's SWAMP THING. Since then, he has provided covers and interiors for Marvel and DC Comics, most notably on titles like HELLBLAZER, THE INTIMATES, *Daken: Dark Wolverine*, *Superior Spider-Man* and *The Amazing Spider-Man*. BATMAN: EUROPA is his first painted book. He lives in Reggio Emilia, Italy, with his wife, Jessica, and his daughter, Martina.

DIEGO LATORRE is a Spanish comic book artist, film director and designer. His American comic book work has been published by DC, Marvel and Dark Horse. Other clients include MTV, Diesel, Virgin, EA Games, Fox, Zero and Perspective Studios.

As a film director, he has directed the multi-award-winning short film *Blink*, as well a several music videos for top Spanish rock bands. His design work was exhibited several consecutive years at Milan Design Week. He lives on the Mediterranean coast with his son, Hugo.

French artist **GERALD PAREL** first became prominent in the United States for his work as a Marvel cover artist, lending iconic covers to such superhero titles as *Iron Man*, *Captain America*, and *S.H.I.E.L.D.* as well as literary comic adaptations *The Picture of Dorian Gray*, *The Three Musketeers* and *The Last of the Mohicans*, among others. His first American interior art was for the 2012 original graphic novel *Iron Man: Season One* (written by Howard Chaykin). BATMAN: EUROPA marks the artist's first work for DC Comics.